THE MANAGER'S GUIDE TO
REWARDS

THE MANAGER'S GUIDE TO
REWARDS

What You Need to Know to
Get the Best for—and from—Your Employees

Doug Jensen, Tom McMullen
and Mel Stark

HAY GROUP

AMACOM

American Management Association

New York • Atlanta • Brussels • Chicago • Mexico City • San Francisco
Shanghai • Tokyo • Toronto • Washington, D.C.

This publication is designed to provide accurate and authoritative information in regard to the subject matter covered. It is sold with the understanding that the publisher is not engaged in rendering legal, accounting, or other professional service. If legal advice or other expert assistance is required, the services of a competent professional person should be sought.

Library of Congress Cataloging-in-Publication Data

Jensen, Doug, 1945–
    The manager's guide to rewards : what you need to know to get the best for—and from—your employees / Doug Jensen, Tom McMullen, Mel Stark.
        p.   cm.
    Includes index.
    ISBN-10: 0-8144-0886-9 (hardcover)
    ISBN-13: 978-0-8144-0886-5 (hardcover)
    1. Incentive awards.   2. Incentives in industry.   3. Employee motivation.
    I. McMullen, Tom, 1962–   II. Stark, Mel, 1948–   III. Title.

    HF5549.5.I5.J463   2007
    658.3'124—dc22

                                                                        2006012222

Printing number

10   9   8   7   6   5   4   3   2   1

Contents

Foreword

I WISH I COULD TELL YOU that there is a secret formula for a successful rewards program. It takes a lot of hard work from a lot of people to make a total rewards program work within an organization. It seems to me that the key to a successful rewards program isn't so much about a sophisticated or elegant design as it is about making sure that it fits with the organization's business strategy and work culture and that people believe it makes sense to them.

I think the idea of this book is on target. I strongly believe that the unit manager is the key in terms of making things happen in an organization and is the key differentiator in the effective implementation of a company's set of rewards programs. One of the things I've learned in my career is that outstanding performance comes from managers who connect with and engage their employees—engaging the heart as well as the head. This is a simple but little appreciated maxim.

Perhaps one of the most important things that a manager does is to set the work climate within his or her part of the organization. This climate can either strengthen or weaken the organization. The manager's role is critical for us, because we have found that many of our people work at Applebee's because they want a genuinely good place to go to work, they want flexible hours, and they want to be treated with respect. Establishing this climate is critical to our ability to retain our best people. Our best people want to be on a winning team and they want to perform well. We do not underestimate the role that managers have in setting the climate or tone of their part of the organization.

While senior executives and the human resources team might take the lead role in the design of the various forms of rewards programs within the organization, it is really the collective group of managers who are instrumental in making the program work effectively. The role of line manager is critical, because it is the line manager whom employees tend to believe and trust above all others.

A few years ago at Applebee's, it often happened that the human resources team might design something that they worked very hard on—and it may have been the absolute right thing to do—but line managers didn't always make the connection or see it as advantageous to them. Over the past several years, we've turned the corner on this. Today, we have what I would call a "culture of testing" any significant changes to our rewards programs. Before we undertake any major change, we make sure that we engage and align with our managers by getting their input and direction first. We also try to hedge our bets by piloting programs in certain areas before we do a broader launch.

At Applebee's our store managers are highly empowered to reward and recognize performance. Our Apple Bucks Program is a way for managers to hand out spot rewards. Apple Bucks are essentially points that employees can redeem for cash or merchandise. We aren't talking small dollars either—we spend over $1 million on noncash awards and gifts for a payroll of approximately $100 million. Our employee satisfaction surveys show that these noncash rewards are quite meaningful and important. We've also found that just giving people the choice to participate in a program like this is very valuable in our culture.

It's also important to point out that although many people think about rewards as the traditional components of a compensation program—that is, base, bonus, and benefits—the intangible or indirect forms of rewards, such as a fulfilling job, future career opportunities, and recognition and development programs are all important parts of the tool kit that the manager has available to make a real impact on engaging employees and developing a high-performing organization.

As you read this book, I encourage you to take a fresh perspective on your role as a manager and how you reward and recognize your employees. The effective use of these tools is a win-win for all of us—employees, managers, and shareholders.

Lloyd Hill
Chairman and CEO of Applebee's International

Preface

By Murray Dalziel, Managing Director,
Global Practices, Hay Group

THE WORLD IS CHANGING and the world of business is changing along with it. Improvements in technology and a deeper understanding of human psychology have led to "flatter" organizations that get things done with greater speed than ever before. These new organizations have the potential for transparency—an atmosphere in which each work group knows what the other groups are up to, in which unit heads communicate openly with one another, and in which every employee understands the organization's mission, its goals, and its strategies.

In this brave new world, line managers are often called upon to act in roles previously filled by human resources (HR) professionals. They are now communicating about benefits, talking about pay, measuring performance, and designing jobs (which change more frequently than ever)—roles for which they may not have been prepared. Yet research suggests that managers—not HR professionals—are the best people to communicate with workers about rewards. That's because people trust their bosses; most people will even tell you they work for their bosses, not for their organizations. However, with the rapid pace of today's demands and changes, there's little time either for line managers to learn new skills or for important messages about rewards to cascade down the organization to line managers.

The purpose of this book is to help managers understand the components of "total rewards"—cash, incentives, benefits, perquisites, and intangible rewards—or everything employees can earn in exchange for the work they do. With the valuable skills discussed in this book, and with HR as an advocate and guiding force, line managers should be able to play a key role in attracting, retaining, motivating, and engaging their employees.

The authors' intention is certainly not that this book alienate HR personnel. Rather, it's their goal to help managers become more effective at motivating employees to keep pace with their units, companies, industries, and the world as a whole.

Acknowledgments

A CLICHÉ THOUGH TRUE, we could not have written this book without the help and commitment of a number of people who shared their expertise and experiences, and especially their time. We would like to thank a number of our clients, who stimulated our thinking and shared their insights and stories in support of this work. Their accounts and perspectives provided context and examples for many of the topics.

Many of our colleagues at Hay Group gave their personal and professional support and were indispensable in the creation of this book. Thanks especially to Murray Dalziel for his vision and articulation of the need and opportunity to communicate with managers. In addition, the following colleagues provided substantial expertise throughout the book: Paul Clifford on reward design and architecture; Kevin Seaweard on market pricing and job evaluation processes; Rob Colenbaugh on base salary management systems; Bill Reigel and Brian Tobin on variable pay; Ron Garonzik and Geoff Nethersell on the effective design of career paths and George McCormick on job and work design; Michael Jensen and Tony Faron on performance management; Karl Aboud, Jim Bowers, and Phil Johnson on performance measures; Vasu Mirmira on pay-for-performance linkages; Mark Royal on total rewards; Michael Cotter and Marie Dufresne on leveraging the value of benefits programs;

Rich Sperling on compensation program return on investment; and Doran Twer on communications.

Several colleagues were instrumental in critiquing and improving the manuscript, especially Bill Reigel, Vasu Mirmira, Martin Meerkerk, Geoff Nethersell, Jim Bowers, and Craig Rowley. In addition, several other colleagues contributed significantly to developing and producing the book, especially Jeff Meyers for working with us from concept formation through manuscript completion and promotion, and in keeping us on track; Sarah Massari, who helped to coordinate the project; Winnie Lucchesi for adapting and formatting the figures and tables; and Claire DiPardo for her help in researching and documenting many of the references. We'd also like to acknowledge Gene Bauer for his ongoing support and allocation of resources.

We would also like to thank a number of clients and friends in line management and human resources leadership roles who gave their time and agreed to be interviewed for this book. Their perspective and insights help make this book more meaningful and real to the audience. These individuals include Scott White at Applebee's International, Terri Francino at Southco, Rich Johnson at The Home Depot, Lis Baldock and Alisa Poe at American Modern Insurance Group, Kelly Smith at Replacements Ltd., Jane Vassil at Saint Vincent's Health System, John Leinart at John Deere, Al Kluz and Gloria Venski at Northwestern Mutual, Greg Folley and Carl Smith at Caterpillar, Dennis George at Bridgestone Americas, K. Dow Scott, Ph.D., at Loyola University Chicago, Bruce Lasko at Avaya, Amy Nenner at Heineken USA, and Kelly Logan at the Pennsylvania Higher Education Assistance Authority.

Special thanks go to Louis Greenstein, whose invaluable expertise and perseverance made this concept a reality through his significant editorial skills. Thanks also go to Allan Wittman for his steady guidance and support in developing the proposal and manuscript, and to Adrienne Hickey and Erika Spelman, our editors at AMACOM, whose attention to detail and expertise in publishing matters were critical.

The Manager's Guide to

REWARDS

CHAPTER 1

Why This Book Is Important

MOST BOOKS WRITTEN about compensation are targeted to human resources (HR) professionals or senior executives. As a result, they are often conceptual or theoretical, or they focus on technical and compliance-oriented matters with little attention to practical implementation. But today more than ever, decisions for managing rewards programs are being made by line managers, not by the HR department. We believe there's an unmet need to inform and educate managers about how to reward their employees most effectively to achieve their organization's goals. This book bridges the gap between designing reward programs and making them work.

Throughout this book, we provide practical guidance on compensation-related topics for line managers (managers with profit-and-loss accountability in their organization). We use actual client cases and tell "war stories" to examine real-life experiences. And we draw from our research in partnership with *Fortune* magazine on its annual World's and America's Most Admired Companies lists, as well as our research partnership with WorldatWork and Loyola University Chicago in the rewards practices of effective organizations. We also reference findings from our global Hay Group Insight employee database of employee opinions, which is one of the largest databases of employee opinions in the world today.

The Problems with Compensation Programs

Ask most managers in companies today about their organizations' compensation programs and you'll hear sharp criticisms about how they are not working. Our consulting experience and research support this general reaction. Do the following statements sound familiar? Do they describe your reactions or your employees' feelings about your organization's compensation programs?

- *Available Funding:* "How can I motivate and keep my best people when I can give my employees only a 3.5 percent salary increase?"
- *Appropriate Authority:* "I'm allowed to make major business decisions costing hundreds of thousands of dollars, but I can't spend $10,000 to reward my best people. Something is wrong with the pay program here."
- *Line of Sight:* "The bonus plan doesn't work. My employees see no connection between what they achieve and how much in bonuses they are paid."
- *Performance Orientation:* "Pay here is unfair. Your salary is more a function of how long you've been around and what department you work in than what you contribute."
- *Market Measurement:* "I am told that we must pay the market rate, but the market values don't reflect what I know my key employees are worth."
- *Compliance:* "It's more important that I comply with the compensation budget than deliver superior results."

Today's managers generally don't believe that their company's compensation programs are effective in helping get the results for which they're held accountable. Yet this perceived inability of rewards programs to deliver superior results signals an enormous missed opportunity. That's because, for most managers, compensation is their largest controllable operating expense. Indeed, other programs would likely be cancelled if they cost as much and delivered as little. If you believe the opportunity to earn more money can influence employees' behavior and performance, then figuring out how to manage compensation should be a priority for you. Successfully managing the compensation you offer your employees gives you an incredible tool to achieve improved business results.

If compensation is a large cost of doing business, and compensation is linked to employee motivation, then what's the problem? Is it one of design or of implementation? How do you make your company's investment in compensation work for the company instead of against it? Why is compensation not held to the same return-on-investment (ROI) standard as other business costs? Do we believe employees are an asset or an expense?

Most organizations do one of two things when it comes to compensation:

1. *Follow the herd:* Many organizations go to great lengths to understand the market and then follow it pretty much blindly. If they applied this logic to other aspects of their business, they would pay market rates for their supplies, charge market rates for their products and services, and advertise their products using "Me too!" ads. Ironically, companies strive to distinguish themselves when it comes to products, services, and price, but when it comes to managing their investment in human capital, most strive to be in the middle of the pack.

2. *Reach for the stars:* While it's laudable that some organizations innovate the way they manage compensation, often they merely go after something promoted as new and different rather than sort out whether these new programs are aligned with their business strategy and work culture. Unfortunately, a lot of organizations are interested in doing something different just to be different, rather than ensuring their compensation programs are successful. Many innovative programs fail because they don't align with business needs or the way they get things done.

As a manager, you may be faced with having to live with "Me too" and "New and improved" programs that haven't been well thought out. It's no wonder that you are confused about how best to use compensation to support business success. So, if your compensation programs are problematic, what constitutes "best practice"? Simply stated, best practice is what works for you and your organization.

Our research and experience with clients suggest that best practice is often not so much about sophisticated and different design as about effective alignment and execution. Jeffrey Pfeffer, professor at the Stanford University School of Business, agrees, saying, "A knowledge of what constitutes best practices in all domains, and certainly in the area of managing the employment relation, is transmitted with increasing rapidity. The source of real competitive advantage resides in the ability to actually implement practices that other organizations find difficult."[1]

Sports teams rarely win based on new plays. They win with great players, great coaches, and the ability to execute as a team. Likewise in business, compensation can and does play an important supportive role in achieving success, but it rarely causes performance. In our experience, too much weight is placed on compensation, yet not enough is placed on alignment; there's too little focus on what's truly important. Moreover, the KISS principle (Keep It Simple, Stupid) is very important if compensation programs are to have true motivational value.

Compensation to Align with Culture

Line managers have more impact on an organization's rewards program than they may realize. In fact, Hay Group research has shown that up to a 30 percent variance in business results can be explained by differences in the work climate as created by the manager.[2]

Work climate comprises individual, manager-specific behaviors and styles that set the tone for a work unit, group, or department. Accordingly, climate is measured at the individual-manager level by direct subordinates. Employees in positive work climates are more likely to undertake discretionary efforts in support of their work units. This suggests that managers who are attuned to the climate and who can enhance the work environment create an aspect of total rewards that money can't buy. And those rewards are significant in terms of retention.

In addition, a positive work climate inspires unusual commitment on the part of employees, who in turn deliver discretionary effort—a valuable return on the investment made by a manager to create a robust and engaging work climate. Thus, this book is a practical guide to help managers get more out of their organization's rewards system. Using compensation techniques common to most companies, it shows managers what they can do to leverage their rewards program and help achieve success.

We want to make it clear: There are no "silver bullet" compensation programs. There is no one best approach to reward employees that is right for all organizations and for all employees. When Jack Welch retired as CEO at General Electric (GE) and wrote his book *Jack—Straight from the Gut*, which included his approach to rewards, many managers tried to replicate it. Most failed. Why? Because they adopted the mechanics of the GE reward system but they didn't have the capability and cultural alignment to support it.

Compensation must be aligned with organizational culture. It's akin to putting your money where your mouth is. For example, if you preach the importance of being a team player and of achieving quality standards, but you rank order employees based only on their individual quantitative results, you can't expect the compensation to support these goals. For compensation to be effective, you need to identify what drives value in the organization and then relentlessly and consistently reward these outcomes.

Total Rewards—It's More Than Money

When managers criticize their organization's rewards programs, they usually focus on money. But people are motivated by more than money. In fact, some people say that money is not a motivator for them at all. So before pointing the finger at how unfairly money is allocated to employees, managers should consider how to use intangible rewards as well as monetary ones. For example, you can get a lot of mileage out of structuring jobs and career paths so that employees understand what they need to do to progress to the next level, as well as ensure that only individuals who demonstrate these capabilities are promoted. If you promote people because of tenure and then complain about the inability to reward your best people, you're missing an easy fix.

This book is about how to use rewards in their broadest context to achieve business success. Thus, rewards include both tangible monetary rewards and intangible (nonmonetary) rewards such as meaningful job designs, career development opportunities, work culture and climate, and work-life balance. So, for most of this book we talk about how managers can impact the total rewards programs, as opposed to the monetary compensation programs alone. Figure 1-1 illustrates this model of a total rewards program, which includes both tangible rewards, such as base salary, incentives, and benefits, and intangible rewards.

The Manager's Tool Kit

While we're concerned here about the impact a manager can have on an organization's rewards programs, managers have many other tools at their disposal to drive organizational success and achieve a positive return on their investment in people. The model in Figure 1-2 provides a

FIGURE 1-1. MODEL OF A TOTAL REWARDS PROGRAM

	Common Examples	Reward Elements	Definition
Intangible Internal value or motivation	• Work Culture & Climate • Leadership & Direction • Career/Growth Opportunities • Work/Life Balance • Job Enablement • Recognition	Intangibles (typically intrinsically valued)	TOTAL REWARD
Tangible Rewards to which an objective dollar value can be assigned	• Cars • Clubs • Physical Exams	Perquisites	TOTAL REMUNERATION
	• Retirement • Health & Welfare • Time Off with Pay • Statutory Programs • Income Replacement	Benefits	
	• Stock/Equity • Performance Shares	Long-term Incentives	TOTAL DIRECT COMPENSATION
	• Annual Incentive • Bonus/Spot Awards	Short-term Variable	TOTAL CASH COMPENSATION
	• Base Salary • Hourly Wage	Base Cash	

Source: Hay Group

FIGURE 1-2. SEVEN ORGANIZATION PEOPLE LEVERS

Source: Hay Group

useful way of thinking about the levers an organization has to translate business strategy to end results. They all relate to people. Managers who achieve the highest level of success are the ones who align these levers with one another. Managing people effectively is hard work, but it's the kind of work that rewards organizations who do it well.

A summary of each of these seven organization people levers follows.

1. *Leadership:* The leadership group knows its own goals, roles, and processes. There's a united and compelling vision that inspires the new organization. Individual leaders know how to "walk the talk" and create clear expectations for others.

2. *Values and Culture:* Culture is shaped by those activities, operations, and behaviors that the organization supports, encourages, and rewards. It's specific enough to lead to behavior changes. Managers take steps to create understanding and buy-in, and the "new employment contract" is understood and accepted.

3. *Work Processes and Business Systems:* People know how to sustain process improvements for new ways of working. Work processes flow across organizational boundaries to cross-pollinate and take hold in departments, work groups, or business units. Rewards and behaviors support and reinforce this. Information flows to where it's needed, when it's needed.

4. *Organization, Team, and Job Design:* Jobs are defined and designed; there's clarity about how roles are valued and measured. People know what success looks like and how it links to work culture and business strategy. Teams and individuals understand their roles and accountabilities. There are optimum layers and levels of management throughout the organization.

5. *Individual and Team Competencies:* Individual and team competencies (valued and desired behaviors) have been identified. The right people are being attracted and retained, and outstanding performers have been matched to pivotal roles.

6. *Management Processes and Systems:* The business strategy has been translated into specific performance measures. Scorecards are in place for key jobs. Performance planning, coaching, and review processes are linked to reward programs.

7. *Rewards and Recognition:* Reward systems and processes support business direction, work culture, business processes, and job design. There's a clear tie between rewards and performance measurement. Work is valued and rewarded according to its contribution to the organization. The organization recognizes results attained and how they were achieved. Individual and team contributions are valued and appropriately rewarded.

We spend quite a bit of time discussing the rewards and recognition area, but it's important to realize that rewards and recognition cannot be considered as separate and distinct from the other six people levers. A work unit's performance is optimized and human capital ROI is increased when the supporting people systems in these seven areas are aligned and reinforcing each other as opposed to working in isolation.

A lack of integration and alignment can lead to poor results for the manager and the organization. For example, if an organization has spent a fair amount of time, energy, and resources upgrading its performance management, rewards, and employee development systems, but hasn't aligned its senior leaders to these programs, these initiatives may be viewed as merely HR moves that don't connect to an important organizational goal.

The Structure of This Book

Chapters 2 through 5 of this book focus on macro, overarching rewards program matters. For instance, Chapter 2 addresses the question of how to think about and measure the ROI of rewards programs. Chapter 3 discusses the architecture of rewards programs and their links to business strategy and organization culture. Chapter 4 reviews how to connect performance measures to the rewards program, and Chapter 5 covers the concept of a total rewards program—both the tangible and the intangible elements.

Chapters 6 through 9 cover the core dimensions of compensation and benefits programs. Chapters 6 and 7 focus on determining the market value of work and base salary programs. Chapter 8 covers variable pay, and Chapter 9 discusses the hidden value of benefits.

Chapters 10 through 13 cover key programs that are linked to the compensation program and constitute many of the related levers of the reward program. Chapter 10 discusses performance management and how individuals can be managed and coached to achieve success—and then rewarded for it. Chapter 11 provides a discussion of career paths and the effective alignment of work to employee capabilities, as well as its importance in the total rewards package. Chapter 12 reviews practical ideas on what works (and what doesn't work) in communicating reward programs to employees. We wrap up with Chapter 13, on the significant impact that recognition plays in the manager's rewards portfolio.

We want to reinforce the idea that this is not a book about sophisticated compensation program design. Rather, it is a manager's guide to using rewards programs to achieve competitive advantage and organizational success, in both the short and long term. We believe that the ideas presented in this book, if incorporated into your management practice, will lead you to greater personal success. If practiced broadly, they will also bring you a healthier, more successful organization where reward programs are part of the solution, not the problem.

Ensuring an ROI on Your Rewards Programs

YOU MIGHT THINK that it's silly to ask whether organizations measure the ROI of their compensation programs. Most of us would assume they do. After all, compensation is one of the largest controllable expenditures an employer makes—sometimes up to 70 percent of its total costs. Yet fewer than 20 percent of organizations report using a formal ROI analysis for making compensation decisions.

Throughout this book we discuss reward strategies and actions that managers can take to significantly increase the return on the investment in their people. This chapter begins that process with a perspective on ROI—specifically, how to identify what to measure and how to measure it.

What? Me Measure?

Even though relatively few organizations actually measure their HR return on investment, most HR functions are generally satisfied with the effectiveness of their compensation programs. In a survey of professionals in the compensation management field, most felt that their budgeting and planning, as well as administration and control processes, are generally effective.[1]

A big question for line managers (as well as HR leadership) is, "How can people in an organization believe a program is effective if they aren't even measuring its ROI?"

If an organization's business strategy is its plan for allocating its resources to win in the marketplace, then a compensation strategy is a plan for allocating its compensation resources to help the business execute its strategy. Therefore, if you, as a manager in the organization, don't know the total value of your compensation programs vis-à-vis the appropriate markets, plus their effectiveness in delivering key messages and their alignment with desired business outcomes, how can you claim to be maximizing the return on your rewards investment?

Most organizations wouldn't purchase a $10,000 copier without calculating its ROI, but many will spend hundreds of millions of dollars on their compensation programs without considering an ROI analysis. In recent research conducted by Hay Group, WorldatWork, and Loyola University Chicago, we found that approximately 62 percent of employers in a general industry survey reported that they don't even attempt to measure the ROI of their compensation programs. Of the 38 percent that do, most do it informally by talking with managers and employees about their perceptions of the program's effectiveness. The balance of organizations that measure ROI (18 percent) use formal measures such as employee opinion surveys and comparisons of the investment in people and their productivity.[2]

We also found that America's Most Admired Companies (according to *Fortune* magazine/Hay Group research) are much more likely to measure ROI (formally and informally) than are other organizations. Also, those who perceive they have effective compensation management processes are more likely to measure ROI, whereas those who perceive they have ineffective compensation management processes are highly unlikely to measure compensation ROI. All of this suggests that actual measurement of ROI is a best practice (see Figure 2-1).

Why Organizations Don't Measure ROI

So why don't most organizations measure the ROI of their compensation programs? There are a number of possible answers. For some organizations, the compensation function may not be involved in the ROI activity; measuring ROI may be up to finance or operations. For others, measuring ROI may not be feasible; for example, if financial and HR

FIGURE 2-1. COMPARISON OF COMPANIES MONITORING THE ROI OF THEIR COMPENSATION PROGRAMS

	All	Most Admired Companies
We do this informally via discussions with management and employees.	20%	21%
We do this formally via comparing our investment in human capital to financial and productivity measures.	9%	21%
We do this formally via assessment of employee and management attitudinal data.	9%	18%
Not applicable. We do not attempt to assess ROI.	62%	36%

Source: Hay Group/Loyola University Chicago/WorldatWork Research on the Fiscal Management of Compensation Programs (2005)

measurement and reporting systems aren't in place, it's too difficult and time-consuming.

Part of the answer, however, can be found in the role and strategic orientation of the HR or compensation function within the organization. The compensation function usually has a shared or advisory role in measuring and monitoring the level of investment in compensation. This includes reporting and interpreting the compensation program's direct expenditures. But given the functional silo orientation of many HR departments ("functional silos" operate as isolated islands, often out of communication with other departments), investments in human capital are analyzed on a line-item basis—that is, the compensation staff focuses on direct compensation, the benefits group focuses on benefits costs, and the training and development staff focuses on employee training costs. This can mean that no one in HR actually takes on the accountability of the organization's total investment in human capital.

Moreover, compensation staff and HR have typically focused more on measuring and monitoring the investments in compensation programs than on their returns. A more detailed treatment on what is meant by "investments" and "returns" follows, but suffice it to say that compensation professionals who don't understand and measure the returns (or end results) aren't taken seriously by line managers.

Also, according to Dow Scott, professor of HR at Loyola University Chicago, "An organization may have a culture where compensation is viewed more as a sunk cost of doing business than as an investment that can or should provide a return. If this is the orientation of senior leadership, it might explain the high percentage of organizations that choose not to measure ROI."

What Should Be Measured? The Investments

When considering your organization's investment in a compensation program, you must think about *all* aspects of the total rewards package provided to employees. *Total rewards* go far beyond direct cash compensation. Figure 1-1 showed that there are other elements beyond the direct compensation package that determine why employees choose to work for one employer instead of another—and why they choose to remain with one employer year after year.

As discussed earlier, *intangible rewards* include all rewards other than tangible rewards. Intangibles are the reasons employees choose to work at a particular organization over another when both employers offer the same tangible rewards. Indeed, intangible rewards are critically important to the organization's ability to attract, retain, and motivate talent. Don't view them as incidental. Intangible rewards can be core to "employee branding" and make up the backbone of the employer's "value proposition" offered to current and future employees, especially if those employees are skeptical of the overall recruiting and retention strategy.

Although pay is often a factor in people's decisions to resign, it's seldom the only factor. Dissatisfaction with pay is typically not what leads employees to begin exploring alternatives, though the prospect of better compensation elsewhere may solidify their decision to leave once they have started their search. Nonetheless, retention strategies often mistakenly focus solely on compensation such as higher base salaries, retention bonuses, and more stock options. In contrast, many employees would welcome opportunities for personal development and growth. Aware that they're responsible for managing their own careers, they know that their futures depend on continuously improving their skills. If they don't expand their capabilities, they risk compromising their employability where they currently work—and elsewhere.

There are two more essentials for employees today: understanding the organization's strategic direction and having confidence in senior management. Being in charge of their own careers, employees want to know where their organizations are headed—not out of casual interest but to ensure that their skills will continue to be valued. With job security uncertain even in the best of circumstances, betting on a winner is all the more important. Figure 2-2 underscores these points by comparing the employee satisfaction levels of people planning to stay at their organizations for the next two years to those planning to leave their organizations in the next two years.

These findings aren't representative of only the U.S. marketplace. In a survey conducted in June 2001, Hay Group Europe research found that approximately one-third of all employees plan to quit their job within the next two years, with sales and information technology staff being the most mobile. The top five reasons cited for employees wanting to leave are (in order of importance):

1. Dissatisfaction with manager
2. Lack of career opportunities
3. Job not "stretching" enough
4. Personal reasons (spouse, partner moving on, maternity, etc.)
5. Compensation

Figure 2-3 also reinforces the importance of intangible rewards in retention.[3] So it should come as no surprise that many of the most effective programs used today to retain talent do not involve direct compensation. Figure 2-3 identifies the most effective types of programs in use

FIGURE 2-2. DIFFERENCES IN SATISFACTION LEVEL: EMPLOYEES PLANNING TO STAY VS. THOSE PLANNING TO LEAVE

	Total Percent Satisfied		
Satisfaction with:	Employees planning to stay for more than two years	Employees planning to leave in less than two years	Gap (%)
Use of my skills and abilities	83%	49%	34%
Ability of top management	74%	41%	33%
Company sense of direction	57%	27%	30%
Advancement opportunities	50%	22%	28%
Opportunity to learn new skills	66%	38%	28%
Coaching and counseling from supervisor	54%	26%	28%
Pay	51%	25%	26%
Training	54%	36%	18%

Source: Hay Group Insight Database

FIGURE 2-3. EFFECTIVENESS OF PROGRAMS TO RETAIN TALENT

Program	Effective/ Very Effective
Has identified key employees who are essential to the business	54%
Keeps key employees apprised of their future opportunities with the organization	42%
Monitors satisfaction of key employees concerning their pay and work situation	41%
Actively develops employees who may replace key employees	37%
Has a succession plan to fill positions or replace individuals critical to success	36%
Pays key employees substantially above the labor market	28%
Provides mentors for key employees	23%
Provides retention bonuses to key employees	14%
Provides loans that are forgiven after given periods of time for key employees	1%
Other	0%

Source: 2004 Hay Group/Loyola University Chicago Counter-Offer Research. Reprinted with permission, WorldatWork, © 2004.

by organizations to retain talent, per a 2004 Hay Group study on counteroffer practices. As shown, programs rated as most effective in retaining talent tend to focus on intangible rewards such as career development opportunities. Programs focused on direct tangible rewards, although important, are rated as less effective.

What Should Be Measured? The Returns

As we mentioned earlier, organizations that measure ROI tend to be split on doing it formally or informally. They're also split on whether to measure qualitative employee opinions or quantitative financial/productivity measures. Ultimately, your organization should measure what is most meaningful regarding its investment in people and its impact on stakeholders. Of organizations that measure compensation program ROI, most view top-line business operating results, employee retention, and controlled labor costs as the most important factors. Figure 2-4 shows the prevalence and perceived importance of various measures used to assess the ROI of compensation programs

If you measure only qualitative opinion or only financial return

FIGURE 2-4. PREVALENCE AND IMPORTANCE OF MEASURES USED TO ASSESS ROI

	Prevalence	Importance
Top-line business operating results—i.e., revenues	High	High
Employee retention	High	Med.
Controlled or lowered labor costs	Med.	High
Employee productivity metrics	Med.	Med.
Bottom-line business operating results—i.e., profits	Med.	Med.
Employee satisfaction survey measures	Mod.	Med.
Informal opinion gathering from senior leaders	Med.	Med.
Informal opinion gathering from employees	Low	Low
Ability to recruit employees	Low	Low

Source: 2005 Hay Group/WorldatWork/Loyola University Chicago Research on Fiscal Management of Compensation Practices. Reprinted with permission, WorldatWork, © 2005.

metrics, you probably won't get a good reading. For a well-rounded view of your program's effectiveness, measure both. We believe, and our research shows, that measuring top-line and bottom-line business results, productivity, and employee retention is as important as measuring survey results and opinions from senior leadership and employees.

Also, some assessment measures are appropriate for some specific compensation programs and inconclusive for others. For example, the effectiveness of a base salary program is typically assessed against employee retention criteria and employee satisfaction, while variable pay programs tend to be assessed against business operating results.

An Employee Perspective on ROI

Consider the notion of ROI from an employee's point of view. That is, as an employee, will you be better rewarded if you invest more of yourself in the organization? Hay Group Insight's rolling database of employee attitudes found that only about 40 percent of employees believed they would earn more compensation if they improved their performance. As a result, most employees are skeptical about the link between pay and performance, and therefore also about achieving an improved ROI as it relates to them.

There are several reasons for so much skepticism on the part of employees, as follows:

Limitations in Base Salary Increase Pools: For many organizations, there are significant limitations to merit-based salary increases. As we noted, many organizations try to reward performance solely through merit pay programs. But economic influences and internal equity corrections limit the merit pay's effectiveness as a pay-for-performance vehicle. Rather than being solely based on an employee's performance and pay relative to the market, merit increases are heavily influenced by an organization's overall salary budget. This, in turn, is influenced by industry conditions and general economic factors, such as the unemployment rate. In effect, employees expect a salary increase each year that is at least the size of the average salary increase budget. As a result, wage inflation consumes merit pay budgets.

Lack of Differentiation: Inadequate differentiation of performance is a major cause of skepticism. Organizations have a tough time meaningfully differentiating employees' performance. It's a cruel irony when most employees exceed expectations yet the organization's overall performance flounders. But there is an interesting parallel between managers and parents: Just as few parents would admit that their children are "below average," managers exhibit a similar tendency with their employees. While we would expect performance within a group to represent a normal distribution, the performance curve is often skewed to higher ratings because managers lack the will or the know-how to evaluate their employees' performance properly.

Former General Electric CEO Jack Welch says, "The A's (the top 20%) should be getting raises that are two-to-three times the size given to the B's. B's should get solid increases recognizing their contributions every year. C's (the bottom 10%) must get nothing."[4]

And mechanical differentiation isn't much better than poor differentiation. When the focus is on forms and ratings scales, managers put too much stress on the process and not enough on coaching and developing their people. The result is largely window dressing.

Even when organizations achieve differentiated performance, they still struggle to translate this into differentiated pay. Higher performers deserve the highest rewards, and organizations need the courage to not spread incentive pay like peanut butter—that is, evenly over the organization. This is essential, even when an incentive program receives adequate focus and funding. Similarly, they need the courage to pay lower performers lower incentive pay—if anything at all. Unfortunately, many managers would rather settle for mediocrity than make waves or encounter difficulties with low performers disappointed about their payouts. As a result, the message doesn't motivate and align employees in the effort for greater productivity.

Overlapping Objectives: Another factor that causes employee distrust for the pay-for-performance link is overlapping objectives. Many organizations confuse the objectives with the measures of their merit pay and incentive pay programs. As a result, organizations pay employees multiple times for achieving the same outcomes, thereby diluting the funds available to motivate and align efforts. The lack of clear objectives and measures also affects employees, who run the risk of misinterpreting what their employers expect of them.

What Can Managers Really Influence?

Which of the possible investments in compensation can line managers most effectively impact to enhance the return on a rewards investment? Most line managers can't do much to adjust benefits and perquisites. Usually, these rewards are tied to employment, tenure, or job level rather than to individual performance. However, line managers are often able to impact long-term incentive compensation. Payouts in these programs are usually linked to organization or group performance, but the programs themselves often allow for adjustments to reflect individual performances or contributions. Line managers are most able to alter the base and variable cash programs and the intangible rewards areas. And, remember, employees say the intangibles are among the most important benefits of working.

In his book *The ROI of Human Capital,* Jac Fitz-enz describes the results of extensive, long-term studies by the Saratoga Institute that looked at what employees valued in the workplace. He found that the principal driver of human performance and retention was the immediate supervisor or manager.[5] Cash compensation was the last item on Saratoga's list of seven employee expectations, which Fitz-enz describes as:

1. Receive job-related training.
2. Receive career-development support.
3. Have advancement opportunity.
4. Be treated as contributing adults.

5. Have personal knowledge and experience put to use.
6. Be kept informed about company matters and changes.
7. Be compensated fairly and equitably.

Considering the rewards elements that matter most to employees, and those that line managers can most effectively address, the question remains, "How can line managers use rewards to improve employee performance and contribution to the organization?" Making a clear and strong link between rewards and performance seems the most obvious way to increase the return-on-rewards investment. Let's look first at the return from increased performance and then work backward to the investments that will produce that increased performance.

How Does Improved Performance Increase ROI?

What's the value of improved employee performance? The metrics vary for individual jobs based on specific job content, but whatever the job, there's a clear increase in output for superior performers. In pioneering research by Hunter, Schmidt, and Judiesch as reported in their article "Individual Differences in Output Variability as a Function of Job Complexity," there are significant differences between average and superior performers. Moreover, the differences in performance increased for jobs of greater complexity. Lower-complexity jobs, such as lower-level support jobs, had an approximate 20 percent difference in performance output between average and superior performers. Higher-complexity jobs, such as management and professional jobs, approached 50 percent differences in output between average and superior performers. The most pronounced differences were in sales jobs, where there could be upward of a two-times difference in performance variation between average and superior performers.[6]

Productivity, quality, and other output measures generally are available so that the return side of the ROI equation can be assessed. And there are less direct return measures to use as well, including flexibility, reliability, continuity, innovation, and customer satisfaction. Although less direct, these latter measures are part of the total return on the rewards investment, typically part of balanced scorecard measures, and shouldn't be ignored.

Some of the investments to improve performance are also easy to identify and quantify. For example, the cost of developing and delivering training, and the pay for employees while attending training sessions (and for substitute workers, if needed), are direct investments. The return on an investment in training is also direct. But for training to have an ROI, employees must perform better after the training than they did before it; that is, productivity, quality, or other performance metrics must be higher. Some of the improvements may take some time to show up, but their presence is an indication of the ROI for the training.

Managerial training is also an investment in improved employee performance. As we discussed in Chapter 1, Hay Group research finds that the culture and climate of an organization—which are directly impacted by the immediate supervisor or manager—account for 30 percent of the discretionary effort of employees.[7] Investing in manager development produces direct returns in enhanced employee performance.

But what is the return on increased employee retention and reduced unwanted turnover? According to conventional wisdom, every 1 percent of unwanted turnover costs a company between 0.5 and 1 percent of total salary. So reducing unwanted turnover by even one percentage point makes significantly more funds available for other uses. In manufacturing companies, employee compensation typically represents 20 to 30 percent of revenues; in service organizations, it can reach up to 80 percent.[8] In fact, for individual managers, employee compensation may be the single largest controllable item in their budget!

For example, if employee compensation is 50 percent of a manager's budget and he reduces unwanted turnover by two percentage points, that manager's overall expenditures are reduced by up to 1 percent. This may not seem like much, but consider that:

- Every dollar of reduced expenses equals a dollar of increased profits; if a company's operating margin is 20 percent, it takes a $5 increase in revenues to produce an additional $1 of profits; if the operating margin is lower, it takes a higher increase in revenue.
- Making 1 percent more of a manager's budget available for discretionary spending enables the manager to give substantially higher salary increases to employees—especially if the higher increases were given only to the best performers.

Thus, if improving intangible rewards results in improved performance, the manager has the added result of more funds available for additional rewards, both intangible and tangible.

There is also an opportunity to improve performance and ROI by managing tangible rewards. Usually, base salary, annual incentives, and bonus/spot awards are linked directly to individual performance and contribution. Managers can use these measures to reward employees who provide more value to the organization.

Managers can use available merit increase funds to recognize and reinforce superior employee contributions—or they can miss this opportunity altogether by giving all employees the same increase. Figure 2-5 shows the typical relationship that organizations say they want to have between performance and pay. The diagonal line shows pay as matching performance. Pay at the top of the salary range goes with high levels of performance, and pay at the bottom of the range corresponds to low levels of performance. In theory, employees who are already paid along the diagonal line should receive salary increases that keep them on the line when ranges are increased or performance improves. Employees paid above the line should receive smaller increases or no increases at all, and those paid below the line should receive larger increases to move them to the line.

Let's now add some employees and look at the relationship of pay to performance for each of them, and how managers can effectively discuss performance, pay levels, and salary increases. In Figure 2-5:

- Employee 1 performs at entry level for the job and pay is low in the range.
- Employee 2 performs at target level and pay is in the middle of the range.

FIGURE 2-5. THE PERFORMANCE-PAY RELATIONSHIP

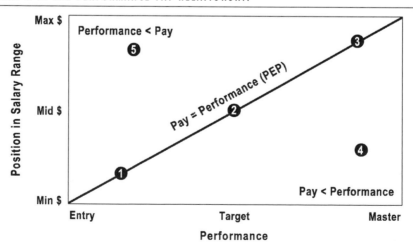

• Employee 3 performs at high level and pay is high in the range.

All three of these employees are paid at levels appropriate to their performance. Each of them should receive a salary increase (if the salary range moves up) that will keep them on the Pay = Performance line. Manager–employee conversations will be different despite the apparent similarity in their salary increases. For Employee 1, the conversation will likely emphasize the opportunity for larger salary increases as performance improves over time. For Employee 2, the conversation will balance discussion of the fit between target performance and target pay, with a discussion of what the employee can do to improve beyond the target performance and receive larger salary increases. And for Employee 3, the conversation will likely focus on the fact that current pay is high in the range (a pay premium compared to the range midpoint) to reward the employee's high level of performance; future pay increases will maintain that pay premium, but the range does have a maximum.

Employees 4 and 5 present very different situations. Employee 4, probably recently promoted or hired, has achieved a high level of performance that exceeds current pay. The conversation with this employee probably will focus on matching pay to sustained performance over time and the likelihood of larger-than-average salary increases if performance continues. At the same time, there's a question of how long Employee 4 will be patient if the manager says, "I would have given you more, but I couldn't because of the budget limits for salary increases." Managers need to find ways to reward employees whose performance far exceeds their pay, despite budget limitations. To paraphrase *60 Minutes*'s Andy Rooney, "Did you ever notice how there's never enough money for increases but we always find enough to hire replacements?"

There are two ways to look at the relationship between pay and performance for Employee 5. We can say the employee is overpaid, which makes everybody unhappy and is unlikely to lead to a productive solution. Or we can say that Employee 5 isn't currently performing up to pay level. With this view, the conversation between the manager and the employee will focus on ways the employee can contribute more. There may be something getting in the way of this employee's performing better. It could be a matter of training or of poor fit between person and job. If this approach helps the employee to perform better, both the employee and the organization are better off. If it doesn't work, we may indeed conclude that the employee is overpaid. Having tried performance improvement first, though, both the employee and the manager will understand the disconnect between current performance and pay, and a productive solution is more likely.

That's the way it works in theory—but not often in practice. In a survey of WorldatWork members representing more than 1,000 organizations, 68 percent reported that they give increases to 95 percent or more of their employees. And 68 percent of the respondents reported that their increases to top performers were less than or equal to 1.5 times their increases to middle performers.[9]

Let's look at two different approaches to planning for salary increases. For instance, Companies A and B have budgets of 4 percent and middle performers receive average increases that match the budget numbers. Company A practices what most of the organizations in the aforementioned study do: All employees receive increases, and top performers receive 1.5 times the average increase of middle performers. Company B, however, gives no increases to the 20 percent of employees who are farthest above the diagonal line in Figure 2-5. This enables Company B to give the 20 percent of employees farthest below the line increases that average two or more times the increase for middle performers. Company B sends the very clear message that performance drives pay!

Having looked at the ROI on reducing turnover, you might question whether Company B would, in fact, be encouraging turnover by giving no increases to some employees. Company B might be encouraging turnover, but it's encouraging turnover among those who are paid more than the value of their performance. The difference is between unwanted and desirable turnover.

Five Principles for a System of Differentiated Rewards

So what can managers do to improve their employee-rewards ROI? There are five principles that can help managers establish a system of differentiated rewards:

1. *Remember the* **management** *in performance management:* Managers spend significant time and energy trying to figure out the best system for rating and evaluating their employees. However, in the absence of a silver bullet, it's important to note the essential components

of effective performance management (which are covered in more detail in Chapter 10): clarity of goals, frequency of dialogue, and differentiated performance and rewards.

Effective management is the thread that binds these three factors together. We've found that managers comply with pretty much any ratings scales that are handed to them. But the most capable managers differentiate performance, and they subsequently get the kind of results that the performance management process was intended to produce.

2. *Money talks, so secure funding:* For the most part, good managers can clarify goals, create a "culture of dialogue," and differentiate performers. However, if funding isn't in place, they won't be able to differentiate rewards significantly enough to recognize outstanding performers. Organizations that establish funds to differentiate rewards are more likely to get a more significant return on their rewards investment. If an organization is truly committed to paying for performance, then a program of primarily promotion increases and base salary merit increases probably won't work.

Many organizations know this and find ways to go beyond the traditional merit budget as a way to differentiate performance. Research conducted by Hay Group, Loyola University Chicago, and Worldat-Work found that a significant majority of organizations offer special internal equity adjustments for high-potential or key contributors in addition to the traditional base salary increases and promotion increases.[10] Given the conventional constraints of merit pay, organizations may want to consider allocating a portion of their compensation investment to reward those who have truly achieved outstanding performance.

3. *Differentiate rewards, not just performance ratings:* Organizations need to ensure that performance ratings translate into differentiated rewards. Many organizations agonize over ensuring that managers comply with some sort of a distribution curve of performance ratings. But what value is this if the highest performer still receives only marginally more rewards, whether it's merit pay, incentive pay, or options? The ratings are merely a means to an end, and the end is higher rewards for the highest performance, not a perfect performance rating distribution curve.

Most managers and employees agree that rewards differentiations should be based on performance, leading to better execution and employee attitudes. At many organizations, managers want to give their stars bigger increases, but others see that as a zero sum game. Giving larger increases to certain employees means that other employees get much less, which requires managers making some difficult decisions. As we saw earlier, nearly half of the workers surveyed by Hay Group agreed that poor performance is tolerated in their organization. This implies that many managers choose the path of least resistance, giving employees roughly the same increase, rather than confront poor performers. This situation can be avoided by having dialogues throughout the year and by truly differentiating the rewards. Ongoing dialogue eliminates the element of surprise, which can lessen the impact of receiving a smaller increase. Managers weak in conducting performance-oriented discussions should seek coaching to improve their skills. This management "courage" can go a long way toward improving the climate of the organization.

Some top-performing organizations believe that well-differentiated rewards—even forced ranking of employees—leads to better execution. But unless managers are willing to do the "heavy lifting" of holding those often difficult dialogues with their employees, effective reward policies won't happen.

"It used to be that we were given the merit-increase money and we distributed it to our folks largely via formula based on where they were in the salary range," says Gloria Venski, a human resources coordinator at Northwestern Mutual, a large financial services organization. "Today things are different. Now managers have more latitude in terms of how we distribute the money. For instance, managers meet in a group and have good, open conversations about pay and how to best reward people. It's more effective to have a group of managers discussing pay and performance issues as a group than it is for me to have those discussions with them individually. We can better guide and direct employees when we can say, 'here's what you need to do to improve, and here's how I'll reward you for doing it.'" The result, according to Venski, is "more satisfied employees who see the link between pay and performance."

4. *Make clear performance-reward linkages:* Organizations must ensure that their employees understand what they're being asked to do to earn their rewards and that their individual goals are based on a realistic view of the future and are connected to what the organization needs to do to succeed. Furthermore, the magnitude of the rewards must be consistent with the value of the organization's goals.

Employees at all levels are more motivated to put discretionary efforts into their jobs when they feel connected to the bigger picture and they understand how their actions contribute. This is both a rewards issue and a communications issue. Goals and measures have little value if employees are unaware of how they're progressing toward meeting the goal until they have either met it or missed it. At its best, performance management becomes the way an organization achieves strategic change. When this happens, business drivers (such as customer service or quality improvement) go from being mere words to being active elements of each person's job.

5. *Communicate, communicate, communicate:* Anything concerning compensation is a sensitive internal issue. For good or for bad, it's the most prominent concrete measure of an employee's worth to an organization. Compensation decisions and compensation changes are always highly charged. While managers overwhelmingly acknowledge this, they struggle mightily to communicate the rewards program to employees. According to Hay Group research, most organizations (over 90 percent) have a compensation philosophy that identifies the key principles of the program. However, when it comes to communicating about that compensation, most organizations get a failing grade.[11] Most employees don't understand what the compensation program is designed to do (as seen in Figure 2-6).

At a more local level, some managers expect merit increases and incentive payments (or the lack of increases/payments) to take the place of an active performance-management process. However, merit pay increases aren't significant enough to manage poor performers out of the

FIGURE 2-6. PERCENTAGE OF EMPLOYEES WHO UNDERSTAND THEIR COMPANIES' COMPENSATION PHILOSOPHY

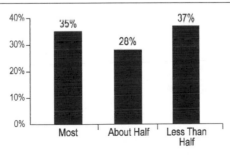

Source: 2003 Hay Group/Loyola University Chicago/WorldatWork Research; Linking Compensation Policies and Programs to Organization Effectiveness (2003). Reprinted with permission, WorldatWork, © 2003.

organization, encourage the potential of high performers, or motivate employees to acquire the skills and competencies to perform more effectively in their roles. Effective communications among the organization, the managers, and the employees are essential to effect change. The goal isn't necessarily a high volume of interaction; communications "by the pound" generally result in diminished returns. And make no mistake: No amount of communication—no matter how well focused or elegant—can rescue an ill-conceived compensation program. Yet many sound programs flounder when employees don't get the right information in the right way and at the right time.

Summary: A Checklist for Ensuring a Return on Investment in People

Whether or not managers actually calculate the ROIs in rewards, they can make effective decisions by thinking about the returns that will result from each rewards choice they do make. Managers can and should look at all of the rewards elements they can use as investment tools—and they should consider the likely returns whenever they make these investment decisions on employee rewards.

Managers who use all of the rewards elements available to them, and who clearly link rewards to performance, ensure that they get an appropriate ROI from their people. When determining an ROI for your organization's total rewards budget, keep the following in mind:

- Many of the most effective retention programs do not involve direct compensation—they involve intangible rewards.
- Line managers may have the most control over intangible pay elements such as work environment, development opportunities, and spot awards; what's more, employees and job candidates highly value these intangibles.
- As a manager in an organization, you cannot hope to maximize the ROI of your tangible and intangible reward programs if you don't know their total value, their effectiveness in delivering key messages, and their alignment with desired business outcomes.
- To get a well-rounded view of a program's effectiveness, measure *both* quantitative financial return metrics *and* qualitative opinion metrics.

- Establish clear performance-reward links and ensure that employees understand how their contributions connect to the bigger picture.
- Consider multiple ways of differentiating rewards, not just in the base salary increase program.
- Communicate, communicate, and communicate!

CHAPTER 3

The Link Between Rewards and Business Objectives

"IF YOU BUILD IT, THEY WILL COME." Thinking back to this famous line from the movie *Field of Dreams*, you may recall that the baseball field Ray Kinsella built in Iowa became a magnet for the old and the young, the living and the dead, with a love for the game. Building the field was Ray Kinsella's way of fulfilling his dream of watching the baseball greats in action. He built it; they came; and his dream came true.

We may be stretching the analogy a bit, but we think it's much the same for an organization. Its founders or leaders had visions: Build a company that will go where we want it to go and the customers will take us there. Accordingly, they set out to build the best organization they could. And if they built it correctly, their dreams should come true. But when you are building a company, an organizational chart with its various functions and roles is only a starting point. You must develop an appropriate business strategy and an operational plan. And you need a human resources strategy that aligns with and helps activate the organizational and operational plans.

As presented in Chapter 1, the seven levers model (Figure 1-2) suggests a variety of organizational components, management systems, and HR elements that need to relate to one another in order for the organization to move from strategy to execution. Within HR, as Figure 1-2 highlights, the rewards program is just one of many tools working in concert to help ensure the successful execution of the business strategy. "If you build it . . ." certainly applies to the rewards programs. Build it correctly, based on your organization's needs and in the right spirit, and it will help recruit, motivate, and retain the talent you need to accomplish your goals.

This chapter provides the background and perspective on how to examine the architecture of your rewards program and link it to your business strategy and work culture. In addition, we lay out the key components that constitute an effective rewards strategy.

A Blueprint for Your Rewards Program

Architects like to say that form follows function. In other words, how a building looks is a consequence of the reason it was built. All barns have big doors, for example, because without big doors a farmer couldn't move the livestock in and out and the barn couldn't fulfill its function of housing large animals. This principle also applies to how and why you build the organization as well as how and why you build your rewards program. In other words, the way your rewards program looks is a result of what you want from it. Your blueprint will outline the design requirements to make everything work.

What are the "must get it right" critical success factors and overriding strategy of the organization? How and why is the organization structured the way it is, and how is work organized and likely to flow? And based on those answers, what types of people are likely to have the "right stuff" for your organization? What behaviors do you expect of individuals or, where appropriate, of teams? Will your operations require close supervision, or will people have wide discretion for problem solving and decision making? What are you trying to accomplish? How will you accomplish it? And what should be in place to help ensure the success of your organization and its programs? What will your rewards blueprint look like and how will it help support your HR and organizational objectives?

To ensure that the rewards program is an effective tool for its managers, a company may take great pains that the program is right for the business, its strategy, its operational plans, and its culture. This means ensuring that the rewards program does the following:

- It reflects the company's values and philosophy about people management.

- It is aligned with the company's other management systems and processes to support strategic alignment and employee engagement, especially the organization structure, employee relations strategy, selection goals, and performance management and succession processes.
- It makes effective use of the unique opportunities and intangible rewards that the company can offer its employees.
- It is appropriately competitive compared with the general labor market in which the company competes.

We should be clear here that a rewards program won't change a poor business strategy into an effective one. But it can provide essential support to the organization's strategy by helping people deliver results more efficiently and cost effectively. And while any aspect of a rewards program may be pursued as an independent entity, and worked on at the same time as other organization efforts, it's likely that the planning of rewards will require an iterative approach: looking back to explore the rationale for previous decisions, and adjusting to changes and new situations as the company moves forward.

Organizational Culture as a Foundation for Rewards Design

By answering the questions posed earlier, an organization can begin to understand its particular work culture and lay the foundation for the rewards strategy that will be most effective. We will use them to illustrate how different rewards strategies may be applied in different work culture environments.

Figures 3-1 and 3-2 emphasize how organizational culture can help shape your rewards program offerings.

The Functional Work Culture

Industry in the post–World War II U.S. economy was dominated by highly structured and hierarchical companies where function was the key driver. Consider Detroit's automobile industry, or even the motion picture industry, where studios owned and managed all the resources for production. Respect for the chain of command, with clear lines of authority and accountability, was a key characteristic of these work en-

FIGURE 3-1. COMPENSATION-CULTURE MATRIX

Compensation Elements	Work Cultures			
	Functional	**Process**	**Time Based**	**Network**
Base Salary	Standard job grades Moderate variability in base pay	Broader salary bands Low-to-moderate variability in base pay	Very broad salary bands High variability in base pay	One salary band High variability in base pay
Individual Incentives	Limited use of incentives Paid annually	Wide use of incentives Interim payments	Moderate use of incentives Paid after program success	Low to moderate use of incentives Paid after phase of venture completion
Team-Based Pay	Recognition for exceptional success	Gainsharing Group/team incentives	Program profit sharing	Venture profit sharing
Other Compensation Elements	Pay for competencies Pay for skills	Pay for competencies Pay for skills	Pay for competencies	(Critical competency for individuals gives them entree to venture team and sharing in venture profit)

FIGURE 3-2. INCENTIVE-CULTURE MATRIX

Incentive Elements	Work Cultures			
	Functional	**Process**	**Time Based**	**Network**
% Eligible	20% of employees or less	80%–100% of employees	60%–80% of employees	20%–40% of employees
Target Payout to …	60%–80% of eligibles	80%–100% of eligibles	40%–60% of eligibles	20%–40% of eligibles
Target Payout Level	25%–40% of base	10%–25% of base	40%–60% of base	60% or more of base
Payout Timing	Annually	Quarterly	Ad hoc + post project completion	Post phase or venture completion

vironments. Proven methods and clear, well-established, and documented work processes guided the operations; and the underlying cultural bedrock provided secure employment and fair and consistent treatment of employees.

In this environment, the simple concept of a fair day's pay for a fair day's work characterized the rewards philosophy. Emphasis was on the individual as a work unit and base pay was the predominant element; salaries for jobholders in the same position varied only moderately.

The Process Work Culture

In the 1980s, rapid advances in information technology had a dramatic impact on the business landscape. One result was new ways of organizing work, which subsequently changed the relationships between functions in an organization and the organization's customers.

Culturally, the customer became king and maximizing customer service and satisfaction became key performance indicators. Customer satisfaction was measured, in part, by delivering reliably on commitments made to customers and gaining their confidence. Instead of rigid operating guidelines, employees were given the resources necessary to satisfy customers, to respond to their feedback, and to maintain their accounts. In this environment—with more moving parts, greater flexibility, the need to work in teams cross-functionally, and the ability to create new processes and solutions on the fly—there was a need for a new design principle for rewards that would have greater variability, link rewards with performance, widen opportunities for base pay differentiation, and make greater use of incentive compensation. Team-based assessments, performance metrics, and new rewards programs became much more prevalent.

To illustrate how one organization attempted to align its operating model and culture with its rewards program, consider the health insurance company that chose the commitment to improve customer service by making a heavy investment in a training program for customer service representatives. The reps learned better voice technique, interviewing skills that would better ferret out customer needs, and up-selling methods. Yet the company kept the same rewards system as before, basing its incentive pay on the number of calls completed.

When management got its first set of customer satisfaction surveys, the results were bleak: Customers widely agreed that, although it was courteous, the staff was remarkably unhelpful in resolving problems. Why? Because, as one rep put it, "If we spend more than four minutes on a call, we would never get our bonus." The new business strategy required that reps engage in longer, more in-depth conversations with customers. But as the rep pointed out, the dysfunctional rewards system punished those reps for doing so. The intent was right and the training was essential, but by not having an integrated and appropriately designed rewards program, the organization fell short of meeting its operational commitment to improved customer service.

The Time-Based Work Culture

As the world has continued to shrink, and as global commerce has become more the norm than the exception, quality and customer satisfaction, although still important, have given way to greater emphasis on reducing costs and finding new sources for the manufacture, sale, and movement of products with ever-quickening pace. This cultural dynamic is referred to as time based.

Flexible thinking and the ability to adapt quickly to change are critical skills now, as shifts in the business environment need to be anticipated well in advance. Identifying opportunities and increasing decision-making speed are critical, as the need to produce a product and make it available sooner and cheaper than the competition creates a high sense of urgency for companies that want to compete in this time-based environment. For example, General Electric often is seen as having the cultural attributes driven by its desire, on a global basis, to be number 1 or 2 in each of its lines of business. When Chrysler took on the Neon project—producing the first true economy car made in Detroit—it assembled a "best of the best" project team whose work processes were characteristic of the time-based culture.

In the time-based culture, base pay is often geared to the capability of high-performance individuals and the anticipation of their success. That's why it's common to see large variations in the salary levels between high performers and other employees. However, when it comes to variable pay, there may be some emphasis on individual performance but greater degrees of opportunity are geared to after-the-fact assessments and the success of the mission for those involved.

The Network Culture

Now, let's fast-forward to the age of the Internet: Just as technology created new internal working relationships more than 25 years ago, the Internet and other electronic communications tools have opened up opportunities for people from almost anywhere to work together any-time—what has been termed the network culture. As illustrated in one particular TV commercial, this global networking allows a small auto parts distributor in Texas to do business with a large manufacturing company in Asia. And it enables a one-man professional services operation to compete realistically with larger organizations doing the same work.

The idea of outsourcing is characteristic of this network culture, as access to resources is broadened to a global extent. Not unlike the time-based culture, the companies with the network culture can move quickly and capitalize on creativity and innovation. Speed and the ability to create new ventures and new lines of business, and to build multiple strategic alliances simultaneously have led to pioneering new ways of working and doing business. And there's no turning back.

Rewards today are a negotiable piece of the employment puzzle, based on supply and demand, the unique capabilities of individuals, and what the market will bear. While we characterized the 1940s motion picture industry as a functional culture, today that industry reflects a network culture where independent producers, directors, writers, actors, and other professionals come together at various points in time, on various projects, and in different alliances. Independence is acknowledged and respected. Risk is rewarded, and compensation varies significantly on all fronts. The spoils of the venture are shared by all participants.

To illustrate how the work culture impacts a company's rewards program, consider what Al Kluz, director of compensation and benefits at Northwestern Mutual, has to say about its environment and program:

"We have a fairly egalitarian work culture; therefore we do not have many special or one-off compensation programs. We have a core incentive program, and everyone participates. Going forward, it is a challenge for us because we are competing in an increasingly specialized marketplace and our managers are feeling pressure in certain pockets of the organization. It's forcing us to change. We're starting to develop specialized pay programs for certain hot jobs.

"But that can be a challenge. People will see different treatment for one position that a co-worker might be in and say, 'But what about my job?' The pay programs can be very different between insurance organizations and brokerage organizations, for example. While we have some specialized pay programs for certain jobs, this is uncomfortable for many of our managers. Some fear that some of our best people will be attracted out of some parts of the organization into other parts of the Northwestern Mutual organization."

One Size Never Fits All

So what is a manager to do about rewards? A manager in today's network culture business world must be aware of the organization's culture and its HR and operating needs in order to develop a fair and successful rewards program strategy. Recognize, however, that one organization's best practice may be another's poison. Many organizations have tried and failed at broadbanding, forced performance distributions, or competency-based pay because it was the "program of the day." Just because something works well elsewhere doesn't mean it will work well for your organization. Although the design of these programs may be sound, more often than not it's the organization's culture and management's alignment around its business processes that are the "glue" in any successful implementation.

Although your organization is likely to have a dominant cultural style, it's unlikely that style holds up in all areas of the business or, at least, that it holds up to the same degree. At best, cultural models are caricatures, highlighting prominent features of a work environment. Organizations are dynamic, so your approach to a rewards strategy must be also.

The following case study illustrates the need to tie compensation programs to the specific work culture.

A Case Study: Arbella Insurance

Arbella used to be a traditional, Boston-based property/casualty insurer with about $660 million in annual revenues. However, in the late 1990s, new competition from the e-commerce and banking sectors threatened the company's status quo.

The workforce was entrenched in a culture of entitlement. Each of the company's approximately 1,100 employees earned a fairly automatic 4 percent annual merit increase. It was believed that high achievers weren't adequately rewarded and low achievers weren't discouraged. Most employees resisted change and innovation. Management described the workforce as "sleepwalking, day in and day out." Yet, regular salary increases were the largest annual expense. And by rewarding sleepwalkers, Arbella wasted about 1 percent of its merit pay budget—$600,000 to $700,000 per year—just to maintain the status quo.

Arbella needed to restructure its pay program to distinguish itself in the marketplace as a company that rewards excellence, not one that doles out entitlements. Management wanted employees to cut costs, embrace new methods and technologies, and eliminate bureaucracy. But Arbella couldn't afford to pay bonuses to its top performers. The new program had to reward the best employees, but not cost more money. The new program would need to support Arbella's objectives, which included:

- Maximizing return on compensation investment
- Focusing on individual performance, encouraging employees to think outside the box
- Supporting cross-functional teamwork and synergy across departments
- Investing in manager development so line managers would have the skills and knowledge to make the right pay decisions

Arbella wanted the new salary program to drive change, but management could not articulate what changes it wanted. Knowing that a successful salary program must be tied to its work culture, Arbella used a targeted culture modeling process—an assessment tool also known as a C-Sort—to help it identify the necessary changes. Using the C-Sort tool, Arbella surveyed its top management on 56 key attributes that defined its culture. Respondents ranked each attribute by level of priority in the current and desired cultures. Sample attributes included:

- Encouraging teamwork
- Supporting the boss's decisions
- Rewarding superior performance

- Pushing decision making to lower levels
- Maximizing customer satisfaction

In spite of some initial skepticism about the culture-assessment process, the C-Sort had a big impact. It showed that Arbella recognized the need for a performance-based culture. On the other hand, the suggestion that a more results-oriented Arbella would appear less loyal to its employees was an emotional sore spot for the "old school" leadership.

The executives were fully engaged in discussions about where to take the organization. The team eventually agreed that average performance would not result in dismissal, but above-average performance would be rewarded much more than it had been previously. That settled the loyalty issue. Finally, everyone bought into changing the entitlement-based culture to a performance-based one. "This was the toughest thing we had to do," according to one executive, "but it was the right thing to do."

Next, the management team tackled the challenge of tying the desired culture changes to a new salary program. Prior to the change, the base salary program resulted in virtually everyone's receiving a 4 percent annual increase. In the new cultural context, average-performing employees would receive 3 percent (still within acceptable industry norms); above-average employees would receive 4 percent or more; and top achievers would receive an average of 7 percent. Based on performance instead of entitlement, the new program would cost no more than the old one.

Arbella knew that it needed to talk to lower-level managers about the importance of change. These managers learned to identify and reward their best people. And they learned how to explain to disgruntled employees why some would receive smaller raises than in previous years. That conversation was difficult, but necessary. The workforce heard this message: "Things are changing. If you step up and embrace the changes, you will be rewarded." Personal underwriters who got more involved in commercial underwriting were rewarded for their initiative. Clerks who learned new claims-processing methods instead of asking, "What's wrong with the old way of doing things?" were rewarded for facilitating change. Marketing personnel who were proactive with agents instead of merely functioning as service providers were recognized for changing the culture.

Arbella awarded the top 25 percent of its employees a 7 percent or greater merit increase without spending any more on payroll. Attrition remained low. No one left the company because of the new salary program. Today, Arbella's work culture emphasizes performance much more than job security, loyalty, or consistency. Management sees the workforce as more adaptable, able to use limited resources more effectively, and interested in improving operations. Arbella's people are more committed to the company's long-term success than ever before. In the context of reward, all Arbella previously got for its merit-pay ROI was the maintenance of the status quo. Now, Arbella's merit-pay ROI includes recognizing its best performers, retaining its top contributors, building teamwork, and providing a real incentive for improving performance.[1]

The Total Rewards Strategy

To set the right framework for meeting company objectives and to align with the predominant culture of the organization, management typically establishes a total rewards strategy that, not unlike an architectural blueprint, articulates how the company will use the various tangible and intangible rewards to provide a compelling total package for current and future employees. It expresses the company's value proposition to its workforce.

A Hay Group client, Fidelity Investments, based in Boston, reinforces its strategic objectives and rewards outstanding performance by distinguishing and leveraging many of the traditional compensation elements. For example, the company determines merit increases (which reflect overall performance as measured against job standards and development in a role) separately from incentive payouts (which reward performance as measured by established annual goals). The company further reinforces this separation by initiating merit increases in July and paying out incentives in December. This helps Fidelity ensure that it doesn't pay for the same thing twice.

Thus, a total rewards strategy should spell out the basic role and emphasis of each element of the cash compensation and benefits plan, and discuss how they work together to provide competitive and fair rewards opportunities that help meet the company's talent needs. This will require defining (1) the external labor markets where the company competes for talent; (2) how high, compared to the market, the company wants to pay people who can meet its talent requirements; and (3) the mix of reward types—that is, the portion of total rewards consisting of performance-linked variable pay plans like incentives and stock and the portion consisting of relatively stable and secure "fixed" programs like base pay and benefits.

Likewise, the total rewards strategy should also:

- Communicate the overall philosophy of how organizational, team, and individual performance are linked with the rewards program.
- Address how the rewards program supports the company's culture and management processes.
- Describe how the rewards program aligns with job design, selection and recruiting, performance management, development and succession, and employee relations.
- Describe how the rewards offered to employees relate to the company's employee-branding strategy to attract, retain, and motivate the people the company has targeted.

Ideally, the reward-branding link reflects the company's best thinking about the tangible and intangible rewards it can offer, and how these offerings will be valued by current and future employees. Figure 3-3 offers 10 examples of intangible rewards that fit a total rewards strategy.

From Strategy to Structure

The tangible rewards structure is a visible tool for implementing a total rewards strategy. The structure or schedule specifies the link between reward opportunities and the jobs, and it establishes the process for ongoing rewards administration. The rewards structure specifies the targeted rewards dollars for each job in the organization, typically the salary range midpoint or market reference point, the target incentive opportunities, the equity grant guidelines, and the benefits provisions. It also defines the range of opportunities (minimums and maximums) within which the company will pay jobholders.

The dollar values given in the rewards structure reflect the internal and external values of the jobs, defined in the guidelines set by the rewards strategy. They are a picture of the company's expected employee contributions and talent requirements, and they help ensure that managers' pay decisions align with the organization's plans and business strategy.

FIGURE 3-3. TEN EXAMPLES OF INTANGIBLE REWARDS THAT IMPACT A TOTAL REWARDS STRATEGY

---

1. Moral/Political/Social Affiliation: "We're doing something important."

2. Ego benefit, such as an opportunity to perform a glamorous role that others admire or be associated with a powerful image, industry leader, or celebrity.

3. Opportunity to get rich if everything goes right.

4. Excitement: "We are cutting-edge/fast-paced—we're not your father's company."

5. Career growth opportunities: "Come to our company and we'll provide you with a more responsible—and better-paying—position."

6. Training opportunities: "Work with us for three years and you'll become highly marketable."

7. Professional development opportunities—e.g., opportunity to work in a learning environment with leading technology and/or world-class colleagues.

8. Sound management/sane work-life balance: "We're a well-run company and know what we're doing, not a screwed-up outfit that will drive you crazy. You can have a life with us!"

9. Stable employment/income at a substantial growing concern.

10. Lifestyle benefits—e.g., desirable location.

Now, let's consider the definitions of key terms regarding the rewards structure:

• The *internal value* for a job is the dollar value of a position based on its responsibilities and requirements as compared to those of other jobs in the company. It's typically represented by a grade or band assignment. The internal value is driven by the organization's structure and how the company has allocated accountability. It also reflects the talent and know-how that the company deems appropriate given the expected contribution of people in that position.

• The *external value* is the dollar value associated with a job given the organization's rewards strategy. This value is the amount that the company is willing to pay based on competing offers in similar functions with comparable responsibilities and requirements.

At most companies, the rewards structure has corresponding administration procedures. These include base pay guidelines, incentive compensation eligibility rules and funding guidelines, promotional increases policies, administrative governance accountabilities, and related measures and procedures. Having clear and consistent policies and procedures helps ensure that rewards processes run as smoothly as possible, and are in alignment with other ongoing management processes.

Summary: A Checklist for Designing a Rewards Program

The ultimate success of a total rewards program is the degree to which it can attract, retain, and motivate employees. Said another way, the best rewards programs do the best job at rewarding the right people the right amounts for doing the right things. While a total rewards program certainly helps create the environment in which an organization can be successful, it's up to individual managers to use the program to get results. Leaders committed to the organization's success create a rewarding and engaging work experience for their people. This is the most important determinant of whether employees stay and whether they make a maximum effort to achieve company success.

To take full advantage of your organization's rewards structure, as a manager you need to:

- Know the business of your business. How does work get done and how does the company create economic value?
- Know who the high performers are and why. What is it that they do and how does that make a difference?
- Recognize your company's predominant culture and understand its attributes. How can you use it to achieve greater results?
- Consider what reward elements work best, in what combination, with what degree of emphasis, and how best delivered. What is most likely to effectively attract, retain, and motivate your staff?

Performance Measures That Motivate

PERFORMANCE GOALS AND MEASURES have a significant impact on the way people work. If the manager sets the right goals, those goals provide direction for employees about what's important for the organization; in essence, people know what's expected of them and they're motivated to achieve those desired outcomes. On the other hand, if the manager fails to set goals, there will be confusion, a lack of motivation, and dysfunctional behavior.

The performance puzzle has two primary pieces. The first is the *right measures* and the second is the *appropriate targets* (or standards of performance). Essentially, the manager says to the employees: "Here's what we believe is important to accomplish and the target you should aim for." Both pieces of the puzzle need to be in place to ensure the organization gets the results it needs.

When employees are doing the right things to the best of their abilities, customers are likely to be satisfied, resulting in more profitable business for the organization and the increased likelihood of long-lasting, well-paid jobs for employees. This is the premise behind models such as the "balanced scorecard," which suggests that value is created by employees working effectively to produce products and offer services that meet customer needs, and that added value generates profitable growth for the company.

This chapter explains how to set the goals for your employees to meet and how to monitor their progress, recognize their achievements, and reward their performance. We believe managers can establish relevant performance measures that, if accepted by employees, lead to higher individual (and organizational) performance. It's a win-win-win situation where employees, customers, and employers all benefit.

Setting the Goals

We offer nine propositions that demonstrate that the ability to set effective goals is a critical skill for managers. Goals should:

1. *Create focus:* People's performance is a reflection of the goals they set or that others set for them. Goals affect performance by directing the employees' attention and actions, mobilizing and prolonging the work effort, and motivating them to develop reasonable strategies to attain the goals.

2. *Be reasonable:* General acceptance that the goals are reasonable, attainable, and appropriate for the job is necessary for those goals to have a positive impact on performance.

3. *Be measurable:* Goals are only effective if their achievement can be measured. Measures are often quantitative (for example, financial goals), but they can also be qualitative (for example, achievement of project milestones).

4. *Be achievable:* Individuals must have (or believe that they have) the ability and the available resources to deliver high performance and achieve the goals.

5. *Offer challenges:* Higher goals yield higher performance. By setting the goals so that employees have to "stretch" a little to meet them, you'll get better performance than simply by asking them to "do their best." But only up to a point—see numbers 2 and 4 above.

6. *Provide feedback:* Employees need regular and timely feedback to keep on track and so you can get the most of your goal setting.

7. *Include tangible rewards:* Offering money and other concrete rewards will increase commitment to and reinforce the importance of the goal.

8. *Require participation:* Employee participation in the goal-setting process can encourage acceptance of the goals.

9. *Be personality neutral:* The positive impact of goal setting applies to all types of people. If the goal is appropriate, and the employee wants to succeed, then the personality of the individual has little impact on the result.

These propositions are valid regardless of the rewards program, whether base salary progression, short-term incentive, long-term incentive, or recognition. What matters is that employees know what the goals are, how they will be measured, and what the rewards are when the goals are met.[1]

Thus, in order for people to be successful in meeting their goals, three components must be in place:

1. Clarity—people need to know what to do, what is expected of them.
2. Capability—people need to know how to do what is expected of them and have the tools to get the job done.
3. Commitment—people must accept that the job needs to be done; they should feel engaged in the effort and understand that they'll be compensated for their efforts.

In summary, goals define what is expected of employees. They clarify and prioritize what's important. They identify the capabilities needed to do the job. If a designer, for example, isn't up to speed on the latest graphics software, production could be slower than it needs to be. In this way, setting goals can coincide with employee development.

Commitment to the goals can be easier to get if the employees are involved in setting the goals. Indeed, defining the goals facilitates employee commitment. But regardless of whether employees participate in setting the goals, they should always be involved in discussions of why the goals are important and why meeting the deadlines is critical. This information helps employees see how they can contribute individually to the organization's success.

Finally, goals serve as a template for providing feedback. One of the most common failings among those managing performance is to select one set of measures for the compensation program and another set for feedback. At the very least, this is confusing and frustrating for employees.

Choosing the Right Incentive Measures

As a manager, you should choose measures of work that individual employees have the ability to control and that contribute to the organization's overall success. This is termed "alignment"—that is, employees' individual and departmental goals are in accord with the goals of the organization. If you don't have alignment of goals, you've got a problem. You'll find that employee commitment to your measurement system is greatest when individual goals are aligned with the needs of the organization. Likewise, employees will commit to incentive measures if they believe them to be important and they feel they have reasonable control over achieving them.

It's All About Alignment

Figure 4-1 illustrates the concept of alignment via what we refer to as the Alignment Matrix. This simple framework displays the typical employee reactions to goals, based on how well the goals demonstrate the two attributes of impact on the organization and individual control. As shown, it's not enough for one of the attributes to be in place. For example, if measures are linked to the organization's performance, but employees feel that it's beyond their control to "measure up," the natural reaction will be, "But what can I do about this?" This often happens

FIGURE 4-1. PERFORMANCE MEASUREMENT MATRIX

		Individual Control	
		Low	**High**
Impact on Organization	**High**	**ORGANIZATION:** Good organization measure, but no individual impact *"Why me?"*	**ALIGNMENT:** Meets organizational and individual needs *"Makes sense!"*
	Low	**NOT APPLICABLE:** Neither organization nor individual benefits *"Why bother?"*	**INDIVIDUAL:** Good individual measure, but how does the organization benefit? *"Is this right?"*

when high-level business enterprise measures are used. High-level measures, such as company profit, may be appropriate for creating a sense of organizational belonging, but they aren't likely to motivate individual employees, since those employees' "line of sight" is often limited to their division or department.

In a 1,000-person organization, typically a midlevel employee's efforts won't have a significant impact on corporate profits. So, even if employees accept that meeting a goal is important, they won't see how their efforts will have a significant impact. In some cases (research and development, for example), there's an inverse relationship between departmental and corporate profitability objectives. For example, money spent on developing new products reduces current profits. Therefore, when enterprise measurements are used, it's important to apply a balanced approach so that there are unit and employee measures that they can relate to.

So does this mean that corporate profit-sharing plans are not appropriate? No. Profit-sharing plans can help employees understand that variable compensation, not entitlement, is rooted in the organization's profitability. According to Starbuck's Chairman and CEO Howard Schultz:

> We believed very early on that people's interaction with the Starbuck's experience was going to determine the success of the brand. The culture and values of how we related to our customers, which is reflected in how the company relates to our employees, would determine our success. And we thought the best way to have those kinds of universal values was to build around company-owned stores and then to provide stock options to every employee, to give them a financial and psychological stake in the company. . . . As a result, Starbucks has the lowest employee turnover of any food and beverage company.[2]

John Chambers, CEO of Cisco Systems, agrees: "There's not been a single successful company in the history of high-tech in the last two decades that has done that [been successful] without broad-based stock option plans. When I originally heard about that in school, I would have called it socialism, when in fact it is the ultimate form of capitalism. It is a very effective way to align interests."[3]

But Money Is a Factor, Too

Employees may have direct control over certain local measures, but since they can't see how achieving those measures would benefit the organization, they may be hesitant to make the extra effort—and, more important, the organization will be wasting money. This wasteful situation often arises when measures are chosen simply because they're easy to identify.

For example, sometimes measures relate more to a prior organizational value than to a current one. Other times they may seem intuitively appropriate, but they produce unintended consequences. One example of this situation is a steel company that paid its employees based on production volume. The company found it achieved high volume—but at the expense of quality. As a result, the incentive program was linked to the number of rejects in the production process: the fewer rejects, the bigger the reward. But since employees had control over what was deemed a reject, they had the incentive to let marginal products pass. After numerous Total Quality and reengineering initiatives, the incentive measure became "the number of quality pieces produced," not "the number of rejected pieces." This way, quality was built into the system and the rejection rate was no longer relevant.

Thus, the right incentive measures depend on the type of reward vehicle (tangible, intangible, short-term, long-term), the type of business (business model and culture), and the type of job. Each of these factors is worth exploring individually, but real success comes from achieving the right balance of all three.

The Architecture of Your Measurement System

The system of performance measures that most appropriately applies to a particular situation will depend on the following key factors: (1) the organization's culture, (2) the rewards vehicles, and (3) the overall business strategy.

Living Your Values

A business organization is founded on an understanding of the company's mission and values—the drivers of its culture. Once these concepts are understood and acknowledged, the proper HR programs for the company—including the best ways to measure and motivate employee performance—are those that enhance and support those drivers. Managers then consider the rewards vehicles that are possible (for example, base-salary increases, incentive awards, recognition awards) and think about the measures that might work best within the culture. They then turn their attention to finding the right balance of top-down (business-plan driven) and bottom-up (job-accountability driven) measures.

The culture of an organization is defined in part by its business model but also by its values—strongly held beliefs or principles held by the company on how it conducts its affairs. Some organizations view living up to their values as the stakes for their employees. That is, they don't use values as measures of work effort but, rather, as rules for conduct or performance. For example, "Either you demonstrate the right values or you're out of here!" Other organizations measure the *extent* to which employees model the company's values. This may be an evaluation of how well a person's behavior embodies all the values.

Assessing values is a complex and confusing assignment. For example, integrity might be considered a value, but how do you measure it and how do you set targets for showing integrity? Values assessment may be more about how people behave than about what they accomplish. Some managers call this the "how" of job performance as opposed to the "what." But the "how" is hard to define, let alone measure. And such assessments may not be much help in providing feedback to employees unless examples are backed by clear standards of behavior. Indeed, measuring a value such as integrity requires some sort of behavioral rating scale so that assessments can be based on demonstrable, observable behaviors and can be supported by instances when such behaviors were used or not used. We believe that assessing values is important for both individual development and determining promotability, but it is not important for determining incentive compensation.

Having a Rewards Philosophy

Earlier, we argued that there are benefits to setting appropriate performance goals regardless of the type of rewards offered. However, different types of rewards serve different purposes and produce different results. Managers need to have a clear idea of what they are getting for the base salaries, incentives, benefits, perquisites, and recognition they offer employees.

Figure 4-2 illustrates the purposes of various types of rewards. Because the purpose of each reward is different, managers need to understand their applications. Remember, benefits are compensation: They require monetary investment and provide value to employees. However, they are not programs that typically align with business performance objectives (except retirement benefits, which may contain profit sharing). As a result, we do not deal with employee benefits programs in this section. Chapter 9 discusses how managers can unlock the hidden value of employee benefit programs.

Base Salary: Base salary is the rewards vehicle that recognizes an employee's present value and may also reflect the individual's potential and future worth to the organization. Consider the situation when you hire a new employee and have to settle on a starting salary. There are four key factors: the value the person will be adding to the team (special skills and experiences), how much the person is currently earning (his or her value to someone else), the earnings of other employees doing similar work (internal equity), and what you can afford. Essentially, the new employee is an investment, and you need to determine a fair price for this investment, given the likely returns and the price you're paying for similar investments.

As employees acquire better skills, greater competence, and more experience, their value grows. Of course, there are other factors affecting employees' value: how they're rewarded, for one thing, and whether

FIGURE 4-2. SPECTRUM OF REWARDS AND THEIR PURPOSE

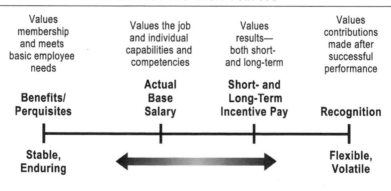

people with those skills and competencies are in short supply, for another.

Essentially, there are two ways to determine increases in base salary once the employee is on the job: ability to grow in the job and demonstrated job performance. Growing ability refers to an employee's acquiring new skills, greater competencies, and more experience—and demonstrating the ability to apply that knowledge on the job.

Past performance is a reliable predictor of future performance—most of the time. We recommend increasing base salary to reflect sustained levels of on-the-job performance. But to do this, assess job performance on the basis of ongoing accountability rather than short-term projects and brief objectives. For example, when you look at the employee's output for a job, consider each of the role's key accountabilities—usually specified in the job description—and assess whether the person met, exceeded, or fell short of expectations. The overall rating is an aggregate of accountabilities. Remember that when managing employee performance, it's important to consider both results and capabilities.

Incentive Compensation: Short- and long-term incentives provide employees with significant motivational focus and also offer a way to measure their efforts. Incentives typically are focused on organizational, team, and individual objectives.

It's important to ensure the right mix of incentives as well as the degree to which the incentives are either organization based (tied to the company's bottom line, for example) or more narrowly focused, such as on the current jobholder (meeting individual deadlines in a quality manner).

When developing an incentive plan, it's important to balance the objectives. There's a tendency to focus on financial performance, but balance includes criteria that occur earlier in the value chain, such as employee learning and growth and operational effectiveness. Our research with *Fortune* magazine's Most Admired Companies shows that these organizations balance their performance incentives. They include more customer, operational, and employee learning and growth measures than do the peer group, which focus on financial measures alone. In addition, these Most Admired organizations balance the time frames for their incentives; that is, their incentives address both short-term and long-term goals, whereas the peer group is more focused on short-term measures. Additional discussion of variable incentive pay is provided in Chapter 8.

Recognition: Recognition and nonmonetary rewards can be very effective motivators and can help drive business performance. Encouraging employees to put their discretionary effort into their work and to deliver superior performance with the chance to make a difference and be recognized is a very powerful management tool that is often not utilized enough.

Recognition programs can also reinforce desired behaviors and work cultures that can enhance the employer's brand and promote the organization as an employer of choice. See Chapter 13 for an additional discussion on recognition programs.

Linking Performance with Strategy

As mentioned at the beginning of this section, for performance incentives to be effective, they need to be aligned with the business strategy and the culture of the organization. That is, properly established performance objectives need to address both culture and strategy. Strategy addresses the "what" of performance and culture addresses the "how." However, culture can help establish the "what." For example, in a process culture, the "what" of performance may address the need for superior customer service and satisfaction. The "how" may relate to the need for cross-functional teamwork.

Figure 4-3 shows the typical types of performance measures for an organization.

There are different types of performance measures that an organization can utilize. Some of these measures, such as human capital or research, are leading indicators of performance, in that strong performance in these measures should impact performance in the future. Economic measures, such as profit or revenue growth, are trailing measures in that they reflect past performance. As described in the balanced scorecard model, positive performance in leading indicators such as investment measures and improvement measures positively impact the trailing indicators such as customer and economic measures.

All of the categories are important, however not all can easily be quantified to serve as measures. Leading performance indicators do not have an immediate impact on financial performance, but they're impor-

FIGURE 4-3. TYPICAL PERFORMANCE MEASURES

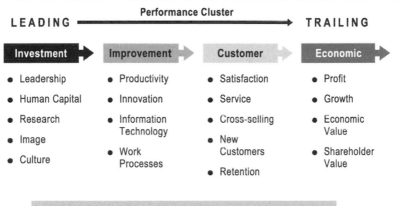

Paying for performance requires measuring the right things and paying for achieving them. "What gets measured gets managed."

tant if value is to be maintained. Profits don't just happen! As Lou Gerstner, former CEO of IBM says, "People don't do what you expect but what you inspect."[4]

As was described in Chapter 3, work culture plays an important role in the design of reward systems. It also has an impact on the types of performance measures that an organization will focus on. For example, companies with a time-based work culture that emphasizes the quick commercialization of new products and services may adopt a customer measure of increasing market share relative to competition. An organization with a process-based work culture may likely focus on maximizing customer satisfaction.

Figure 4-4 shows how to align an organization's culture with its performance metrics.

Top Down or Bottom Up?

As mentioned earlier in this chapter business strategy is a key top-down driver for performance measures. To choose measures that will have a high impact on organizational success, start with the business strategy as defined in the most recent business plan. At any point in time, an organization will be working toward a set of strategic objectives, so this is a great place to start. If the strategic objectives define the steps the organization should take, any employee contribution to those initiatives will likely have traction. Even the janitor, with accountability for ensur-

FIGURE 4-4. PERFORMANCE MEASUREMENT RELATIVE TO WORK CULTURE

		Work Culture			
		Functional	**Process**	**Time Based**	**Network**
Performance Measurements	**Key Measurements**	Functional Measures	Work Team Measures	Project Measures	Alliance Measures
	Investment	Career Progression	Culture Measures	Innovation Measures	Ad Hoc
	Improvement	Functional Excellence	Operational Measures	Operational Measures	Ad Hoc
	Customer	Sales vs. Budget	Customer Satisfaction	Market Share	Ad Hoc
	Economic	Profitable Growth	Sustainability of Value	Beat the Competition	Adhere to the Contract

ing that washrooms for workers are kept clean and well stocked with soap, towels, and toilet paper, can affect plant productivity.

So far, we've looked for performance measures from the perspective of the organization—its strategy, business model, and culture. But it is equally important to think from the bottom up—that is, from the stated requirements of the individual job to the corporate strategy. And the best place to begin is with the job description.

Job descriptions serve many purposes, but most include a section that lists the main tasks that the jobholder is supposed to do. These may be labeled "key duties" or "major responsibilities" or "principal accountabilities"—the heading doesn't matter. The important thing is that there is a listing of what is expected. The primary benefit of a job description is that it provides clarity as to what is expected by the employee in the job. For each of the items in the list, the manager can ask, "What's the most appropriate way to measure whether the jobholder has done that?"

A plant manager may have a major responsibility to "provide quality product to meet customer requirements." How do you know whether the plant manager is being effective? Some likely measures are (1) the time it takes to fill orders, (2) the percentage of orders filled correctly the first time, and (3) the number of quality problems uncovered by customers. In addition, many organizations conduct customer surveys to learn how effective they are at meeting customer needs.

In some instances the accountability is not limited to one function;

in a team environment, accountabilities must be clear. You don't want a football team where everyone goes out for a pass. The same is true of business organizations. Saying that the objective is to win the game does not differentiate between individual responsibilities. In sports, teams win when the members execute their individual jobs well (or at least better than the opposition). The same is true for business organizations.

So the process of identifying the most appropriate measures is almost always a combined top-down and bottom-up approach. A manager uses the objectives set for the department and perhaps identifies a particular job that has a primary or shared impact. The manager then looks to the job description and identifies the priority tasks (given the business model and the organization culture). With this combined approach the manager can generate a short list of contributions that employees are expected to make and then pare this down to an acceptable number of the most important for the purpose of setting objectives.

But My Employees Are a Team!

Depending on the organization's business model, employees may work as individuals, in small teams, or in large teams. Just to make matters more complex, they might even work in all three scenarios. Is there a difference in choosing measures for an individual or for a team? Let's consider four different team scenarios and compare them to the sports world:

1. *Individual:* This describes an environment in which employees are best considered as acting in an independent fashion (they fully control the process in which they perform their duties). Wrestling or gymnastics teams operate like this. You add up individual scores to get the team score.

2. *Small Teams:* This describes an environment in which employees are best considered as members of a project and/or team. Track teams have elements of the individual as well as a small team (relay teams, for example).

3. *Bigger Teams:* This describes an environment in which employees are best considered as contributors to a department or business unit. Football teams fit this model because the whole team is composed of smaller offensive, defensive, and special teams.

4. *Integrated Teams:* This describes an environment in which employees are best considered as contributors to the corporate enterprise. Basketball or soccer—games in which teams operate in an integrated fashion to achieve results—are good examples of integrated teams.

Again, the essential principle is alignment. Whatever the scenario, the manager measures the most important tasks of the job, using the measures over which employees have the most control. In football, kickers are measured by how far and how accurately they kick the ball, not by how many touchdowns their team scores.

A Framework of Measures

Virtually all executive positions require a combination of measures. These could be individual, corporate, and maybe also team based. For example, a manager of corporate accounting may establish measures linked to corporate financial performance, department-specific project objectives, and individual objectives. Sometimes an organization imposes a framework of measures that managers must work within. This framework could be in the form of specific measures that apply to everyone (for example, we are all "leaders," so how we demonstrate our leadership ability should be measured).

Another relatively common approach is to use a balanced scorecard for cascading accountabilities, from the team level down to the individual employee level. A balanced scorecard might use metrics with predetermined criteria. For example, four segments could be identified as follows:

1. *Person/Job:* Delivers the key output of the job while expanding personal capability to add value to the organization.

2. *Productivity:* Improves productivity in the core job processes.

3. *Customer:* Improves the level of customer service (internal or external customers).

4. *Financial:* Ensures that the focus of the job supports growth, profit, or both.

The idea is to set one or two measures within each of the segments. The advantage of this framework is that the totality of the job is considered. The manager doesn't run the risk of focusing on only one or two segments of the job, can apply the measures more consistently, and can identify the tools necessary to support the position. In some cases, only one of the segments applies to an individual job, but most jobs can be linked to broader objectives.

Setting Targets That Motivate

If the first part of the puzzle is choosing the right measures, the second part is setting the appropriate targets or objectives in terms of those measures. We found that *Fortune* magazine's America's Most Admired Companies had performance goals with three key attributes: they were clearer, more challenging, and more realistic than the performance goals for the peer group. At first, this may seem contradictory. How can a Most Admired Company report that its goals are both more challenging and more realistic than those of other companies? The answer lies in the self-confidence of the organization's managers and its employees. The best companies do not take the easy way out and set soft goals. They want to win and they do win. These organizations stretch themselves by setting their expectations ahead of their competitors, and they have the right people, the right processes, and the right structures in place to win.

For setting goals at the employee level, the SMART goal-setting process is a time-proven technique. The definitions of SMART may vary slightly from source to source, but the typical meaning is:

- *Specific:* Be clear on what you're trying to achieve.
- *Measurable:* Ensure that you have good data on how you're doing.
- *Achievable:* Don't try to achieve too much; ensure that you have adequate resources to achieve your goal.
- *Relevant:* Ensure that your goal aligns with broader organizational goals.
- *Time Based:* Know when you want to achieve the goal.

The SMART approach is a framework for establishing quantifiable, results-oriented goals that are well recognized by most line managers. A more detailed treatment of the SMART goal-setting process is given in Chapter 10.

A word of caution: Don't set lower goals just because the employee is less capable and has a history of low performance. This is counterproductive. The question that must be answered is: How challenging is the goal for any reasonably competent employee? Do, however, establish more challenging objectives for more capable employees as long as they are also more highly compensated.

Summary: A Checklist for Performance Measures That Motivate

Whether you manage steel production, a sales organization, a restaurant, or a creative department, you'll find that leading is like coaching. If you were the coach of a sports team, you wouldn't merely assign the players to positions and develop a playbook. You'd work with your team to ensure it has the skills to win. You would drill, you would practice, and you would keep them focused. You don't go away during the season, come back at the end to find out how everyone did, and hand out awards to the best players. The same is true for managers. Set SMART goals, manage for performance improvement, and use compensation to focus your players and encourage their development. For your performance measures to motivate, you must do the following:

- Choose the right measures by using both top-down and bottom-up analyses of the work that needs to be done.
- Ensure that the measures you choose align with the organization's goals, offer individual control, and support the organization's values.
- Set appropriate targets that motivate employees.
- Select appropriate rewards vehicles that drive performance and recognize achievement.

CHAPTER 5

Getting Employee Commitment with "Total Rewards"

ALTHOUGH MANY ORGANIZATIONS BOAST that their people are their most important assets, a good many fail to act as though they believe it. In fact, an organization's people *are* its best competitive advantage. Strategies, business models, products, and services can all be readily copied, but it's much harder for competitors to replicate the talent and engagement of employees working together for competitive advantage. That's why human capital helps a business distinguish itself from the competition.

Herb Kelleher, founder of Southwest Airlines, attributes his airline's consistently strong performance to its unique culture. "It's the intangibles that are the hardest things for a competitor to imitate," he says. "You can get airplanes, you can get ticket counter space, you can get tugs, and you can get baggage conveyors. But the spirit of Southwest is the most difficult thing to emulate. If we ever do lose that, we will have lost our most valuable competitive asset."[1]

A "total rewards" approach to performance management recognizes that when it comes to developing a motivated and committed workforce, the tangible rewards of compensation and benefits are necessary but are not sufficient. Think of these tangible rewards as the entrance fee to a tournament. Winning the game requires you to think more broadly, to consider the "value propositions" you are offering the employees—that is, the total returns the employees can expect to receive based on their contributions.

Rewards means different things to different people, depending on the context in which the word is used. (Just think about old TV Westerns and those "reward" posters!) While some days business can often feel like it's the Wild West, most companies traditionally interpret *rewards* as the employee's pay (base salary, incentives, or bonuses) and the value of the benefit plans. These reward elements, individually and collectively, are discussed in other chapters in this book. However, when you hear the term *total rewards*, the connotation goes beyond these tangibles. Total rewards also includes the intangible elements—the rewards that are harder to see and touch but real enough to affect an employee's level of engagement in and satisfaction with the job, not to mention the possible means of attracting and retaining new talent.

Accordingly, this chapter focuses on those intangible elements of which every manager must be aware. Because of their importance as key employee-retention tools, it becomes the manager's obligation to shape and use these intangible rewards in combination with tangibles to influence employees' desire to stay, learn, and grow with the organization—and thereby add value to the company.

Why Is a Total Rewards Approach So Vital Today?

Figure 1-1 highlighted the tangible and intangible elements of a total rewards model. In this model, base salary is the foundation for all other tangible rewards. Beyond the base salary, there can be bonuses, long- and short-term incentives, and a variety of benefit plans. The total rewards approach broadens the concept of rewards to include culture, leadership, opportunities for career growth, job enablement, and recognition. The increasing importance of these elements can be attributed to the changing dynamics of today's organizations.

What are these changing dynamics? Here are just a few of the factors that enter the employment picture:

The War for Talent: A soft labor market may have held down turnover rates in some companies in recent years, but retention is rapidly becoming a high-priority issue again. In the 2005 U.S. Job Recovery and Retention Survey conducted by the Society of Human Resources Management and Career Journal.com in November 2005, 36 percent of people currently employed indicated they were actively searching for a new job. An additional 40 percent of people currently employed were passively searching for a new job. Moreover, 80 percent of people currently employed indicated that they would be at least somewhat likely to begin a job search once the economy and job market improves.[2] These statistics are not lost on HR, as two-thirds of surveyed HR professionals report being concerned about the number of voluntary resignations reported in the 2005 survey. And demographic trends suggest that the war for talent will continue well into the future. Indeed, the Bureau of Labor Statistics data indicate that the pool of U.S. workers between the ages of 35 and 44 will shrink by 15 percent over the next 15 years.[3]

A 2005 Accenture study of executive priorities in companies worldwide indicates that "attracting and retaining skilled staff" ranks at the top of managers' present agendas, followed by "changing organizational culture and employee attitudes."[4] Unfortunately for managers, competition for employees is increasing just as compensation budgets are becoming more constrained. To cope with this squeeze, managers must consider intangible rewards as well as tangible ones in attracting and holding on to employees.

Increasing Focus on Employee Engagement: Hay Group defines *employee engagement* as "a result that is achieved by stimulating employees' enthusiasm for their work and directing it toward organizational success." By making work more meaningful and rewarding, then, managers can encourage employees to put discretionary effort into their jobs and deliver superior performance. In fact, promoting high levels of employee engagement is critical today. In the rapidly changing environments that most businesses now operate, management must count on employees to act on their own in ways consistent with the company's culture, objectives, and values. Faced with a challenging global economic environment, many organizations need to do more with less, which makes the discretionary efforts of employees willing to "go the extra mile" all the more important. And to foster maximum employee engagement, managers need to understand and take advantage of the tangible and intangible rewards that motivate employees.

A More Diverse Workforce: Today's workforce is more diverse than ever. The globalization of the marketplace, the flow of talent across national borders, and an increasing awareness of the benefits of varied perspectives have led to more cultural and ethnic diversity in the workplace. In addition, the numbers of women who work have grown. Social changes and demographic trends have also contributed to greater diversity; for example, both men and women enter and exit the workforce more frequently in the course of their working lives, primarily in response to personal situations and higher priorities. Likewise, the concept of retirement has changed: More people view retirement as a time of part-time work or for launching a second career, rather than as total withdrawal from the workforce.

As the workforce has grown more diverse, so have employee interests and needs. Today's managers need a flexible approach to rewards programs that will foster employee engagement and greater commitment to a wider group of workers.

The Total Rewards Palette

In his *Harvard Business Review* article "Leadership That Gets Results," Dan Goleman makes an analogy between professional golfers and high-impact leaders. Golf pros are armed with an array of clubs. Over the course of a match, a pro chooses clubs based on the demands of the shot, sometimes pondering the options and sometimes making an automatic or instinctive selection. The same, Goleman says, is true of the high-impact leader who can choose among managerial styles, making conscious or automatic decisions about the best approach to managing different situations depending on the circumstances.[5]

Goleman's analogy can be extended to the various elements of total rewards. When the elements are used artfully and with knowledge in differing situations, a manager can manage the total rewards palette to make the most of the intangible, intrinsic elements of rewards.

The employment relationship is an exchange between a company and its employee. A company rewards employees either for performing a service (such as answering phones or operating a machine) or for attaining something (such as a sales quota or a production goal). Employees agree to take on certain responsibilities and work in return for those rewards. In numerous research studies that Hay Group has conducted, however, we've found that the real value of this "reward contract" is in the management of the intangible elements and in its ability to generate commitment and discretionary effort from employees. Therefore, while the tangible platform for rewards must be solid, a company cannot maximize its return on the rewards investment without managing its total rewards package. The key dimensions of the work environment that constitute the intangible rewards framework are depicted in Figure 5-1.

Work Culture and Values

As was discussed in Chapter 3, *culture* is a term used by many businesses to describe the overall tone of an organization or business unit. It is the set of signals that an organization emits regarding ways for its employees to think and act. It is the tone for how the company does business. An organization's culture comprises attributes that have been set down by an organization's leadership. The corporate culture, therefore, and the values that it reflects, is essentially a code of conduct that the organization supports, encourages, and rewards.

In a 2001 Conference Board research report, corporate culture is identified as one of the key resources of a business, along with capital, labor, products, services, profits, and an operational infrastructure that finances, builds, markets, sells, and delivers.[6] But managers should be aware that work culture can be managed. An effective manager recognizes what and how to change when change is necessary and has a powerful role in guiding the organization's performance in a shifting market.

What we mean here is that work culture is not something a manager

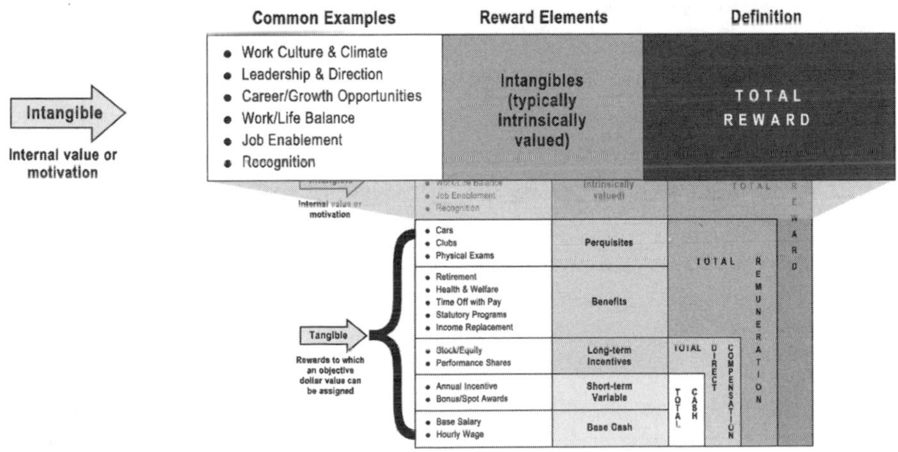

FIGURE 5-1. INTANGIBLE REWARDS PORTION OF TOTAL REWARDS MODEL

can decide to have or not have; it cannot be turned on or off. Rather, culture exists and will continue to grow and evolve in the organization. The question is whether you as a manager will plan that growth and nurture it as you would a garden, or whether you'll simply let it grow wild. Amazon.com chief Jeff Bezos says, "Cultures aren't so much planned as they evolve from that early set of people that are hired. I'd rather interview 50 people and not hire anyone than hire the wrong person." According to Bezos, new employees either dislike the culture and leave or feel comfortable and stay. So the culture becomes "self-reinforcing" and "very stable."[7]

Another example can be seen as part of the "Star Design" initiative, a Heineken USA–branded change to channel-focused selling. The largest importer of beers in the United States, Heineken USA has a 500-person sales organization that distributes its brands, including Amstel Light, Heineken Premium Light, and Heineken. Within Heineken's broader context of building autonomous regional units and reshaping roles within the U.S. sales organization, there was also an investment of $1 million in the Heineken Sales Campus, a two-week residential program for sales professionals. "It's created a culture we never had before," says Amy Nenner, vice president of human resources at Heineken USA. "It reinforces our corporate values—a passion for quality, respect for one another, performance, and enjoyment."

The Sales Campus exceeded management's expectations. Most Heineken USA salespeople work from their homes and out of their cars, so it is difficult for employees to stay committed to those corporate values. The Campus is a way to reach out, to connect people to values, and to encourage a professional support network where the company's culture can resonate. "The campus creates a bond," says Nenner. "People graduate, then they stick with their classmates; they lean on one another." Recently, the Heineken Sales Campus was recognized as The Most Innovative Corporate University by the Best Practices Institute of the United States.[8]

Managers who want to take advantage of all the rewards resources at their disposal should watch for the signals and behaviors coming from senior management, as well as be synchronized with the organization's code of conduct. While culture is not something that any one individual in a business defines, controls, or activates, being aware of what it strives to be, what is encouraged, and what is not tolerated can work to any manager's advantage.

Work Climate

If corporate culture is an organizationwide set of characteristics, *climate* consists of individual, manager-specific behaviors and styles that set the tone for a particular work unit, group, or department. While culture is a collective effort, climate is a function of the manager's activities. Climate describes the work environment created by an individual manager; it is a reflection of the unit's employee engagement, organizational commitment, productivity, and discretionary effort. And, in this regard, climate can be measured, influenced, and redirected by a manager.

Climate is measured at the individual manager level by direct subordinates. Hay Group has identified six dimensions that characterize the climate that can be set by a manager: flexibility, responsibility, standards, rewards, clarity, and team commitment. As discussed in Chapter 1, our research has shown that climate accounts for up to 30 percent of the variance seen in performance. That is, employees in positive work climates are more likely to spend their discretionary effort in support of their work units.

From a total rewards perspective, the implications are twofold. First, a positive climate is an intangible reward, not a tangible one. Second, a positive climate is easily perceived and highly regarded. We're sure you know people who enjoy not only what they do for a living but also being at their workplace and with their coworkers. Managers who create an unparalleled work environment can leverage this intangible reward to gain employees who think twice about departing the organization.

Scott White, vice president of Performance and People Systems at Applebees, the restaurant chain, underscores the importance of climate, saying, "Perhaps the most important thing in this whole area of rewards is having a good boss because they set the right kind of work climate in the organization." Says White, "We have found that many people work here because they want a genuinely good place to go to work, they want flexible hours, and they want to be treated with respect in a culture of pride. People who work at Applebees want to be on a winning team and to do well."

Leadership and Direction

Hay Group has done extensive research to identify the factors that determine employee commitment, drawing on data collected through our global Hay Group Insight database of employee opinions collected in hundreds of organizations. Our findings suggest that employee confidence in the ability of top management is among the most important predictors of turnover. The relationship between employee confidence and worker retention shouldn't be surprising, though. Today's employees recognize that their prospects for continued employment, career development, and advancement depend on their organization remaining healthy and stable. Increasingly taking charge of their own career, employees can't be expected to bind their future to that of their employer unless they can be confident that the organization is well managed and headed in the right direction.

In most organizations, employee understanding of an organization's strategic objectives drops off markedly when descending from the senior management ranks to middle management levels. Yet middle managers bear responsibility for implementing those strategic plans and communicating them to employees at yet lower levels. Is it any wonder that the understanding of strategic objectives is even weaker in the broader employee population? Hay Group's Insight employee opinion database suggests that knowledge of, and confidence in, the strategic objectives of a company is a major driver of employee engagement and commitment.

Growth and Development Opportunities

Employees are increasingly responsible for managing their own careers and they know that their futures depend on improving their skills. If they aren't *expanding* their capabilities, they risk compromising their employability; there's no standing still in this world. Accordingly, opportunities for growth and development are among the most consistent predictors of employee commitment. As one Fortune 100 CEO recently told us, "The number one question I get asked as I visit my company's facilities around the country is, 'What do I have to do to get ahead? What do I have to do to move up in this company?'" To retain key talent, managers need to identify the potential career paths, especially early in an employee's tenure with the organization.

Indeed, managers play a critical role in determining employees' career paths in the organization. Through coaching and regular feedback, supervisors can help employees identify developmental needs and enhance their skills. Managers also often serve as mentors for their employees, helping them understand organizational expectations and develop supportive networks. Finally, managers act as sponsors for their employees, helping them take on additional responsibilities, get promoted, or in other ways "work the system."

Overall, most employees view their managers positively. Hay Group employee opinion norms suggest, however, that many aren't getting the advancement support they need. For example, our global Hay Group Insight employee opinion database shows that only 41 percent of nonmanagement employees, and just 47 percent of managers, consider their supervisors to be offering good counseling in career development. To keep more of their best people, organizations need to direct their managers more toward the development of their employees.

Texas Instruments (TI) does just that. In quarterly performance discussions and career-planning sessions with their employees, managers consider assignment changes that would make the best use of individuals' skills. Since managers are judged on how successful they are at getting top performers to stay, "you cannot fall asleep at the wheel," says Steve Lyle, TI's director of worldwide staffing. This has resulted in a reduction of turnover for many TI business units.[9]

Conversely, lack of managerial oversight for career development is especially evident where high turnover amid high costs can have a significant impact on the bottom line. This problem is highlighted by Ben Johnson, managing partner at the law firm of Alston & Bird, where it costs up to $300,000 to replace each associate. Johnson says that "partners understand that if they get a reputation for running associates off, they're going to get a lot of personal counseling."[10]

Work/Life Balance

Numerous studies point to the fact that U.S. employees work longer hours than ever before. Couple that trend with the prevalence of two-career families and the demands of caring for aging parents, and you have a recipe for work/life balance concerns. Hay Group Insight employee opinion norms confirm that many employees are struggling to balance responsibilities at work and at home. For instance, just 37 percent of employees in our database surveyed indicate that staffing levels are adequate to get the work done in their areas, and only 52 percent indicated that their work and personal lives are in balance. Not surprisingly, nearly 70 percent indicated problems in managing the stress associated with their jobs.

Part of the solution to a work/life imbalance is more flexible work arrangements. But equally important is ensuring that managers are supportive of such work arrangements. A huge investment in greater work/life benefits can nevertheless generate a substantial negative return for the organization if its managers send messages that are inconsistent with policy. For example, if flextime is instituted, allowing employees to work varying hours to better accommodate their personal lives, but productivity and quality both suffer as a result, the blame does not necessarily lay with flextime per se. It might mean that managers did not clarify their performance expectations in conjunction with the new policy. Managers sometimes send subtle (or not so subtle) messages that they would prefer employees not use a flextime program. The result is a negative return on an intangible rewards investment.

Job Enablement

At Hay Group, we often survey our clients' employees to identify the critical drivers of job satisfaction. While many factors vary from industry to industry and organization to organization, what we call *job enablement* factors typically emerge as key considerations across all industries and all types of businesses. In other words, there are some universals, among which is the perception that the organization is providing the authority, information, and resources employees need to do their job effectively.

At the very least, people need to feel that employers aren't introducing barriers to their personal success. Ideally, they should have the sense that the organization is doing *all it can* to promote their success. After all, if organizations want to encourage high levels of employee engagement, they have to demonstrate that employees' discretionary efforts will be used productively. Job enablement factors are particularly important in high-workload environments. That is, when employees are asked to work hard, it's understandable that they want to feel as though they're working smart, too.

Recognition

Numerous studies conducted over the last several decades have suggested that nonmonetary rewards and recognition can be much more effective motivators than cash. It's not that money doesn't matter; it's just that it tends to be what is termed a *deficiency need*. If employees feel that they're significantly underpaid—that their pay does not reflect their contributions to the organization—their motivation is likely to suffer. But when it comes to encouraging employees to put discretionary effort into their work and to deliver superior performance, the chance to make a difference and be recognized for it is likely to provide a very strong incentive. As Harvard Business School professor Rosabeth Moss Kanter puts it, "Compensation is a right. Recognition is a gift."

Patting employees' backs may be a more effective form of positive motivation than padding their wallets, and that is good news for an organization, especially in a difficult economy when budgets are stretched to the limit. Unlike compensation, recognition is inexpensive—indeed, often it's free! Hay Group employee opinion surveys suggest, however, that too few organizations take advantage of the motivational power of nonmonetary rewards. For example, in our Hay Group Insight employee opinion survey database, we found that only 44 percent of nonmanagement employees and just 56 percent of managers reported that their contributions are recognized when they have performed well. Chapter 13 provides a more in-depth discussion of this important component of the rewards program.

The Links Between the Reward Elements

Is all of this total rewards stuff sounding a bit too soft? Are you skeptical because what your bottom-line-focused employees seem to want most of all is for you to show them the money? It may appear as though we're implying that employees have lost their emphasis on financial well-being, but that's not the case. For most of us, earning our living ranks very high on our list of reasons for getting out of bed and going to work every day. And when it comes to tangible rewards, most individuals want the best compensation and benefits they can get in return for their skills, time, and efforts.

A total rewards approach, to the extent that it focuses on the intrinsic returns that organizations can offer employees, should be viewed as a complement to, rather than a substitute for, tangible rewards. Many rewards logically tie to Maslow's hierarchy of human needs, as illustrated in Figure 5-2. According to Maslow's theory, once a person has satisfied his or her basic physiological and safety needs, the attention is then focused on social and ego needs, with self-actualization being the

FIGURE 5-2. HUMAN NEEDS VS. TOTAL REWARDS

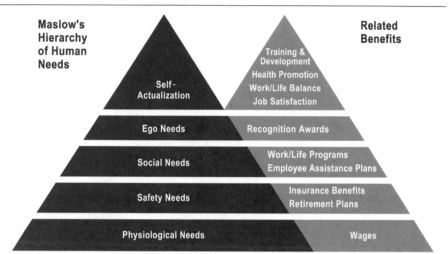

pinnacle of achievement. Figure 5-2 shows how tangible and intangible rewards parallel the levels of Maslow's hierarchy of needs.

Many of the intangible rewards in a total rewards framework have implications for employees' compensation over the long term. We've mentioned, for instance, that the intangibles of opportunities for growth and development are among the major drivers of employee commitment, once the tangibles of fair base salary and benefits are established. This is because employees recognize that upgrading their skills adds value while enhancing their employability, job security, and compensation. The compensation implications of working for an organization that is well led and headed in the right direction are clear. If employees know they're playing for a winner, they can expect greater opportunities, greater employment stability, and better base pay and incentive compensation (e.g., bonuses, appreciation in the value of stock options). Because the bottom line for the organization is ultimately the bottom line for all of us, a total rewards approach is a vital tool for everyone's benefit.

Developing a Total Rewards Strategy

We've discussed the opportunities associated with a broadened perspective on rewards. But before you begin building a total rewards plan for your organization, let's briefly consider two challenges that task presents.

1. *Fostering Leadership Commitment:* Ironically, increasing the intangible rewards available to employees often involves a tangible investment on the part of the employer. Expanding career development opportunities for employees or launching work/life balance programs may require investments of both money and time. If you're looking for a commitment from leadership to explore alternative compensation, you'll want to make a strong case for the likely benefits of increased employee commitment, lower absenteeism, reduced turnover, and the like. And it's essential to include up-front strategies for measuring the return on the investments. We discuss options for measuring and monitoring the impact of a total rewards program later.

2. *Ensuring Alignment with Organizational Objectives:* Rewards, whether tangible or intangible, are tools for increasing organizational effectiveness. The employment relationship involves an exchange: organizational inducements for employee contributions. A well-designed rewards program chooses inducements that will attract and retain the talent needed. Accordingly, your total rewards approach should be based on organizational needs and be balanced with employee wants. Later, we discuss ways you can ensure that your total rewards program makes your team not only happier but also more productive.

With these cautions in mind, we offer a four-phase approach to designing and implementing a total rewards program in your organization. Then we discuss options for telling your employees about that new total rewards program, along with strategies for evaluating its success and managing and enhancing the program over time.

Step 1: Take Stock

As with any journey, you need to know where you are before you plot a route to your intended destination. Accordingly, your initial step should be to inventory all existing rewards components, measuring them against the total rewards framework outlined earlier (see Figure 1-1).

Begin by taking stock of the tangible compensation and benefits you're offering to employees right now. What are your policies regarding base pay and incentives? Which of these policies seem to be working? Which could stand improvement? How effectively does your current system link compensation to performance? How flexible are your benefits offerings, and to what extent do they meet employees' needs?

After considering current tangible rewards offerings, turn your focus to any intangible rewards. These are harder to assess; to identify them, consider the following:

- How would you characterize the image and reputation of your organization and its leadership?
- To what extent are employees excited about the company's business prospects? In what areas do employees have concerns—and how might these concerns be addressed?
- How would you describe the culture of the organization and the climate of your work unit?
- What are the key elements of the work climate that managers create for their teams?
- How effective is the organization in creating growth and development opportunities for employees, either by promoting them or by assigning them new or different job responsibilities?
- When employees succeed, how often are their contributions recognized, either formally or informally?
- What programs or resources are available to help employees balance their work and personal responsibilities?
- Is the organization providing employees with the resources they need for optimal effectiveness, and are there any barriers to individual performance?

In your assessment, try to identify the strengths in your current situation as well as the opportunities for improvement. Take careful note of the strengths, as these will be important to emphasize later in your communications to employees. In your list of areas for improvement, consider how much flexibility you have as a manager to deviate from current practice. And where you see a need for change, note what support you will need to make improvements.

Unless you're a very senior decision maker, you're unlikely to be able to act on all of your ideas—at least right away. So, prioritize your recommendations. Which do you see as the most important? Which would be easiest to implement in the short term and which require more time and effort?

Since ultimately your total rewards offerings will represent the "value proposition" you offer employees, think about this value as your "employment brand." Just as your marketing colleagues position products and services in the marketplace in terms of key benefits and differentiators, position your total rewards approach to differentiate the benefits of employment in your organization. If possible, conduct a competitive employment analysis to consider what your company currently stands for as an employer and how its rewards stack up against those of others in the industry. What are your competitive strengths? What are your vulnerabilities?

As a last task in this phase, work with others in your organization to quantify the costs of your current rewards offerings. For most organizations, employees are not only the most important asset but also one of the biggest expenses. Documenting just how much the organization is spending (on a per-employee basis and in aggregate) on both tangible and intangible rewards is likely to reveal a considerable current investment in total rewards—whether that investment is guided by strategy or not. Armed with these figures, you can build a case for improving your rewards. For example, a $20,000 investment in improving career development resources may sound like a lot of money, but set against the backdrop of a multi-million-dollar expenditure on rewards, it may be a modest step that can enhance the return on the company's investment in people.

You may also want to calculate the costs of *not* taking action. For instance, how much unwanted turnover is there in your organization? Most studies estimate the cost of replacing employees to be between 50 and 150 percent of salary. For an organization with 2,000 employees and an annual turnover rate of 5 percent, that translates to approximately $3.5 million in turnover costs (assuming an average salary of $35,000). And the hidden costs of turnover may be even greater: disrupted customer relationships, lost organization- and job-specific knowledge, and increased strain on remaining employees. Again, that $20,000 investment in career development may appear daunting at first, but if it was to help retain even one valued employee who might otherwise leave the organization, it would more than pay for itself.

Step 2: Sharpen Your Focus

Having assembled an inventory of current rewards offerings, you're now ready to work toward a specific action plan. As discussed earlier, that plan requires assessing both what employees want and what the organization needs.

In Step 1, you made observations about the strengths of existing rewards practices, as well as the opportunities for improvement. Those observations were derived from your own perceptions. No doubt your perceptions have been formed by your understanding of what employees want from the organization. But if your perception is based on incomplete or anecdotal information, you'll want to conduct a more systematic assessment. Then you can proceed with confidence as you make recommendations, allocate resources, and implement your plan.

Consider gathering feedback from employees on the current rewards offered and their motivational impact. Specially designed employee surveys can be useful in this context, along with small-group discussions or one-on-one interviews. Recognizing that your resources are finite, you should design these activities to manage the trade-offs between investment in one type of reward versus another. Along with assessing employee satisfaction with the current compensation and benefits package, for instance, you may want to assess whether, if given the choice, employees would prefer an increase in pay, a reduction in work hours, and/or additional vacation time. Or, suppose that an e-learning training course were to be offered for employees to complete on their own time; how many would be inclined to take advantage of such an offering?

In gathering feedback from employees, remember that one size is unlikely to fit all. What motivates a late-career manager may not be the same as what motivates a new hire. Whether you reach out to your team through surveys or more informal dialogue, be attentive to the different perspectives. Ultimately you want to tailor the rewards offerings to the unique interests of particular employees in order to realize the greatest return on investment.

Consider, also, what the organization seeks from its employees. Outline the objectives for your organization and your unit, along with their operating styles and cultures. Then work back from those objectives and determine the implications for your rewards strategy. For instance, suppose that your organization is characterized by what Hay Group has termed a network culture (see Chapter 3). In this environment—typical of, say, consulting projects or movie making—teams of individuals come together for a project and then disband once the work is completed. Given that the success of a network culture typically depends on "star" contributors, the approach to compensation makes heavy use of incentives to reward individual achievements. Since employees may move in and out of the organization frequently, benefits programs are likely to place a premium on individual flexibility and deemphasize retirement programs and long-term disability options. And training and development programs are likely to promote self-directed learning over more formalized learning.

Step 3: Take Action

Now that you've customized your approach, you're ready to begin implementing your plan. Implementation may involve a wholesale rollout of new programs or an incremental phase-in approach. Either way, view yourself as an agent of change. And as with any type of change, communication—or better yet, marketing—is critical. To gain buy-in, you'll need to show that planned changes hold additional benefits for the organization and for individual employees.

Unfortunately, most managers struggle to explain their rewards programs. A Hay Group/Loyola University Chicago and WorldatWork research study of 1,200 compensation professionals found that more than two-thirds of respondents rated their communications about pay to be "not effective" or only "marginally effective." While most respondents (91 percent) indicated that their organizations have a pay philosophy, nearly two-thirds indicated that "about half" or "less than half" of employees actually understand them.[11]

Given that the same initiative can be expected to impact different employees in different ways, building support for change means engaging the unique interests of different employee groups. Take advantage of what you learned in Step 2: Focus on the extent to which the changes you're proposing are responses to what employees told you about their interests and needs. Employee buy-in of your plan will be enhanced if you give them an opportunity to shape your recommendations.

In implementing your approaches, express the rationale behind the changes. You're likely to need the support of leaders, and here the Step 2 efforts will be helpful. Position your recommendations as supportive of the objectives of the organization, and it should be much easier to encourage leaders to get behind them.

Step 4: Measure the Results

You can leverage your earlier efforts to help monitor and manage the total rewards program as it is implemented. With a handle on past reward expenditures, you'll be able to gauge how the allocation of the rewards budget will evolve over time. By sharpening your focus on a more optimal rewards mix, you may be able to reduce costs in some areas at the same time as you increase investments in others. And with a knowledge of past turnover costs, you're in a position to assess potential cost savings as a means of determining ROI.

You may also want to leverage your Step 2 efforts to help keep open the dialogue with employees as you move beyond implementation. Surveying employees or interviewing them in small groups can provide additional ways to assess whether the plan is a good response to employee concerns and whether it increases the levels of commitment and engagement.

As your plan takes hold, return to the competitive analysis you conducted earlier. Consider new implications for your "employment brand." With knowledge of what rewards you're offering and why, you can set realistic job expectations for new employees and sell existing employees on the competitiveness of their positions; that will assist you with retention of key talent.

Philips, the consumer electronics giant, thinks exactly this way. According to Brenda van Leeuwen, the company's employer-branding manager, "From the start, we took the approach of considering recruitment as a sales and marketing function, and thinking of the employee experience in terms of the customer experience. If we were to attract and retain the best people we needed to 'sell' Philips to them as an employer they would find attractive. This meant we first needed to know how existing and potential employees regarded the company as an employer. The questions we asked ourselves were 'what does the company want to be recognized for, and how docs it differ from its competitors in the labor market?' "[12]

Your focus on the value proposition to employees will have implications for recruitment and selection. As we've said several times, tailoring rewards to employee needs is critical for fostering high levels of commitment and engagement. But equally important is bringing into the organization people who will be energized by the work environment. It's often difficult for employees to determine before joining an organization what it'll "feel" like to work there. But the retention literature clearly confirms the importance of person-organization fit in determining success in a job. With a total rewards package, you'll be able, during hiring conversations, to make a determination regarding the likelihood of a productive match.

Summary: A Checklist for Total Rewards

To build a total rewards program for your organization, use the following checklist as a guide. Knowing what levers are available to you and being on the lookout for opportunities, you can reward and manage your staff effectively:

- Know your organization's pay philosophy, its reward program, and how the various reward elements operate.
- Identify employee attributes that the company encourages, supports, and rewards; these could constitute the organization's culture.
- Understand your company's leadership and people approach—whether it's top-down or inclusive, whether it's focused on managing functions/individuals or teams/units.
- Be aware of how you lead others and the impact you have on your staff, its development, and the work environment.
- Look for opportunities for staff development, whether they're onetime work assignments, new positions, or new responsibilities.
- Be sensitive to staff members' needs and flexible in how you engage them.
- Recognize staff for some of the everyday things that often go unnoticed and, when necessary, provide feedback and coaching on how individuals can do things better.

CHAPTER 6

Putting a Price Tag on Work

A KEY PLANK of an organization's rewards platform is to pay the right people the right amount for doing the right things. This chapter covers the middle part of this phrase—paying the right amount—and explains how organizations determine the value of their employees' work. It provides an understanding of common work-valuing processes in use today, offers a recommended approach, and details the manager's key role in this process.

The Value of Work

Managers are accountable to both the organization and their employees in determining the value of work and in providing fair compensation in return for the work. In order to offer employees pay that is competitive with other companies' and appropriate for the duties involved, a manager needs to understand the real value of the work. Many organizations today determine the value of their employees' work by matching job titles to external compensation surveys. However, this method is of limited use because it does not reflect the true value of the work to specific employers. For instance, the data provide information on how much is paid industrywide, but not all of the value that attaches to each job.

The *value* of work is twofold: internal and external. The manager plays a key role in determining the internal value. After all, who better knows about the content of the job—the mix of responsibilities and the impact of that job on the organization's success? Who better to advise HR in determining the worth of particular work in the external market, and what components of the work make the job worth more or less to the market and to the company?

A Work-Valuing Timeline

The way we assign value to work has evolved over time, with most of the discussion, research, and actual change occurring in only the last 50 years. Before the nineteenth century, there was no formal approach to estimating the value of work (and subsequently to paying employees, which was what assigning value to work was all about initially). The industrial revolution, along with labor laws that came about in the early twentieth century, drove this change initially, and it has continued to this day, subsequently influencing global practices. Figure 6-1 is a time line showing the evolution of work-valuing systems in the United States from the 1920s until almost the present.

For many years in a majority of organizations, base salary compensation levels and job values were determined using *point-factor* methods that we'll discuss in more detail later in this chapter. These were the most influential compensation tools, used from the 1940s through the 1980s, because they could be applied to organizations of all sizes and types. In fact, the point-factor method, also referred to as *job evaluation*, continues to dominate job valuing today, especially in developing nations and in Europe. The most popular form of point-factor valuation is the Hay Group Guide Chart methodology.[1]

The point-factor approach to valuing work focused primarily on internal value. Market pricing was integrated into this system by pricing comparable jobs at each level. Management determined a pay line, which in effect offered all jobs at a certain level (usually represented by a grade or a job point range) the same compensation opportunity. Most companies created committees of key line managers and executives to evaluate the organization's jobs, with HR functioning as facilitator. This process often demanded substantial time from managers—often two days a week

FIGURE 6-1. OUTLINE OF JOB VALUATION HISTORY

1925 to 1950

- Government social legislation and public works programs
- Stronger unions; collective bargaining agreements
- Fair Labor Standards Act of 1938 (FLSA—which governs overtime laws)
- First formal approach to job evaluation developed by Ned Hay (founder of Hay Group)

1950 to 1975

- Wage and price controls regulated compensation decision making
- Equal Pay Amendment to FLSA of 1963 and Title VII of the Civil Rights Acts of 1964 (antidiscrimination laws governing pay and employment practices)
- Use of individual incentive plans declines
- Merit increase grids, seniority-based increases, cost of living adjustment (COLA) clauses were all supporting increasingly detailed job analysis and job evaluation

1975 to 1990

- Individualized variable pay based on performance
- Intense competition for highly skilled workers
- Compensation remains a critical part of the employee relationship

1990 to 2000

- Economic expansion, mergers and acquisitions, international competition
- Intense competition for highly skilled mobile workforce creating stronger emphasis on attraction/retention of key employees
- Increased use of broad-based equity programs to better compete for talent and resources by viewing employer/employee relationship as a strategic advantage
- Government regulations such as Americans with Disabilities Act of 1990 (ADA) and the Family and Medical Leave Act of 1993 (FMLA)

Source: Hay Group. Adapted from WorldatWork. Reprinted with permission from WorldatWork.

during implementation of the program and one day a month to review changes or new job requests.

Why were executives willing to invest so much time in this process? Before the 1990s, there were two predominant employment themes: (1) people had a fair amount of job security—a "job for life" with one company, and (2) management jobs were largely filled from within. So the major sources of an organization's talent were its internal candidates. Thus, point-factor analysis, or job valuation, wasn't entirely about classifying jobs into grades for pay purposes, but about establishing career paths to grow and move talent through the organization. Job valuation gave the organization an internal language to discuss why some jobs were bigger or smaller than others, and to identify the criteria that differentiated jobs. Market data were directly linked to internal equity, so job values were less likely to be linked to functional and job-specific market factors.

The 1990s brought a shift in thinking. Many U.S. organizations adjusted their compensation philosophies to reflect *market pricing* as a means to value work. With market pricing, data from a compensation survey and the organization's size are compared only to the external market (i.e., external value), not to the content or characteristics of the job (i.e., internal value). This changed the focus from internal value to external market conditions as the primary determiner of job value.

What started this shift in outlook? In the 1990s, new technologies began to transform organizations and led to the development of new products, more services, and an overall faster pace of change. New competitors could enter markets more rapidly than before. The recession of 1991 also led to massive layoffs and broke the sacred "employment contract" of a job for life with one company. As the economy picked up, there was aggressive external hiring to fill jobs at all levels.

At the same time, many organizations' compensation-management systems broke down or were unresponsive to the changes occurring. The process for evaluating the content of new jobs was often too slow and too complicated to work in this new environment. Employers also cared less about retaining "career" workers than about obtaining short-term employees to fill immediate needs. Because employees were now working for a series of companies, compensation paid in other organizations became more important than the internal pay picture.

Organizations tended to adopt *market ranking*—a system of comparing jobs to survey descriptions and placing them in ranges or assigning them *market reference values* that approximated the competitive practice.[2] Because many point-factor plans were internally focused, these plans lost some credibility when organizations became more focused on external competitiveness.[3] Market pricing based the value of a job solely on what the external market paid for similar positions. Market pricing was viewed as better at capturing changing pay rates and external supply-demand imbalances. Remember the Y2K programmers? Individuals with COBOL programming skills were unemployable in the early 1990s but worth a lot in the late 1990s as organizations struggled to move their legacy systems from two- to four-digit years! Enterprise resource planning systems (ERPs) are another example of how supply-demand factors cause internal equity values to not fit market conditions.

So What's Different in the 2000s?

Why are the disciplines of compensation management and job measurement moving away from pure market pricing and toward a more balanced approach? Why is market pricing now challenged on a number of fronts as inadequate? One reason is that the external market doesn't necessarily reflect how your own organization values the work. The market data may suggest that job A should be paid more (or is valued higher) than job B, even though job B is seen internally as more complex.

With pure market pricing, company career hierarchies may be turned topsy-turvy. For example, one survey may rank engineer II higher than another survey ranks engineer III. The difference may be in the job model, number of participants in the survey, or quality of the classifications. Compensation market data are like other market research—imperfect. Does this really help managers make sound pay decisions that reflect the organization's values regarding jobs? Although the information may be useful, the decisions should not be driven solely by market reference data. Here's the bottom line on market ranking: It's a judgment call in many instances and does not substitute for a careful analysis of the job elements.[4]

Line managers today need to know what jobs are worth in the job market. What variables (specific accountabilities, experience required, or training needed, for instance) cause a job to command a higher salary? How does this job line up with peer positions? How do the data support career pathing? Management wants to know how to value changes in job content and organizational structure so they can reward employees in the positions that contribute more value to the organization.

Therefore, we suggest a combination of internal value assessment and external market data to determine the value of each job, which we call job-content market pricing. You should know both approaches; one set of facts without the other will give you incomplete answers. How do changes in accountability impact pay levels? How does a manager value jobs that are unique to the organization? Management needs a reliable and consistent method, with the ability to use data globally and across departments, as well as one that uses a common language to describe relative job content. We discuss this approach later in the chapter. At this point, one thing is clear: Valuing work accurately enables organizations to pay individuals in accordance with their contributions while also providing insight into how jobs relate to the organization's goals, objectives, and success.[5]

Why Job Content Matters: Two Examples

As we discussed, understanding the content of jobs is essential for determining market value. Recently, a vice president and divisional merchandising manager of a Fortune 100 retailer asked Hay Group to look into a problem: hiring qualified buyers to support its continued growth. The company had redesigned and flattened the organization and had created buyer jobs with more accountability and decision-making authority. But it couldn't find qualified people for the salary range that HR had assigned to the buyer job. HR was matching the redesigned jobs to market-priced buyers; HR did not take into consideration the redesign of the job, which created a position larger than the market standard. With the position going unfilled, there were bigger workloads for those in existing positions. The situation was beginning to jeopardize sales and profit objectives. Sound familiar?

The first step in working with our client was to ensure that we understood the job in question—not just the qualifications but also the type of work to be performed, the responsibilities, the extent of supervision, the goals, the objectives, the ideal hire's profile, and the customers being targeted. Once the information was gathered, the problem was obvious. This organization was looking to hire people with a skill set that was significantly larger than that for the usual buyer position. Most commonly, this skill set was the requirement for at least a senior buyer or a VP/DMM (divisional merchandising manager).

HR and Compensation had determined the market price for this position by looking at surveys for "buyer" and matching comparable revenue responsibilities where applicable. However, this answered only half the question of value. By ignoring job content, they were undervaluing the position by more than 25 percent. Instead of pricing the job at $90,000 per year, HR should have priced it at $120,000—a recipe for recruiting and retention problems that had a material effect on the business.

When we reported that the job was better matched to a VP/DMM, the organization admitted that its most recent new hires had actually held positions much higher in title in other organizations. HR had been so focused on matching titles that it had overlooked the central problem: a mismatch in job content.

Line managers often tell us that the work for jobs they manage is different from that at the competition, but that HR doesn't get it. Indeed, the vice president of sales at a large global consumer products company described how the data provided by HR were actually too high and that they were creating cost pressures. The position of account manager in her area was actually more like a sales representative, with a focus more on customer service than on sales. At her organization, these account managers performed routine customer support, taking orders and resolving problems, while the sales function operated at the com pany level rather than at the local level. As a result, the required skills and pay level differed from those of a true account manager, whose focus is traditionally on client development and sales. The market value for the account manager in our example company above was closer to $50,000, not the $65,000 that HR's surveys had indicated.

So you can see how important it is to have an adequate understanding of the content of the job so that appropriate external market pricing decisions can be made. Without a clear understanding of job content, you can't accurately value the work being done. Undervalue the jobs and you're likely to increase turnover and create hiring problems. Overvalue the jobs and you risk creating cost pressures and internal discontent.

The Manager's Need to Know

Your HR representative or the compensation analyst supporting your area is probably not going to know as much as you do about how you designed the jobs and why. So explain clearly how the content of the jobs you manage differs from the competition's jobs. According to WorldatWork, the professional association for compensation and benefits professionals:

> Compensation management needs to be "owned" by top management and managed by line managers and supervisors. Top management needs to be involved because compensation is commonly the largest controllable line in the budget. Corporate

leaders need to be confident that the pay system is serving the organization's business needs.

Line managers are in a prime position to decide if their people are paid properly and to make periodic decisions to adjust individual salaries. They know the star performers and the employees and other employers come for to recruit. Even in the smallest firms, line managers have a good sense of what the market is paying for jobs in their fields.[6]

We've touched on the fact that misaligning jobs and pay can create significant internal pressures, as your team members compare the value of their jobs to those in other departments and groups in the organization. This awkward situation can create even bigger headaches than the two previous examples have shown. Thus, the advice to understand how jobs are designed and how those designs impact market values applies not only to existing and new jobs but also to changes that are made in jobs as a result of shifts in business objectives and customer needs. For example, if you add "client analysis" to a customer service job description, it may increase the value of the job and have implications for future recruiting, retention, and pay levels. We will address this more later in this chapter, but for now be aware that you need to be in partnership with those in the organization who determine the value of work. In most organizations, that responsibility is held by HR.

A line manager must understand the methods that HR uses to value jobs, as well as the pros and cons of those methods. This way you can ask the right questions to ensure that your jobs are valued correctly. According to Stephen Fournier, managing editor for *Business & Legal Reports*, a publication focused on legal compliance for HR professionals, "Line managers often find themselves caught in the middle . . . on one side is the candidate, who is expected to disappear promptly if the offer is too low. On the other side are upper management and HR, struggling to maintain a fair, disciplined and defensible structure within budgetary constraints."[7]

In face-to-face discussions with candidates and HR, line managers often find it helpful to know the following:

- How the job fits into the employer's job hierarchy and the basis for determining its relative worth
- Market pay for the job or pay grade: minimum, midpoint, and maximum rates, as calculated from survey data

- How pay raises are distributed and what candidates might expect in recognition of exemplary performance

Do most line managers have this information? Probably not, according to *Business & Legal Reports.* When survey respondents were asked to rate, on a scale of 0 to 5, the level of knowledge attained by their line managers in these areas and the level that should be attained, there was a pronounced gap, with line managers falling short in every area.[8]

New Ways of Assigning Value to Work

As discussed earlier in this chapter, the way of assigning value to different types of work has changed over the years. To review briefly, there are two general approaches used today: market pricing and job evaluation. Both place value on the work being performed, with the former focused on what the external market pays for similar jobs, and the latter on the internal relationships of job content in the organization, with secondary focus on what the external market pays for comparable job content. Both have strengths and weaknesses (see Figure 6-2).

But a third approach is gaining visibility: a merger of market pricing and job evaluation that maximizes the benefits of both while minimizing the downside of either. This approach has been called different things by

FIGURE 6-2. COMPARISON OF TWO APPROACHES TO WORK VALUATION

	Advantages	Disadvantages
Title Match	• Reflects data for jobs of comparable duties and roles or organizations	• Often comparable job titles do not exist
	• Reflects economic issues such as supply and demand of labor	• No formal way to adjust for job content differences or quality of matches
	• Relatively easy to complete	• May not line up with career paths
	• Can often be modified to reflect industry, geography, revenue, or regression based on ad hoc adjustments	• Are modifications reliable and repeatable year over year?
	• Tangible results to share	• Tangible results to share
Job Evaluation	• Reflects job content	• Influenced by quality of evaluations
	• Reflects the organization's culture and values	• Requires evaluations
	• Systematic way to determine how job content impacts market	• May not take into consideration unique differences in pay for functions, titles, or market
	• Supports career progression	• Can be difficult to explain to those not familiar with job evaluation methodology
	• Provides market data where no match exists	

different experts. According to an article in *Human Resource Executive,* "Some HR executives are beginning to question their over-reliance on market data to price jobs, turning instead to a new approach that ties pay to a job's value to the company."[9] But before we discuss this third approach, let's review the two approaches used most often today.

Job Evaluation

Hay Group pioneered the point-factor comparison method of job evaluation in the early 1950s. The approach starts with the assumption that every job exists to add value to the organization by delivering some kind of results. During job evaluation, the content of each job is analyzed relative to three factors and is then given a numerical value for each factor. These factors are broadly defined as know-how, problem solving, and accountability. This approach is also called point-factor because of the assignment of points to these factors. The numbers are then totaled to determine the overall job size. For example, a management job evaluated under this approach may have 400 know-how points, 200 problem-solving points, and 230 accountability points. Total points would add to 830, which may equate to a salary band 10. The salary range for a band 10 job would then be a function of how the organization values its jobs relative to the overall market for jobs requiring similar skills and having accountabilities of similar size and complexity.

With the job evaluation approach, there's less emphasis on specific title-to-title comparisons and more emphasis on how jobs compare relative to skill, effort, and responsibility. This approach requires a solid understanding of the jobs under review, usually derived from job descriptions, questionnaires, interviews, and the like. There are other ways that organizations implement the job evaluation approach, either internally or in collaboration with consulting firms. But all of these methods determine the internal value of a job using specific criteria; the internal value is then linked to market data. For example, another method of job evaluation is a variation of *whole job slotting*, in which jobs at a somewhat qualitative level are compared against each other based on the total attributes of the jobs in an attempt to determine which jobs are more valuable to the organization.

Research conducted by Hay Group, Loyola University Chicago, and WorldatWork shows that point-factor approaches are still viewed as the most effective way to value work.[10] Other approaches rely less on specific title-to-title comparisons and more on how comparable job content is compensated in the market. While job evaluation typically is a primary way to link jobs to compensation, it can also be the foundation for programs that support career development, job-person fit assessment, succession planning, and organization analysis, as the following case illustrates.

Case Study: Deere & Company

Founded in 1837, Deere & Company (John Deere) grew from a one-man blacksmith shop into a worldwide corporation with operations in more than 160 countries and 46,000+ employees. John Deere consists of three equipment operations, a credit division, and four support operations.

In 2000, John Deere's new CEO, Robert W. Lane, challenged his HR department to come up with a global rewards strategy, which would provide global consistency in the way Deere business units assessed performance and rewarded employees. Deere developed a total rewards strategy, but to make it work, Deere needed a way to assess the value-added contribution of roles. According to John Leinart, director of compensation, benefits and integration, "we had a home-grown point factor system and pay was market driven. It was really hard to maintain globally. The first step we took to implement our new system was to gather facts about work globally that allow us to look at jobs via accountabilities, qualifications and competencies." Today managers at John Deere can make apples-to-apples comparisons of qualifications and competencies for all jobs in the organization.

These days, according to Leinart, half of all eligible employees routinely log on to the company's employee-development website, where they can learn about career development and career paths, company-sponsored educational opportunities, diversity matters, staffing needs, and performance management. This website lets employees know what is expected of them in their jobs, where they can get the skills they need to develop further, how they will be measured, and where they can go for help. And the site is consistent for employees across the world.

"We make software to track grain from seed to store," says Leinart. "But before this, we didn't have a job grading system to track people through their careers. This didn't make much sense to us." John Deere's new global rewards strategy has helped the company gain clarity, align jobs globally, and communicate to everyone in the organization just what it takes to succeed in his or her job. The benefits of this program include:

- *Job Alignment:* Today, a grade 7 engineer at one location does the same work as a grade 7 engineer anywhere else in the world. This allows the organization to leverage its people globally, use a common language for work values, and gain tremendous efficiencies.

- *Powerful Methodology:* The new system gives John Deere a work-based, data-rich objective methodology for global talent management.

- *A Legally Defensible System:* With jobs aligned and performance graded with consistent and fair measures, equal-pay lawsuits are less likely.

Market Pricing

The market-pricing approach values jobs based on what other companies pay people in similar positions. This is typically done by comparing an organization's jobs to various salary surveys and making judgment calls on relevant matches, then recording the market pay. Often the relative values in various surveys are merged to determine a single market value. Figure 6-3, for example, shows how the market rate for an accountant has been calculated using three different surveys.

One of the obvious challenges in using this approach is what to do when you don't think the title match is valid—for example, if the companies cited in the surveys are much larger or smaller than your organization, or the job match seems light for the job in your organization. You either accept the data for what it is or you adjust it up or down. In some cases, the surveys may have a high or low match in addition to

FIGURE 6-3. MARKET RATES FOR AN ACCOUNTANT

	Weight	Median Pay
Survey A	50%	$44,000
Survey B	25%	$38,000
Survey C	25%	$52,000
Weighted Average		**$44,500**

various cuts of the data, but when these either don't exist or don't make the appropriate distinctions, many managers will simply add or subtract 10 to 15 percent to the data as an adjustment. The difficulty is in establishing a clear and defensible process you can repeat year after year.

Often you can't make a title comparison, and sometimes there are no market data. Our research suggests that a typical organization can market price no more than 60 percent of its jobs.[11] And often the jobs that can't be market priced are unique in the organization—designed to give it a competitive advantage. Therefore, it's especially important to have a valuing process that ensures these roles are priced appropriately. Since most market-pricing organizations confront this reality regularly, they relate, or "slot," these roles relative to a benchmark that they can price. In other words, they use some form of internal job valuation to determine the relative value of the 40 percent or so of jobs that can't be title matched directly to survey data. Adjustments can be made to market data on a holistic basis, but such judgments are more defensible if made on the basis of solid job evaluation criteria.

The Optimal Approach—Job Content Market Pricing

After reviewing the pros and cons of job evaluation and market pricing, it seems logical to combine the best of both, thus balancing internal value with direct market or title comparisons (when available). We call this approach *job content–based market pricing*. This third approach begins with an evaluation of each job and then applies that information to specific market data.

We make decisions based on price almost every day—for groceries, entertainment, household goods. But we make major purchases based on an often complex set of criteria. After all, what you will pay for a product or service is a function of what you want and the value you will derive from it. We do not decide to just pay a market average for a given product. In fact, always paying market average for everything we buy would be ridiculous, wouldn't it? Rather, you assess your needs and then decide how much the product or service is worth to you and your family.

Likewise, you have particular criteria in mind when you consider the value of a job. You may have jobs that by design are more or less complex or have more of an impact on end results than the industry norm. For example, this could be a sales role that requires advanced skills to close the deal. Is this job worth the same as more traditional sales jobs in your organization? How do you balance the importance of a job to the particular organization with the complexity of other jobs that may differ from the competition? And how does this inequity influence market data unique to these positions?

Figure 6-4 is a comparison of the job values (represented as total points) assigned to the position of safety engineer, determined by using both job evaluation and market-pricing approaches. As the figure shows, the traditional market-pricing (external match) approach produces a salary well above the true value of the job, whereas a traditional job evaluation (internal match) approach may not reflect how this specific market pays for this engineer's skills. So in this case, the market data may need to be adjusted downward, closer to $55,000, or an almost 15 percent difference.

The advantages of this job content market-pricing approach is that it combines the best of both job evaluation and market-pricing approaches. It supplements traditional market pricing because it better reflects the true nature and value of the jobs in your organization. There are trade-offs, however, in that this approach requires an understanding and knowledge of job analysis and job evaluation methodologies. It also requires adequate time and resources to apply these methodologies in determining when jobs should be priced differently from reported market data for generic jobs.

Case Study: JCPenney

The retailer JCPenney recently implemented a job content–based market-pricing philosophy to move away from a fairly paternalistic culture that encouraged internal promotions driven by longevity rather than real changes in job content. JCPenney took the following steps to implement this approach:

- Partnered with an outside consulting firm and thoroughly planned each step of the project

FIGURE 6-4. INTERNAL VS. EXTERNAL WORK VALUES FOR AN ENGINEER POSITION

Internal Match	Evaluation	External Match	Evaluation	Market P50 Pay
Safety Engineer III	417	Sr. Safety Engineer	494	$64,000

- Met with senior organization leaders to understand key issues and obtain buy-in and input
- Worked with line managers and HR to identify and understand the content of benchmark jobs
- Reviewed external market surveys and identified the most relevant sources of comparators
- Matched up benchmark jobs to surveys by job title and job content
- Grouped jobs based on their impact on the company (career banding) to reduce job title proliferation while retaining meaningful career paths
- Slotted remaining nonbenchmark jobs around the benchmarks.
- Implemented and communicated the program

JCPenney found that job evaluation when combined with market pricing could provide much more accurate market data because it:

- Facilitated a more thorough analysis of the content of jobs and how the design of jobs affects their market value
- Provided JC Penney executives with a common language to describe work and an understanding of the criteria that determine the value of work, as well as how some jobs are bigger or smaller than other jobs
- Created a methodology that was consistent and repeatable for obtaining market data on nonbenchmark roles

Donna Graebner, compensation director at JCPenney, credits this system with moving its culture from pay based on effort and tenure to one based on accountability and end results.[12]

Summary: A Checklist for Putting a Price Tag on Work

As we have said, job content does matter in establishing values for the jobs in an organization, and many companies are at least informally incorporating job content into their work-valuation methods. It's clear that line management plays a vital role in the effective valuing of work. Line managers are tasked with designing jobs, so who better to describe that content and, working with HR, determine the value of those jobs than the line manager?

The methods organizations use to place a value on the work their employees do have evolved over time. Employers today realize that a

balanced approach provides the best solution. Line managers will continue to play a critical role in this process. For example, there are four
important ways line managers can play a critical role in determining the
value of work:

1. Be involved in the design of jobs (job analysis, descriptions, etc.)
   and ensure that HR understands the nature of the jobs you create
   or shape and how they relate to other jobs in the organization
   and elsewhere.

2. Be accountable for documentation of the work being performed.
   Often job documents are the primary source of data used in valuing work. Since HR is spending less time on job valuation owing
   to budget constraints and other priorities, it is even more important that line managers take ownership for those documents.

3. Help HR establish and review job content, and subsequent market values, to ensure the values support career development and
   reward employees who have taken on additional responsibilities.
   Line managers must ensure that HR understands the process and
   methodology, as well as how job values ultimately impact pay
   levels.

4. Partner with HR to ensure effective communications with employees. No matter how good the valuing process is, if how the
   values were obtained is not understood, little if any value is created. Line managers need to ensure that appropriate information
   is shared with employees. Communicating with employees about
   job values sets a path for continued employee career development, whereby they take on more responsibilities, for which they
   are justly rewarded.

CHAPTER 7

Base Salary Management: Building the Foundation

EMPLOYEES MAY NOT REMEMBER all of the objectives of their organization's incentive program or be able to recite their employer's core values. But they do know what their base salaries are, they understand what fairness and competitiveness are, and they probably have strong opinions about why their last raises weren't big enough.

Base pay is the foundation of any compensation program and the most visible component to the vast majority of employees. Every paycheck is a reminder of the link between individual efforts and the organization's perception of their value. Clearly there is a critical need to get base pay right and to use it effectively to attract, retain, and motivate staff. In the previous chapter we covered how organizations decide on the value of work, which typically determines the pay range for given jobs. In this chapter, we explain how to use your organization's base salary structure to best position your staff's compensation to recognize and reward performance.

How Base Pay Programs Should Work

To see the importance of base salary to most employees, take a look at Figure 7-1. For the CEO and other senior executives, the variable por-

FIGURE 7-1. PERCENTAGE MIX OF COMPENSATION FOR SEVEN LEVELS OF EMPLOYEES

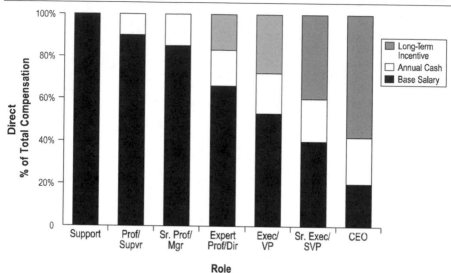

tion of their pay represents most of their compensation. They have more at risk and therefore the link between pay and performance is strongest in the bonuses, long-term incentives, and other compensation they are offered. The opposite is true for employees at support, supervisor, managerial, and professional levels: the individuals who constitute the vast majority of employees in any organization. For them, base pay is the largest component of the pay package: 80 to 100 percent of their total compensation.

In order to manage base pay for your employees, it's important to understand the mechanics of the base pay program where you work and how much latitude you have within that system. Typically, as companies grow and mature, they need to formalize how they manage pay as well as people. As we've stressed throughout this book, the best compensation structure is one that fits your organization's strategy and culture. Decisions about base pay are made not on an individual employee basis but within the context of the organization's needs and operating philosophy.

There are three primary types of compensation structures: individual job pricing, salary grades, and broad bands. While each has different operating mechanisms, all three have some common objectives:

- Recognize the relative value of work within the organization.
- Provide a framework for consistent decisions about pay.
- Manage compensation costs and balance internal equity with external market.

Which structure is right for your organization? That depends on the size and complexity of your organization—and your current and desired work culture. Figure 7-2 shows the basic evolution of base pay at a growing organization. The move is from individual jobs to salary grades and finally to salary bands; as the system evolves, the number of salary levels is reduced and the pay process is streamlined. While some organizations still use individual job pricing, salary grades are the most common type of base pay structure.

Individual Job Pricing

By its very nature, *individual job pricing* is a function of need and circumstance. In a 20-person start-up company, the compensation structure is whatever the individual salaries of the employees happen to be. When new employees arrive, their capabilities and salary requirements are compared to those of the current employees, and their base salaries are established.

FIGURE 7-2. EVOLUTION OF BASE PAY TO SALARY BANDS

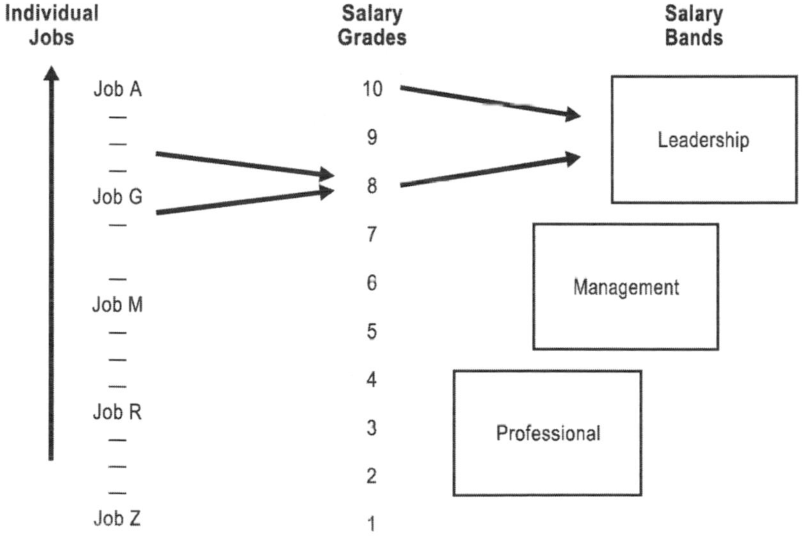

On one hand, the person making the hiring decision might be concerned about creating pay inequities that could upset the budding work environment and whatever teamwork has evolved to make the company successful. On the other hand, the employees may recognize that new people bring needed skills to help the company grow. And since the company may not be relying on data from compensation surveys, the employment market is defined by whatever it takes to get the necessary talent on board.

As organizations grow, it's common to establish a market target for each job (for example, the average or median salary for that position in the labor market) based on public data or proprietary compensation surveys. The addition of minimum and maximum salary caps creates a range of pay that managers can use to make compensation decisions. For example, traditional salary ranges have a minimum at about 80 percent of the market target and a maximum of 120 percent. Accordingly, a salary range with a market target of $100,000 would have a minimum of $80,000 and a maximum of $120,000. See Figure 7-3 for a typical salary range structure for six different jobs.

Salary Grades

In a larger company that has hundreds of jobs and tens of thousands of employees, maintaining distinct market rates of pay and salary ranges for individual jobs would be an administrative nightmare. Accordingly, most large organizations use *salary grades*, which typically group jobs of similar size together for compensation-administrative purposes. As noted in Figure 7-3, the market targets for jobs D and E are only 2.5 percent apart. So combining two or more levels into one level simplifies

FIGURE 7-3. SALARY RANGES FOR SELECTED JOBS

	80% Minimum	Market Target	120% Maximum
Job A	$44,000	$55,000	$66,000
Job B	$38,400	$48,000	$57,600
Job C	$33,600	$42,000	$50,400
Job D	$32,000	$40,000	$48,000
Job E	$31,200	$39,000	$46,800
Job F	$28,000	$35,000	$42,000

administration of the structure and eliminates a small difference that may be difficult to explain.

Salary grades are the most common compensation structure, found in approximately 80 percent of companies.[1] Figure 7-4 shows a sample salary grade structure.

In Figure 7-4, grade levels are grouped or clustered (1–2, 3–6, 7–10). Grades 7–10 may be supervisory and professional jobs that, although varying in scope and complexity, are more similar to one another than they are to other jobs in the organization. Clustering helps employees understand job categories and it helps managers communicate about them.

When you can talk about how your organization's pay is structured—when you can point out why, for example, Bob earns $58,000, Mary Kay earns $48,000, and Christopher and Rachael each earn $40,000—you'll be in a great position to help your employees understand that their own job level reflects their job's scope, complexity, and value to the organization. This is a first step in managing base pay and in managing the expectations around base pay.

When developing a salary grade structure, there are a number of things to consider:

• *The Number of Grades in the Structure:* How many grades should the salary structure have? The number of grades depends on the size of your organization and the range of jobs. Some organizations may have

FIGURE 7-4. TRADITIONAL SALARY STRUCTURE

Grade	80% Minimum	100% Midpoint	120% Maximum	Example Jobs
10	$48,000	$60,000	$72,000	Senior Accountant
9	$41,600	$52,000	$64,400	Accountant
8	$36,000	$45,000	$54,000	Accounting Supervisor
7	$32,600	$40,800	$49,000	Accountant (Entry)
6	$29,600	$37,000	$44,400	Sr. Accounting Technician
5	$26,800	$33,500	$40,200	Sr. Accounting Clerk
4	$24,200	$30,300	$36,400	Accounting Clerk
3	$22,000	$27,500	$33,000	Accounting Clerk (Entry)
2	$20,000	$25,000	$30,000	File Clerk
1	$18,000	$22,500	$27,000	Receptionist

grades from entry-level nonexempt support to CEO. Others may decide to take grades up to senior management levels and use a different structure for top executives. Although there's no universally accepted right number of grades, having too many or too few can pose problems. For example, we've heard many managers say, "I can't tell the difference between the jobs in Grades 6 and 7. I have an employee who thinks his job should be at Grade 7 instead of Grade 6, and I don't know what to tell him." Another common management concern is employees notice that similar jobs in other departments are graded higher than their own. Understanding how your company assigns jobs to grades and the process to review grade levels is important to setting the right pay opportunity for all positions.

• *The Assignment of Jobs to Grades:* Jobs are typically assigned to a salary grade based on their scope, complexity, and market value. Grade 8 in Figure 7-4 could include a range of jobs such as first-line supervisors, financial analysts, and programmers who have the same relative value to the company. Typically, the organization will have a "schema," or a set of criteria, used by HR in concert with line managers to assess, analyze, and evaluate jobs and to assign them to appropriate grades.

• *The Overlap of Salary Ranges:* As noted earlier, with a traditional salary range, the minimum is typically set at approximately 80 percent of the job's midpoint and the maximum at 120 percent. We say this range has a "50 percent spread," since the maximum is 50 percent greater than the minimum. Over the past decade or so, we've observed that salary ranges are getting wider. This means that managers have more flexibility in dealing with market issues and getting the talent they need. In our research with Loyola University Chicago and WorldatWork, we've found that the most common salary range width is now between 50 and 70 percent.[2] It's also common for salary ranges to overlap so that high-performing or long-tenured employees in one range can earn as much as new employees at higher grade levels. That makes it easier to move potential leaders across the organization, giving them experience in different business units while keeping their salaries within established ranges.

Broadbanding

Broadbanding is a response to a management challenge that's bigger and more complex than compensation alone. As organizations have "delayered" and become flatter, leaner, and more customer focused, they are requiring employees to possess a broader range of skills and take on new and changing responsibilities. As a result, some employers are moving away from traditional job classification hierarchy (picture the classic organizational chart with CEO at the top, under which are executive VPs, then senior VPs, then directors, etc.—your basic command-and-control organization). But since flatter organizations offer fewer opportunities to move up the ladder, wider salary bands allow people to earn salary increases without necessarily changing job titles. These organizations de-emphasize upward mobility and offer new reward mechanisms associated with an individual's personal, professional, and career development.

The concept of broadbanding has been used since the early 1990s. It was created to support career management in engineering ladders (for example, the jobs of engineer I, II, and III could all be in the same broadband, providing a manager flexibility to manage compensation and career levels in tandem). In practice, broadbanding results in fewer grades or job classifications than an organization had before. See Figure 7-5 for a sampling of jobs broadbanded by competency level.

Broadbanding tends to work best in fast-paced companies where speed to market is of the essence and where teams of experts are fre-

FIGURE 7-5. SAMPLE JOBS GROUPED BY COMPETENCY LEVEL

Band	Sample Jobs
Leadership/Expert Professional Senior-level Directors/Managers who translate strategic objectives into tactical plans and lead core functions or expert-level professionals.	• Director of Operations • Director of Sales • Director of Technology
Management/Senior Professional Mid/senior-level Managers who develop and implement operational plans for a functional area or highly seasoned professionals.	• Operations Manager • Plant Controller • Senior Systems Analyst
Supervisor/Professional First-line Supervisors/midlevel Managers focused on short-term execution of operational plans or entry- to mid-level professionals. Positions in this Band ensure the delivery of services either by their own effort or through supervision of others.	• Accountant • Production Supervisor • Regional Sales Manager
Specialized Support Positions that provide administrative and/or technical support performing procedures that require specialized knowledge, training, and skill. Mid- to advanced-level nonexempt or entry-level-exempt roles.	• Customer Service Rep • Drafting Technician • Laboratory Technician
Administrative Support Entry-level nonexempt roles that provide basic support to the day-to-day effectiveness of the company.	• Accounting Clerk • Receptionist • Shipping Clerk

quently put together and dismantled to satisfy the organization's constantly changing needs. The structure—with exceptionally wide salary bands often in excess of 100 percent from minimum to maximum—emphasizes career development and lateral moves within and across functions. As such, an employee could spend many years in one band, earning more and more money, gaining new skills, and taking on bigger responsibilities.

In spite of their flexibility, when organizations treat bands like jumbo salary ranges they often run into cost-control problems and other challenges. Typically, a few *market anchors* are introduced within each band to assist managers with administration. These market anchors provide organizations with a way to manage compensation within the broadband by identifying narrower pay zones that allow rewarding for job knowledge and performance, as well as competency growth. For example, if a broadband has a range of $28,000 to $60,000, it's important not to look at it as a salary range in the traditional sense. Rather, within the band some jobs are valued at $35,000 and others at $50,000. Managers need to manage pay in accordance with the market value of a job or compensation costs may get out of control.

The broadband concept is intended to provide greater flexibility to pay outstanding performers above the norm if the company believes there will be a return on its investment in those people. To illustrate this point, refer to Figure 7-5 and see that there may be a number of market anchors within the band. A job might be assigned to Market Anchor X, which represents a market median of $40,000. Pay around the median can be linked to performance, competencies, and other factors—much as in a traditional salary range. One key difference is that unlike salary range, the market anchor doesn't have a minimum or a maximum. The market data are more of a reference point for the manager to make pay decisions. The manager may decide to pay $55,000 for a job assigned to Market Anchor X, assuming the decision has a sound business rationale. This flexibility is one of the key differences between salary grades and broadbands.

Case Study: Home Depot

With more than $73.1 billion in sales, Home Depot is the world's largest home-improvement retailer and the second largest retailer in the United States. The company has more than 1,800 stores and 300,000 associates. Home Depot grew up fast: 1990 saw just 145 stores and $3.8 billion in sales. Over the next decade, the number of stores tripled every three years. By 2002, the organization was opening a new store every 48 hours. "We were an incredible snowball running downhill," recalls Home Depot's director of compensation and performance management, Rich Johnson. "No one else was in our space. All we had to do was get the store open." With its stock price soaring through the 1990s, Home Depot had no trouble attracting high-energy, can-do people to its ranks.

Problem was, by offering desirable job candidates whatever it took to get them aboard, base salaries were all over the map. Eventually the company lacked consistency, fairness, and equity in how it paid people. That created an awkward situation when multiple Home Depot stores opened in the same markets, with associates' salaries differing widely. When that happens, says Johnson, the analysts begin to look at you differently. "You can keep your arms around a few hundred stores that are geographically diverse," he says. But by 2000, things were snowballing out of control.

Home Depot wanted to develop a solution—one that would still give store managers some latitude in hiring but would add more structure to the process. "We wanted a flexible pay system that would allow us to manage people's careers," says Johnson. "That's why we implemented a broadbanding program."

Home Depot developed a broadbanding system that helped transform the home-improvement giant into a more disciplined organization that pays people based on their performance—within reasonable ranges that everyone understands. Under the new plan, minimum, midpoint, and maximum salaries are set for lot associates, cashiers, sales associates, sales specialists, and supervisors. Managers rank employees either "outstanding," "achiever," "performer," or "needs improvement." And merit increases are distributed based on a combination of individual and store performance.

Among its benefits, the plan is credited with improving annual turnover to 40 percent in an industry that averages near 100 percent or more. Today, pay is much more aligned from store to store, generating improved fairness and consistency. In the old days, Home Depot rewarded longevity. Now the culture is more driven by performance. All the while, Home Depot remains a market leader in compensation.

Linking Performance to the Market

The first step in using base pay to attract, retain, and motivate your employees is to understand the type of salary structure in your organization, how jobs are placed within the structure, how it connects to other compensation (such as bonuses, benefits, etc.), and what its focus is (for example, some base pay systems focus on what the competition's paying, some on fairness between jobs within the organization, and others on a balance between the two). With an understanding of the playing field, we can now shift our focus to the general "rules of the game" regarding base pay management.

Regardless of the type of salary structure in your organization, there are two core concepts that are likely part of the design of your compensation program: the relationship between an employee's performance, potential, and salary relative to the market; and a method of allocating salary increases relative to the market. The midpoint of a salary range or a market anchor within a broadband represents an organization's targeted level of compensation for a fully competent employee. This is driven by a company's compensation philosophy and should take into account the total compensation package (base pay, annual incentives, long-term incentives, and benefits).

Base Pay

Many organizations target base pay at the average or median of the market value. In fact, Hay Group research suggests that 80 percent of organizations report positioning base salary targets between the 40th and 60th percentile of the base salary market.[3] Others may have more leverage built into their compensation philosophy, whereby target base pay is below the market average/median. For instance, they may have a more aggressive variable pay program to make up the difference. Historically, public sector employers have strong benefit programs (health care and retirement, for example), which typically allows them to pay base salaries below the private sector.

Understanding your company's compensation philosophy and the market positioning of base pay is important as you communicate with current and prospective employees. Once you understand the intent and foundation of your company's compensation philosophy, the next step is to consider the basic relationship between an employee's performance and potential relative to the market.

We typically think about a portion of the salary range around the midpoint as a *market zone* (in a broadbanding environment this would be a zone around the market target). In the example in Figure 7-6, if an

FIGURE 7-6. MANAGING SALARIES WITHIN A RANGE

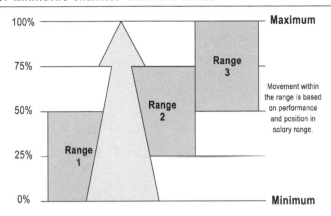

employee's pay falls within 25 to 75 percent (the middle half) of the salary range, the individual would be considered to be "within the market zone." Individual salaries will vary around the market target based on a number of factors, such as performance, tenure, market supply and demand, previous salary, and the employee's potential.

Typically, employees in the lower half of the salary range (0–50 percent) are new hires or employees who are continuing to grow in their capability—newly promoted employees, for example. The top half of the range (50–100 percent) represents above-market pay for consistent high performers or newly hired employees who bring unique and proven skills and experiences to the job—for example, someone hired from a competitor who's been highly successful in a similar job.

The middle half of the range (25–75 percent) represents market pay for solidly performing employees who are competent in the core aspects of their role. Note that there tends to be an obsession with the midpoint of the salary range (100 percent of the market target or 50 percent of the penetration within the range). Sometimes market data may imply a level of precision in measuring the market that doesn't actually exist (a midpoint of $45,352, for example).

While development of a compensation structure is based on a significant amount of data and analysis, there is quite a bit of art to the process as well. Organizations use the *compa-ratio* statistic (an employee's salary divided by the midpoint of the salary range) to determine where someone's pay falls within the range. Over time, companies would like to have a positive correlation between performance and position in the salary range (top performers paid above market, solid performers paid around the market, for example). In reality, though, employees are paid throughout the salary range and their pay at any point may or may not reflect their current level of performance.

Salary Increases

The second core concept in base pay management is allocating salary increases relative to performance. First, organizations need to ensure that performance ratings translate into differentiated rewards. Many organizations spend an agonizing amount of effort to ensure that managers comply with some sort of a distribution curve of performance ratings. But what value is this if the highest performer still receives only marginally more rewards—whether in merit pay, incentive pay, or options—than the average performer? The ratings are merely a means to an end. And the end is higher rewards for the highest performance, not just a perfect distribution curve.

Most managers and employees agree that rewards should be differentiated based on performance, leading to better execution and employee behavior. At many organizations, managers want to give their stars bigger increases. But many see it as a zero-sum game. Providing larger increases to certain employees means that other employees get less, which requires managers to make some difficult decisions. Many managers choose to take the path of least resistance, giving employees roughly the same increase, rather than confront and address poor performance. This can be avoided by having ongoing dialogues with employees and truly differentiating the rewards. Ongoing dialogue eliminates the element of surprise, which can lessen the impact of giving a smaller increase. Managers weak in conducting performance-oriented discussions should seek coaching to improve their skills.

Management "courage" can go a long way toward improving the climate of the organization. As noted in an earlier chapter, nearly a third of workers surveyed by Hay Group agreed that poor performance is tolerated in their organization. The merit matrix (see Figure 7-7) is a tool to allocate a merit budget based on individual performance and the position of employees' salaries relative to the job market.

For example, in Figure 7-7, an employee who "meets expectations" and is currently paid between 93 and 107 percent of the market would be eligible for a merit increase up to 4 percent. This increase will main-

FIGURE 7-7. MERIT INCREASE MATRIX

Performance Rating	Salary as a Percentage of Target		
	80%–93%	93%–107%	107%–120%
4 (Outstanding) Consistently and substantially exceeded position expectations	Up to 9%	Up to 7%	Up to 5%
3 (Exceeds expectations) Consistently met and frequently exceeded position expectations	Up to 7%	Up to 5%	Up to 3%
2 (Meets expectations) Consistently met and sometimes exceeded position expectations	Up to 5%	Up to 4%	Up to 2%
1 (Needs improvement) Met some performance expectations, but total performance was not satisfactory	0%	0%	0%

tain or slightly enhance the individual's position relative to the job market. It reflects an alignment between performance and pay. Using a merit increase matrix results in giving high performers who are low paid relative to their market target larger increases to improve the competitiveness of their pay. And it also results in giving solid performers (those who are high relative to their market target) smaller increases; this has the effect of moving them toward the middle of the pay range.

The concept can work across a large employee population, but because the matrix is pegged to a budgeted amount, every large increase should be offset with a small one. An alternative is to spread increases evenly across the entire organization. But if you do that, people won't recognize a relationship between pay and performance. This is one of the key challenges for managers, and it is a primary reason many view their company's pay-for-performance systems as not working.

One of your primary objectives as a manager is to ensure that the pay for your employees is fair and consistent. By "fair" we mean internally evenhanded and externally competitive. "Fair" also recognizes the performance and contributions of your employees. However, it's important to remember that "fair" does not mean "equal." Accordingly, differentiating pay based on performance is fair; paying a high performer the same as an average performer is unfair to both.

Other Elements of Managing Base Pay

It is hoped that by now you have a better understanding of the types of salary structures organizations use and the concepts employed to link pay and performance. Your organization may have a manual on compensation administration that outlines how to handle a variety of situations regarding base pay management. However, let's look at some typical practices for a number of situations and review several examples of what to consider when you're making pay decisions.

New Hires

As a hiring manager you will be faced with a wide range of candidates (both internally and externally) ranging from individuals whose qualifications are at the minimum required for satisfactory performance to those who bring unique skills and experiences and can "hit the ground running." Typically, most organizations try to hire employees below the market target for the job. This helps preserve internal equity (fairness) while giving new hires the opportunity to earn merit increases. However, sometimes it's necessary to bring in an employee at a higher salary than the market target. Decisions like that are usually driven by market demands for or by the candidate's exceptional qualifications. As a manager, you shouldn't be afraid to make this type of decision, although being aware of and sensitive to other employees' pay and their relative positioning compared to the new hire is critical.

For example, Laura is an external candidate for a payroll supervisor position. She has a B.S. in business administration and seven years of industry experience. Her current salary is $43,500, which is slightly below P50 (median) of the market range. Most other supervisors are currently paid below the 25th percentile (P25), have been recently promoted, and have been in the job less than a year; however, one incumbent, who is paid $38,000, has five years of experience.

The payroll supervisor position has a market range as shown in Figure 7-8. Typically, a company would pay plus or minus the 50th percentile (P50) of the market range for new hires with solid relevant work

FIGURE 7-8. SAMPLE BASE SALARY MARKET RANGE

P10	P25	P50	P75	P90
$36.6	$40.8	$45.7	$51.2	$57.1

experience and who are expected to add immediate value. Given that most current supervisors at this organization have less than one year of experience in the job, their current pay below P25 of the market range is appropriate. It would be acceptable to offer Laura a salary at P50 (around $46,000) based on her transferable skills and valuable work experience.

The hiring manager should also consider developing a plan to review the compensation of the current supervisor with five years of experience, so as to move that associate between P25 and P50 of the market range based on performance; over time, the goal would be to get the associate to somewhere between $41,000 and $46,000, depending on performance, potential, and leadership capabilities.

Promotions

A promotion is traditionally viewed as a move from one position to another of greater authority, impact, complexity, responsibility, and income. As such, a promotional increase should be larger than a normal merit increase or an annual cost-of-living increase. When promotions are implemented at the same time as the annual merit increase, many companies take into account dollars allocated for the employee's annual increases.

There are two types of promotions, which differ in the magnitude of change:

1. *Career Ladder Promotion:* These are mostly job family moves (accountant to senior accountant, for example) that result in a one-grade change or incremental increase in the market value of the job; a promotional increase in the 5 to 10 percent range would be appropriate in most situations.

2. *Role Promotion:* Typically, these are more significant career progressions (hourly employee to manager, for example) involving jobs that are more than one grade apart or have a clear difference in market value; a promotional increase in the 7 to 15 percent range would be appropriate in most situations and in some cases greater than 15 percent if the new role requires a big stretch for the employee.

Demotions

A demotion is usually based on performance or business circumstances (job elimination, etc.). Sometimes it's initiated by the employee (owing to work-life issues). Many organizations are uncomfortable reducing an employee's salary in certain situations, especially when it's caused by a shift in business circumstances. While this may be understandable, it's critical that the organization keep clear records, since a future jobholder should be properly placed in a salary range geared to the job, not relative to the previous jobholder's salary.

Lateral Transfers

A lateral transfer is a move to a new role in the company that's similar in scope and complexity to one's current role. Ordinarily, lateral moves result in the transfer of an employee to a new job within the same pay grade or same band with a similar market anchor. Lateral moves may be employee driven (for example, a personal desire to learn a new area of the business) or company driven owing to a reorganization, owing to the need for employee development, or because a current employee has skills for which the company has critical needs.

A lateral move is an opportunity for an employee to try something new, face new challenges, and add breadth to his or her work experience. And, depending on the nature of the new assignment, it could also help an employee prepare for a bigger role in the organization. Although a lateral move may not automatically result in a pay increase, especially if it's driven by the employee's request, moving people around is an investment in the organization's future. If the value of the development experience is obvious, then base pay increases may also be part of the equation.

Developmental Moves

Developmental moves may be lateral or downward to new roles designed to expand people's capabilities while increasing their value to the organization. Developmental moves help employees prepare for larger roles in the company. These moves are crucial for increasing employees' skills and knowledge by enabling them to take on different challenges and learn new skills. Typically, employees receiving developmental moves are on a fast track and are consistently rated as high performers.

Most developmental moves don't require pay adjustments. However, based on the employee's potential, the level of personal risk being taken, and the expectation of adding significant value in the short term, an employee could be eligible for a nominal increase.

Other Pay Actions

Consider each of the following situations:

• *Employees Paid Below the Minimum:* When a new compensation program is implemented or an employee is promoted, a jobholder's pay may fall below the minimum of what the company thinks the job is worth. Employees who are performing at an acceptable level and are currently paid below the minimum of their salary ranges should be brought to the minimum of the range as soon as possible in a manner consistent with their performance. Most organizations try to accomplish this in a reasonable time period—6 to 12 months. If the employee's salary is considerably below the minimum, it may not be a good idea to make the increase all at once, but in steps until the proper pay level has been attained.

• *Employees Paid Above the Maximum:* Most organizations will hesitate to reduce the pay of individuals who are above the maximum of their salary range. If some people's pay is high relative to others owing to superior performance, they should be promoted to positions that are consistent with their current salaries. But if no such opportunities exist, an individual whose pay is above the range maximum should receive no increases until the pay range has risen appropriately.

• *Upward Reevaluation:* The upward reevaluation of a position can result in a job staying within its existing grade or in the placement of the job into a higher pay grade. The former will likely take place when the reevaluation is a result of changes to the job over a period of time.

Often, a job's scope evolves but the title remains the same. Depending on the scope of this change and the reasons behind it, the result may or may not be considered a promotion. Accordingly, since the newly defined job is in the same salary grade, a traditional promotional increase isn't appropriate. However, some movement up in the salary range may be warranted based on the jobholder's performance and the organization's show of confidence in the individual. But when the reevaluation of a position is the result of significant change at one point in time (such as the creation of a new position as part of a reorganization), this is a more evident promotion, calling for a pay increase in line with the organization's policy.

• *Downward Reevaluation:* When an employee's present position is reevaluated for reasons other than demotion (changes in organizational structure that affect the job's authority and impact, for instance), and the result is the jobholder's placement into a lower pay grade, the employee's salary should not be reduced. And such downward reevaluation should be taken into consideration at the time of the next annual increase.

• *Hot Skills/Geographic Pay Differentials:* Sometimes, established guidelines just won't work for a job: say, when your pay guidelines are established for headquarters in Chattanooga, for example, but you need to hire someone to live and work in New York City; or when you're faced with a hot-skills issue, such as a seller's market for computer programmers with specific skills. In these cases, many organizations simply add a figure—a differential—to the data they're using to determine salaries. Some organizations accommodate the special need by creating a distinct, time-bound contract supplement. If you add a differential, we suggest you keep it as a separate line item so you can manage pay more efficiently when the person moves back to Chattanooga or the programmer market changes.

Five Key Compensation Challenges

As we have worked with organizations of all sizes across a range of industries, certain questions about the effective management of base pay have come up frequently. The following are five of the most common challenges that we encounter and some suggested solutions.

Compensation Challenge #1: "I have a high-performing employee who is currently paid above the market. I would like to give her a meaningful increase, but the guidelines say I should start slowing down pay increases. How do I tell this superstar that she'll be getting a smaller increase?"

This is one of those situations where it seems you might have an employee who could be capable of a bigger role and a chance to have more of an impact. In this case, you might consider ways to reorganize the work so as to optimize the individual's potential, or you might look for a new developmental role. It's bad enough to have to tell a superstar that she'll be getting only a nominal increase; what's worse is that she'll probably get bored in her limited role and move on.

Compensation Challenge #2: "We only have a 3 percent merit budget this year. How can I differentiate pay and performance with such a small budget?"

The truth is that the size of the merit budget really doesn't matter when it comes to relative differentiation of increases. Pay increases were as tightly clustered around the double-digit budgets of the 1980s as they are around the single-digit budgets of today. With a 3 percent merit budget, your top employees can still get a 6 percent (or more) pay increase, assuming that poorer performers get no increase at all. One key characteristic of *Fortune* magazine's America's Most Admired Companies is that they are actually better able to differentiate pay and performance than other companies.[4] Even in times of tight salary increase budgets, these companies still find a way to reward the top performers because they differentiate performance and rewards more than the average organization.

Compensation Challenge #3: "Employees have given me salary data from a headhunter or from the Internet that suggests that they are underpaid. How do I deal with this?"

If only market pricing and determining competitive rates of pay were this simple! Nonetheless, we know this is an everyday occurrence for managers. In responding to this challenge it's first necessary to realize that it will always be possible to find employers and jobs that pay more than yours; that's just a reality. Remember, 50 percent of companies pay more than market median. One question to pose is, "What's it like to work there?" The best way to respond to this is to ensure your employees understand all the different elements that constitute *total* rewards within your organization—both tangible and intangible. It's rare that a website will have all of this information available so your employees will be looking at only one facet of the total rewards equation.

Also realize that recruiters have a vested interest in reporting higher levels of compensation to their clients, and Internet salary survey sites are not viewed as credibly as the proprietary compensation survey sources typically used by HR. However, there are times when it will be necessary to ask HR to assess and validate the company's position on jobs in question.

Compensation Challenge #4: "I'm considering my team in relation to the pay and performance definitions, and there are several people whose current position in the range does not fit the definition. How can I adjust their compensation?"

It's not uncommon to find a high performer who's been promoted several times and is relatively low in salary range, or an average performer with long tenure high in salary range. You can make adjustments over time by slowing or stopping the pay increases for one employee and using those dollars to adjust pay for the other. As a manager, you may be provided with salary increase guidelines by HR. This will help allocate and administer base salary increases within a given year. At the same time, you should view your staff as assets. If you have a finite amount of money to spend (your base salary budget), where do you think you'll get the best return on your investment?

Compensation Challenge #5: "I keep hiring new employees and because of the market I have to pay them more than people who are proven performers in the same job. What should I do about this?"

Here you have to find a balance between the work you need to get done, what it's costing you to hire new employees, and the organization's culture. Some organizations thrive on constantly looking to the market for better and better talent where the implicit message to current staff is to stay current and improve or find another employer. Others, however, have a more loyal approach to how they treat staff. So, the types of decisions posed by this compensation challenge must be made with your company's culture in mind.

That said, if the market rate of pay is increasing at a faster level than your current pay allowances, it could be only a matter of time before your "proven performers" find a more rewarding employer. Unfortunately, many organizations don't realize the cost—real and lost opportunity—of having to go outside to find and hire.

Summary: A Checklist for Managing Base Salaries

Every paycheck is an opportunity for managers to reinforce key messages about the organization's strategies and decisions. When managing base salaries:

- Take the time to learn the mechanics of your organization's base pay program, and how much latitude you have within the system.
- Cluster the job grades to help employees understand categories.
- If your organization is below average in base salaries relative to market and you aren't in a position to change that, be prepared to

discuss benefits and other aspects of total rewards to show employees a complete picture of their true value to the organization.

- Try to hire employees below the market target for the job; this helps preserve internal equity (fairness) in the department while giving new hires the opportunity to earn merit increases.
- If you add a differential to accommodate an employee in a region with a higher cost of living or a desperately needed individual with a hot skill, keep the differential as a line item so you can pull it out of the budget when the situation changes.

Reinforcing Results with Variable Pay

MANY PEOPLE TODAY working in jobs below the executive level have an opportunity to supplement their base salary by earning an incentive or a bonus. Although the size of this additional compensation, which we call variable pay, is usually much less than a person's salary, its ability to influence behavior can be significant—if a manager knows how to use it. Variable pay comes in many different forms, but they have one thing in common: The amount of money varies.

Types of Variable Pay Programs

This chapter addresses many forms of variable pay, but first let's get the terminology and exceptions out of the way.

The Difference Between Bonuses and Incentives

It's important to clarify the difference between bonus pay and incentives. An incentive has a *contractual* connotation: If you do this for me, you'll get a reward. The agreement is made up front, and the criteria and amount of payment are known. A bonus is a *discretionary* reward: Do good things for me and at the end of the year (depending on overall business performance), I'll see that there is something in it for you. With incentives, the measures and targets are explicit; with bonus pay, the measures may (or may not) be established up front, and there are often no specific targets.

Although incentives are generally preferred over bonuses, there are situations where bonuses are appropriate. For example, bonuses are widely used in professional services where the environment is fast paced and it may be difficult to establish objectives that can remain valid for a full year. Since our focus is on choosing the most appropriate measures and targets, most of this chapter deals with incentives.

When Discretionary Plans Are the Better Choice

Sometimes you may not be confident setting performance goals at the beginning of a measurement period because you know from experience that priorities frequently change—and when they do, performance expectations change, too. Or you may know what the objective is—for example, increased profitability—but because there's no performance history, you have no way of knowing how high to set the bar. Maybe you know that results will be influenced by too many factors outside your control, such as market conditions or unforeseen acquisitions. Or you know the right goal but you lack confidence in how performance is tracked.

In these situations, managers should have some discretion—some flexibility—so they can recognize performance without having to aim at moving targets. Discretionary plans are particularly effective in organizations with trustful cultures and when managers are prepared to not pay bonuses when they're not warranted.

Recognition—A Nonfinancial Reward

Besides motivating performance, variable pay plans are effective for recognizing top contributors. Unlike motivation, which requires a defined goal and stated award at the beginning of the measurement period, recognition allows managers to identify outstanding performance at the end of the cycle. This gives managers more flexibility, but it also demands that they have the skills to accurately differentiate the awards among recipients. It is important to note that recognition is a powerful reinforcement mechanism. But recognition obviously is not about financial recognition. In fact, some of the most powerful recognition vehicles are the informal thank-yous that managers give their employees.

Chapter 12 provides a more in-depth treatment of nonfinancial recognition.

Incentives That Motivate

Perhaps the most common approach to variable pay and arguably the most effective in terms of motivation is an incentive plan that defines performance goals and lists the potential earnings for achieving these goals. The performance goals can be individual objectives, team or unit goals, or even company targets. The measurement period can be virtually any length, although it is typically monthly, quarterly, or annual. (See Chapter 4 for details on developing performance measures.)

According to the 2005 *Hay Compensation Planning Guide,* 91 percent of organizations report offering a broad-based annual incentive plan. The trend toward variable pay plans, and particularly incentive plans, is clear, but the reason for implementing such plans varies considerably. According to our research and anecdotal feedback from the marketplace, the most common objectives are to improve organization and team financial performance, improve individual performance or productivity, and create a more competitive total compensation market position.

Ideally, managers and employees ought to like incentives because the rules of the game are clear: I'll give you X if you give me Y results. No difficult judgments to make about how well someone performed and what he or she should receive. And because the ground rules are clear, incentive plans can focus people's behavior on achieving desired results. The key word here is *can*. Whether an incentive plan does in fact change behavior depends on several factors that we'll discuss later. But let's begin by considering the ways an incentive plan can be used to motivate *positive* change.

Types of Variable Pay Rewards

Variable pay programs can vary by the type of reward. Most programs use money; however, ownership shares in the organization are also used. These shares can be real—such as stock in publicly held companies—or virtual shares in a private company or unit within a public company, whose value is determined by factors similar to those for real shares without granting actual ownership rights. As you can see in Figure 8-1, different types of incentive plans are better suited for different kinds of compensation.

FIGURE 8-1. INCENTIVE PLAN: AWARD TYPES AND PLAN PURPOSES

Award Type	Plan Purpose				
	Short-term	Long-term	Recognition	Retention	Motivation
Cash	X		X		X
Equity		X		X	X
Noncash	X		X		X

There are several advantages to using equity instead of cash in your incentive plan:

- You can conserve cash for other purposes, which is often important for small, start-up organizations.
- Equity gives a vested interest in the long-term success of the organization, as the value of the grant will go up or down with the company.
- Equity serves as both a reward and an incentive since the value of the award keeps growing with the performance of the organization.

However, employees may not value equity as much as cash, especially lower-paid or younger employees.

Besides cash and equity, some variable pay programs use merchandise or gifts to reward individuals. These are fairly common in certain industries, such as retail and restaurant, in part because of the administrative challenges of calculating overtime in a variable pay program for nonexempt employees. Some companies use public recognition—president's awards, for example—to distinguish outstanding individual service. These programs, though, tend to be associated more with recognition plans than with variable pay programs.

The Desired Performance Objective

As noted earlier, there are many reasons organizations use variable pay programs. Your purpose for using variable pay should determine the kind of plan you select. In fact, being clear about your objective may be the most important factor in the success of your plan. For the best business results using variable pay, you'll need to prioritize your program objectives and know the role that variable pay will serve versus those played by other programs, such as base salary and recognition.

If asked, most managers would say that the objective of a variable pay program is to motivate or improve performance. This is a reasonable response, but it answers only part of the question. Managers need to be clear about what types of performance the program is intended to motivate. For example, over the course of a year, employees hear many different messages about what's important. There are messages about improving individual job productivity, quality, and on-time performance. There are messages about the importance of completing special projects, identifying opportunities for innovation, enhancing customer satisfaction, and improving efficiencies. In addition to these individual objectives, there may be team goals. That's a lot of messages. No wonder employees often tune out and put their heads down, do their jobs and sit tight, waiting for the next objective du jour.

Variable pay programs can motivate performance if you're clear about *what type of performance* is the priority. How you choose to measure performance should be strategically important to the business. For example, in the early 1990s, Continental Airlines was on the verge of bankruptcy. Part of the strategy to turn around the company was to deliver outstanding customer service, including being on time. These two performance factors—customer service and on-time performance— became a core component of a new all-employee incentive plan.

When you select performance factors that are strategically important, you'll find that people are motivated to perform beyond their job's core responsibilities. At Continental Airlines, for example, mechanics didn't have the incentive to maintain equipment. And pilots didn't have the incentive to follow protocols and complete paperwork on time. Performing these core responsibilities at a satisfactory or exceptional level was necessary, but not sufficient for Continental's success—and not enough to earn mechanic's or pilot's variable pay. Besides, there are ways to reward individuals for doing their jobs—merit pay, for one thing. Selecting performance metrics that are strategically important enables companies with variable pay plans to channel their employees' discretionary efforts into areas that make an actual difference to the company. (See Chapter 4 for more on selecting the right performance measures.)

Besides selecting the right performance measures, managers need to decide *how many* performance goals to include. Having too many goals is like having too many program objectives—the program gets diluted because employees aren't focused. The number of performance goals should depend on the size of the incentive opportunity. As a rule of

thumb, variable pay plans should have a maximum of one or two performance goals for every 5 percent of pay. For example, if an employee
can earn 10 percent of salary for achieving the incentive performance
goals, the plan should be limited to two to four performance goals.

A common critical mistake with discretionary bonus plans is when
managers believe that having flexibility excuses them from needing specific performance measures. Performance measures are still quite necessary if you want to channel your employees' discretionary efforts. For
example, variable pay plans intended to promote customer satisfaction
or improve quality can still focus on employee behaviors in these areas
even though you can't establish specific customer service and quality
goals at the beginning of the performance period. Knowing that discretionary bonuses will hinge on contributions to customer satisfaction or
quality helps focus employee attention on strategically important outcomes.

Rewards Differentiation

The key to using variable pay to recognize top performers is differentiation in the size of the awards. Giving everyone something—which takes
money away from the real top performers—is a common practice that
undermines the plan's objectives. Top performers—for example, the top-
performing 20 to 30 percent of participating employees—should receive
bonuses that are at least 50 to 100 percent above the norm. Likewise, it's
better to give 25 people $1,000 each than it is to give all 50 people $500
each.

The best and easiest way for managers to differentiate variable pay
among recipients is to have clear and easy-to-understand measurements,
as well as tools for tracking people's progress relative to the performance
measurements and relative to one another. The difficulty of creating
meaningful differences in the size of the awards should not be underesti-
mated, however. There are a number of things managers can do to make
this process easier:

• *Manage employee expectations:* Make sure your employees understand the difference between how bonuses are funded and how they are
allocated. And explain the typical award amount. For example, assume
a bonus plan is funded at 10 percent of salary but you want to reward
the top 10 percent of your performers with a bonus equal to 20 percent

of their salary. This means that the typical award for the remaining 90 percent is about 8 percent. Managers should emphasize this amount and explain that additional funding is available for top performers.

• *Maintain an ongoing dialogue about performance:* If you wait until bonuses have to be decided to talk to your employees about their performance, you're too late. Look for opportunities throughout the year to recognize people when they exceed expectations and try to "catch employees doing something right." Likewise, offer constructive feedback when employees fail to meet your expectations. Document these events for use during later performance assessment and bonus discussions. (See Chapter 10 for more on performance management.)

• *Calibrate employee distinctions with peer managers:* It's always easier to make tough decisions when you're not making them alone. Focus your energy on identifying the top performers and then have all managers in the unit review which employees are on everyone's list. A meeting facilitator—for example, someone from HR—can help ensure the meeting goes smoothly. Make certain everyone understands what the person has done or consistently does to warrant inclusion. Assume employees will know who received the largest bonuses and will let you know if they feel it's unfair—so be prepared.

Incentives as the Exception, Not the Rule

Finally, any plan needs to be managed so that employees don't come to think of it as an entitlement. Also, be sure that participants are clear on the link between what they have to do and the impact that will have on the organization. It may also help to discuss what top performers have done to receive higher bonuses. Doing so helps other plan participants understand how they can get larger bonuses in the future. The following case study shows how a company in the southern United States overcame a culture of entitlement.

Case Study: Replacements, Ltd.

Replacements, Ltd. is a Greensboro, North Carolina, provider of out-of-production china, crystal, and silver tableware. The company's buyers scour flea markets, garage sales, antique shops, manufacturers, and other sources for sought-after patterns. Replacements, Ltd. purchases, warehouses, and resells this merchandise. Sometimes the company persuades manufacturers to reissue old patterns based on consumer demand. The privately held 550-person company generates about $70 million in annual sales.

"We used to hand out holiday bonuses," says Chief Financial Officer Kelly Smith. Though "discretionary," virtually every employee earned an annual bonus regardless of his or her performance. "We'd start getting questions in November: 'When are we getting our bonuses?'" Smith recalls. "There was an entitlement mentality."

The problem was that the bonuses did almost nothing to make Replacements employees feel invested in the company. If there was a slight correlation between how much an employee produced and the size of the bonus, few picked up on it. And in any case, managers tended to reward effort, not results. As revenues grew, productivity declined. Replacements executives hoped a variable pay plan would achieve the result they wanted: a pay-for-performance culture where employees would feel that the more they accomplished, the better the rewards.

To kick off the project, Replacements worked with consultants to create a gain-sharing team comprising four senior staff members and two managers with an interest in and knowledge of pay and rewards. In half-day sessions over a number of weeks, the team led the group through a 10-step process leading to the company's first variable pay plan.

There were many issues to tackle. "The biggest," says Smith, "was figuring out how to define gain-sharing calculations." For starters, what should be measured? There are parts of a business employees can control and parts they cannot. For example, employees in the shipping department may have control over the speed and efficiency at which orders are processed. Since each piece of merchandise is individually inspected for flaws, some employees have a hand in ensuring the quality of the company's products. But no one has control over new government regulations that might affect the bottom line—one way or the other. "There are windfalls," says Smith, "and there also things like taxes. We had to get employees to understand that." The project team worked to break down employees' job descriptions to understand how each employee affected the company's bottom line. The gain-sharing calculations came from the team's deeper understanding of the company's business and its people's jobs.

The second part of the design process involved line-of-site issues. For the program to work, employees had to understand the concept of return on capital. And not all did. Replacements published easy-to-read diagrams showing how cash flows through the organization and how everyone can help save money. The diagrams illustrated how even little things such as double-checking an order prior to packing, proofreading shipping labels, performing other quality-control checks, or even turning out the lights when they were the last ones out will save money—and affect the size of a bonus.

Before this plan, different employee groups had different performance measures. For example, buyers were measured by how much product they could find at a good price; shippers were measured by how fast they could dispatch orders. Both groups were measured by quantity, not quality. They lacked a shared vision. Once the company decided how it would calculate the new bonuses and how it would align performance measures, it had an even bigger job ahead of it: communication. Smith spoke about the new gain-sharing plan at company meetings. Managers addressed small groups of workers. The campaign's goal was to educate each employee about how he or she could translate excellent performance into extra money—and not once a year like in the old days, but monthly. The communications were exceedingly difficult. In any given fiscal year, "we could have a profit, but no gain if we have an unexpected windfall," says Smith. When that happened, people became suspicious that finance was cooking the books. Teaching workers about the fine points of finance was a Herculean task.

Over time, Replacements, Ltd.'s variable pay plan has undergone a number of changes, many based on simplifying the communication of the plan for program participants. For internal reasons, it has reverted from a monthly payout to an annual one. But Smith is quick to point out that payout is no longer during the holiday season. Now it's at the end of the fiscal year (September 30) and is not associated with holiday generosity. "It was a great building block," says Smith. "It helped break the chain of entitlement."

Incentives That Encourage Teamwork

In addition to motivating and recognizing individual performance, variable pay can help managers promote teamwork and team results. But be careful about when to use variable pay for this purpose. Variable pay is most appropriately used to encourage teamwork when there's a high degree of interdependence.

How effectively teams hand off work to one another is critical to the success of the entire organization. For example, as part of one financial services firm's growth strategy, existing prequalified customers were targeted for cross-selling opportunities. Management understood that the cooperation between customer service reps and product sales reps would be critical in order to maintain current levels of customer satisfaction and to develop new sales. Call transfers between these two functions had to be seamless. The firm adopted a new team-based variable pay plan that measured both new sales and customer satisfaction as a way of reinforcing the importance of the two groups' working together.

Or consider IBM's experience over the last few years. Before CEO Lou Gerstner arrived, the vast majority of IBM's bonuses to employees were based on individual performance—and consequently the company was almost paralyzed by fiefdoms. According to Gerstner,

> We found, as predicted by economic theory, that the people rewarded for individual performance shared information least; the people rewarded for team performance shared more; and the people rewarded for company performance shared most. In each case, the degree of sharing reflected the sharer's self-interest. If compensation is linked to one's performance relative to others, then employees are likely to hoard information to both maximize their own performance and undermine (or, at least, not benefit) others. But if rewards are tied to firm performance, then individuals stand to gain most from activities—like free knowledge sharing—that benefit the company.[1]

Gerstner made it clear he would discipline or fire anyone who refused to share valuable information, and IBM's executive compensation program subsequently became more focused on team-based measures. The result was improved dialogue and the sharing of information, which positively contributed to IBM's significant growth during the 1990s.[2]

Team-based variable pay programs are less effective when the nature of work is mostly independent, even when the organization's culture values cooperation and teamwork. Team incentives for this purpose are analogous to paying bonuses for showing up at work—behavior is expected as a basis of employment; in these instances, a person is adequately compensated by salary.

Although variable pay can reinforce teamwork and team results, it obviously can't drive it. This is the job of management. Managers need to demonstrate the importance of teamwork in other ways, such as investments in technology, training, and cross-functional problem-solving teams that help individuals work together and break down barriers. Without these management processes and interventions, employees may feel powerless to impact the team results on which variable pay is determined. When this happens, people become frustrated and cynical, not motivated.

The general rule of thumb is that the farther a job is from the CEO, the more the annual incentive should be weighted toward individual performance. This doesn't mean you'll have each individual employee pulling in different directions; it just means that the individual performance being measured can be aggregated as a team goal that everyone at that level can understand. So, the key is to make sure that whatever is being measured individually supports the larger, broader organizational goals and that individual measures don't contradict or offset one another.

Weighted Schedules for the Rewards

Figure 8-2 reflects a simple way to look at different measures for various levels of employees and how much they're typically weighted. There are ranges of weightings because they likely differ between line and staff roles, and among business units, depending on their potential contribution and line of sight to the performance metric. We've typically seen that a minimum weight to place on any one performance metric is 20 to 25 percent since anything less than that either tends not to be meaningful enough to catch a participant's attention or leads to too many performance metrics for a participant to focus on and, thus, it dilutes the type of behavior you want to encourage.

FIGURE 8 2. PERFORMANCE MEASURE WEIGHTS BY EMPLOYEE LEVEL

	Performance Measures		
	Corporate	BU/Div/Dept	Individual
Executive	75%–100%	0–25%	—
Professional/Management	50%–75%	25%–50%	0–25%
Nonexempt/Hourly	0–25%	0–50%	50%–100%

Be Careful What You Ask For

Variable pay can help managers change behaviors, and that's both good and bad news. Employees will change, but sometimes the consequences of the change are greater than the benefits. An extreme example of this is Sears. In the early 1990s, Sears introduced variable pay to its auto mechanics in the hope of encouraging employees to look for other opportunities to service customers. Some employees became too zealous in attempting to find new opportunities—"creating" opportunities where none previously existed. This development became public and it undermined the Sears Auto brand.

Sears's story illustrates another way managers can use variable pay: to help maintain balance between competing objectives. Managers always run a risk that when they tell people to focus on one set of results they'll do so at the expense of other objectives. Examples abound:

- Individual incentives that encourage people to maximize their own results to the detriment of the team
- Units that emphasize financial results at the expense of customer service goals
- Organizations that sacrifice long-term objectives to achieve annual incentive goals

Managers can maintain balance among objectives when using variable pay by doing the following:

- ***Setting Individual Objectives:*** Some variable pay plans require managers to set individual objectives in addition to organizational or unit goals. This is an opportunity to reinforce objectives not reflected in the team-based goals. If these team goals are financial, then individual goals should focus on other objectives, such as safety, customer service, and on-time performance. Shared individual goals—individual objectives that are repeated on multiple or all employee goal sheets—are also effective at achieving balance.
- ***Adopting a Matrix:*** Managers may be able to adopt a variable payout matrix like the one shown in Figure 8-3. This is a simple and effective way to communicate that success is multidimensional. For example, suppose you have two important objectives and you want to ensure that acceptable levels of performance are achieved on both in order to receive payouts. As shown in the example in Figure 8-3, achieving a below-

FIGURE 8-3. VARIABLE PAY MATRIX: PAYOUTS FOR TWO OBJECTIVES

		Objective #1 (Net Income)		
		Threshold Performance at 80% of Target	At Target Performance	Above Target Performance
Objective #2 (Customer Service)	Below Target Performance at 80% of Target	50% Payout	75% Payout	100% Payout
	At Target Performance	75% Payout	100% Payout	125% Payout
	Above Target Performance	100% Payout	125% Payout	150% Payout

target level of customer service and a target level will provide a payout of 75 percent of target.

The Sweet Spot

How much "stretch" is incorporated into the targeted performance objectives is always a factor in variable pay plans. Put too much stretch into the targets and participants will give up when they see there's no chance of getting there; too little stretch and everyone will turn in a stellar performance. Too little stretch also causes shareholders or owners to feel uncomfortable about the reward-return equation. For instance, they may wonder whether they're paying out too much for too little in return. The trick is to find that sweet spot where employees feel the objectives are attainable and the results justify the costs.

Figure 8-4 reflects a level of reasonable stretch for performance goals, showing how often a participant might typically achieve different levels of performance assuming the goals are set appropriately. This would suggest that 80 to 90 percent of the time (or 8 to 9 years out of 10) a participant should be able to reach the minimum or threshold level of performance needed to receive some incentive payout. It also suggests that the target objectives should be able to be met 50 to 60 percent of

FIGURE 8-4. PROBABILITY OF ACHIEVEMENT AND CORRESPONDING PAYOUT

Probability of Achievement		
Threshold	Target	Maximum
80% to 90%	50% to 60%	10% to 20%
Percentage of Target		
Threshold	Target	Maximum
80% to 90%	100%	110% to uncapped
Payout Percentage		
Threshold	Target	Maximum
25% to 50%	100%	150%+

the time (5 to 6 years out of 10), and that a participant should "hit a home run" 10 to 20 percent of the time (1 to 2 years out of 10).

Minimum and Prorated Payouts

When planning variable pay, typically there's a lot of discussion—and a lot of employee concern—about what level of performance will be enough to earn a minimum payout (usually a percentage of the target objective). Employees often feel as strongly about this dynamic as they do about the probability of achieving the target performance. Although the threshold and maximum levels of performance can vary significantly (depending on how much volatility is attached to the specific measure), it usually falls in the 80 to 90 percent of target range as a threshold and 110 percent or more of target as a maximum (if there's a cap at all). The finance people will need to get involved in determining this to ensure that the organization can afford the minimum payouts and is not giving away more than its fair share at some maximum level of performance. It all comes down to what's perceived as fair—both to the organization and to the employee.

The final dynamic concerning probability of achievement is the actual incentive payout percentage relative to the target payout. Again, this can range fairly widely, but in general, participants would receive one-quarter to one-half of their target incentive for attaining the minimum level of performance required to get any money. This is an obvious effort to entice participants to perform at the highest level possible.

There are also different schools of thought on whether to have interpolated (or prorated) payouts between threshold and maximum, or to make them "cliff" payouts (whereby employees earn only the threshold payout until target performance, and only the target payout until maximum performance). Interpolated payouts tend to be more popular with participants as well as more practical, since they can readily associate more incentive dollars with their discretionary efforts. On the upside of the payout percentage, some organizations like to throw a big number on the table (say, 200 percent or more of target payout) to catch people's attention. This usually works for a year or two, and then participants have a better feel for how the game is played (or how targets are set), and they recognize the big number for what it is and start focusing on the target level and its appropriateness.

Unforeseen Outcomes

It's not unusual to see unexpected results—positive or negative—once a variable pay plan is put into place. Figure 8-5 lists some examples. Design teams and management and employee focus groups can often reveal these types of situations before they occur.

Getting the Most Out of a Variable Pay Program

Managers have opportunities every day to influence how well the variable pay program helps them achieve business results. Many of these opportunities are ones that managers should be doing even without a variable pay program. But having money attached to these activities tends to increase their importance.

• *Get serious about performance management:* Start approaching performance management as a business-planning process, not an employee development or HR exercise. This requires that you identify the key outcomes that your unit must produce and then decide on the activities that are critical to achieving those outcomes. Chapter 10 provides more detail about performance management and how to structure it most effectively.

• *No plan is meant to last forever:* As mentioned earlier, plan designs should be reviewed annually to ensure that the plan is driving the right behaviors, that it accounts for changes in how the organization does business, and that the performance metrics are still pertinent or have

FIGURE 8-5. TYPICAL UNFORESEEN OUTCOMES OF VARIABLE PAY PROGRAMS

Issue	Situation
Too Many Measures	An incentive plan for employees in the branches of a retail bank evaluated individual performance relative to a mix of goals and objectives. Because there were so many different measures (tied to the various products and services offered), there was a lack of focus on the more profitable products and services and confusion as to how to balance sales (quantity) vs. service (quality) in their daily activities with customers.
Positive Though Unintended Results	An incentive plan at the business unit level of a medical device manufacturer used a combination of production and financial goals at the business unit level along with specific performance goals for individual participants. This ended up instilling a sense of ownership on the part of plan participants that wasn't even considered by management.
Unclear Purpose	A plan for employees at a utility was funded partially from its merit increase budget. Because the organization did not have a history of using variable pay, had always paid everyone the same level of merit pay, and a compelling reason was not articulated to the participants for its use, employees believed the incentive was an entitlement, too.
Improper Performance Standard Planning	An electrical parts manufacturer wanted to rotate employees, instill a teamwork mentality, and utilize consistent pay-for-performance measures in its organization to improve productivity. The organization's production-level individual incentives worked contrary to those needs because 1) employees who had jobs that they felt were relatively easy did not want to rotate to what they perceived as more demanding jobs because of the potential loss of incentive opportunity, and 2) the individual performance standards were not well maintained, resulting in higher payouts than were warranted.
Poor Funding Design	A chemical manufacturer utilized a variable pay plan that made a payout to employees if they achieved their individual goals even if the organization lost money at a corporate level, even in a down economy. This problem was further exacerbated by employees "sandbagging" during the goal-setting process and not actively participating as a team in trying to solve the problems faced.
Plan Measures Leading to Undesirable Behavior	A food wholesaler based its sales incentive plan solely on volume of new customer sales. This had the dual negative effect of causing the salespeople to spend minimal time managing existing customer relationships (and thereby putting those accounts at risk) and pursuing new sales regardless of how profitable they were and demonstrating behaviors that the company did not value or were counter to its culture (e.g., stepping on internal colleagues' toes in the interest of new business, and dropping the pursuit of new business opportunities at the first challenge).

sufficient "stretch." Too many times we see organizations trying to make their incentive plans work, or expecting the same level of effectiveness year after year. The truth is that in some cases incentive plans have a finite life, and organizations need to either dump them when they have run their course or design new plans.

Gainsharing is a specific example of an incentive plan with a limited useful life. This type funds itself out of efficiency gains or cost reductions that employees generate. The reality is that after a couple of years, the low-hanging fruit has been picked, and it is more and more difficult to achieve any gains, rendering the original plan ineffective as participants conclude that the return on their efforts is not adequate.

• *Communication is the key:* Designing incentive plans is the easy part; communicating and implementing them is where most organizations either make or break it. Remember, incentive plans alone will never drive cultural change in an organization; they only support the various higher-level structural and behavioral initiatives that must be undertaken when an organization is going through change.

Personal Impact Map

We talked earlier about how critical line of sight is for participants in variable pay plans, so that they can see directly how their day-to-day activities and behaviors impact their potential incentive payout. Many organizations design incentive plans with high-level performance goals (higher revenue or profits, for example) for lower-level employees. Without a roadmap to show these employees how their daily activities can impact these high-level goals, the plan quickly loses its punch.

One way to remedy this is through the use of personal impact maps (see Figure 8-6). These diagrams break down various high-level performance goals so that employees at different levels can see (and understand) how they can directly contribute to the impact of the high-level metric.

The cascading levels of the personal impact map identify (or confirm) appropriate incentive plan measures for departments and/or employees at all levels. If you start out by developing a map like this, it may help you avoid setting goals that are too subjective or that conflict with one another.

Ways to Avoid Common Mistakes

Here are some management steps that will help avoid blunders with regard to incentive programs:

FIGURE 8-6. PERSONAL IMPACT MAP

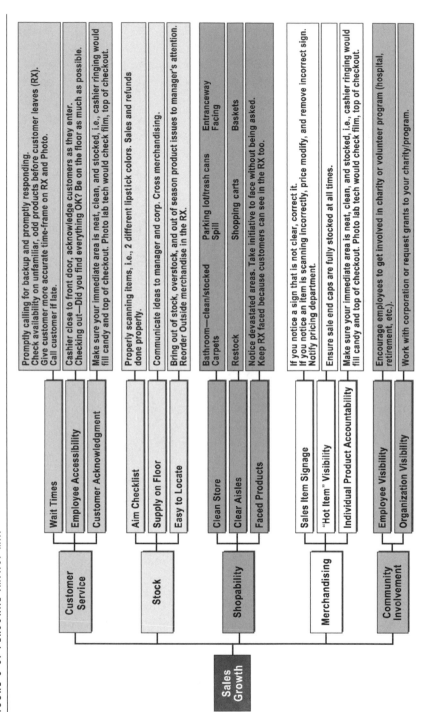

- Establish a "sunset provision" for the plan to ensure its design is revisited every year; good plans still need to be refined, so make sure there's follow-up on plan effectiveness.
- Ensure there's a clear message for variable pay (why you have it, the business case for it, how employees can impact it, etc.).
- Spend the same amount of time on implementation and communication as you did on design.
- Make sure management is committed to the program.
- Generate employee buy-in by developing ways to involve employees in the design (and redesign if necessary).
- Review the effectiveness of the plan each year; good plans need to be adjusted as business plans change and leadership approaches evolve to ensure that they remain relevant and effective.

Maintaining the Plan's Effectiveness

As was the case with Replacements, Ltd., most variable pay plans have a finite time during which they are effective. There will always be examples of plans in certain organizations that seem to go on forever and be consistently effective, but that is typically not the case.

Incentive plans can and should be evaluated on as many of these four different criteria as possible:

1. *Design:* The KISS (Keep It Simple, Stupid) principle is a staple among effective incentive plans. It must be simple and easy for the participants to understand. There's no quicker way for an incentive plan to be disregarded than to make it overly complex or difficult for an employee to determine how to earn a payout. And it has to measure the right things—three or four measures at most. Sometimes the 80/20 rule is the right tack to take; don't spend forever trying to develop the "perfect" plan or else it'll never get implemented and the chances are it will be too complicated, anyway.

2. *Reward/Return:* There should be a direct connection between the bottom-line performance of an organization and the level of payouts provided to participants. Not only will participants disengage if they see the organization doing well and executives reaping rewards when they aren't receiving a payout, but shareholders will be looking for someone

to fry if the payouts are overly generous without a corresponding high performance by the organization.

3. *Administration:* Two items are critical here: First, can you collect performance data without tying up an inordinate amount of time? Second, can the data be distributed to participants within a reasonable time to show how they're doing? Participants should have confidence in the data that impact the incentive payouts. The objectives should also be trackable and accessible.

4. *Employee Satisfaction:* If employees aren't willing to even consider a variable pay plan, you've got a problem. Culturally, some organizations that want to introduce incentives need to take their time, involve employees in the process, and consider whether the culture will support them. In some cases, organizations bent on incentives have had to restaff key roles because the culture against variable pay was so strong. Once the key roles are populated with believers, the rest of the population falls into line or goes elsewhere. Finally, any whiff by employees that the tracking of performance measures is soft or, worse, incorrect, and they will disengage from the plan and likely initiate a drop in employee morale and management trust.

Things to Watch Out For

The following dynamics should be approached very carefully and with a cautious eye when reviewing the effectiveness of variable pay plans. They may all sound and feel good initially, but each has a sordid history relative to effective incentive compensation design and execution.

• *Fashion Models:* What's in fashion may not be what is best for your plan. Just because everyone else bought a leisure suit doesn't mean you have to. Every organization is unique to some degree, whether culturally or operationally, and that's enough to cause an incentive plan that's been successful elsewhere to crash and burn where you work—or vice versa.

• *Manipulators, Opportunists:* Believe it or not, some people will try to manipulate the incentive plan for their own good. Examples include the plant manager who ties the plan to "shipped" goods; the sales manager who manipulates the sales credit database; the business unit head who "lowballs" his unit's goals; the warehouse manager with inventory goals; and the manager with the competitive survey (done by recruiters), or worse, the anecdotal story.

• *Gamers:* These are actions that subvert the incentive plan. Examples include changing the rules of the plan midway through the performance period, changing the eligibility of participants in the plan, and installing "triggers" (threshold levels of performance that must be met before any incentive is paid) that are unrealistic and/or unachievable.

• *Conflict Avoiders:* Examples include: "We treat everyone equally"; "We don't want to hurt anyone's feelings"; "We can't let them earn too much"; and "We can't pay them too little."

A Word About Sales Incentives

Salespeople typically participate in variable pay plans separate and apart from the incentive plans for non-salespeople. Sometimes, sales incentive plans can be more complicated than non-sales plans because there are often more moving parts that can be directly impacted by the participant; for example, sales volume, pricing and profit margin, and different products or services. Then there are the different selling channels (direct to customer, indirect through distributors, dealers or wholesalers, etc.), the different sales cycles (short-, mid-, and long-term), more frequent payout timing, and individual versus team sales efforts. But, just as with non-sales plans, there have to be balanced goals to prevent unintended consequences (such as if top-line sales growth is fine as long as the sales are profitable).

Another big difference between sales and non-sales incentive plans is how much leverage there is between base pay and variable pay. Again, it varies typically based on the type of product, the product cost, and the length of the sales cycle. But it's not unusual to see a sales force with a lower base pay and higher incentive opportunity than its non-sales colleagues. The thought here is that just by changing the mix or leverage of pay (lower base salary/higher incentive opportunity), it will add more incentive to the salesperson to achieve sales goals.

That said, many of the conceptual principles of incentive design are the same for sales and non-sales employees: You not only want to set clear and achievable goals that if met will help the organization, but you want the participant to demonstrate the right kind of behaviors in meeting or exceeding those goals. The classic example of an ill-designed sales incentive plan is the guy who maxes out his incentive payout even though he stepped on his colleagues' toes and upset his customers. If that can happen, your plan design needs an overhaul.

Final Considerations

To have a truly effective variable pay program, organizations have to ask themselves whether participants are motivated to do things they would not otherwise do, whether participants actually have—and feel they have—an impact on the performance of the organization, and whether the participants and organization experience the same level of performance without the incentive plan.

If you can't answer these questions appropriately and accurately, you've got to ask yourself whether the time, effort, and expense that go into designing and implementing your variable pay plan are worth it.

Summary: A Checklist for Variable Pay Programs

Some organizations may feel there's an implicit value in offering a variable pay plan to employees, regardless of its effectiveness. But the downside of a poorly designed incentive plan goes beyond just time, effort, and expense. The negative impact on employee morale and management trust can loom much larger than do quantitative costs. Here are a few things managers should keep in mind about their variable pay plans:

- Ensure there's a clear message for variable pay (for example, short-term results, long-term results, recognition, motivation, retention), and if there's more than one message, explain what they are—good communication is key.
- Maintain balance among objectives to ensure that your plans do what you intend them to do.
- Ensure probability of achievement by finding the sweet spot where employees feel the objectives are attainable and the results justify costs.
- Ensure there is proper differentiation of awards that aligns with differentiated performance and results.
- Establish a sunset provision to force yourself to review the variable pay plan and keep it relevant and effective.

CHAPTER 9

The Hidden Value of Benefits

LONG TAKEN FOR GRANTED, the amount that an organization invests in its benefits programs is getting renewed attention. In fact, many CEOs and HR leaders rank rising benefits costs as one of their biggest concerns today. On average, General Motors spends about $1,360 per car on health-care benefits and pensions—more than it spends per car for steel![1] All industry sectors are feeling the hit: Starbucks Chairman and Chief Global Strategist Howard Schultz told analysts that in the next two years, Starbucks will spend more on employee health care than it does on coffee beans.[2] Between 25 and 30 percent of an employee's total remuneration may likely be in benefits, not cash.

With such a big investment at stake, it's critical for employers to get the biggest bang for their benefits buck: the maximum return on investment. Yet according to Hay Group research and consulting experience, many employees don't even consider their employer's contributions toward health insurance, retirement, workers compensation, company-sponsored life insurance, disability insurance, paid vacation days, and other benefits as part of their pay. Nor do they see other special programs, such as flexible work hours, telecommuting, and on-site day-care centers, as part of their actual compensation. Of even greater concern, they often see their benefits as an entitlement to which they're due no matter what the company's performance or what's happening in the market. In fact, most employees have no idea of the full monetary value of their benefits.

This chapter discusses the full value of benefits, their role in the total rewards program, and the manager's impact in influencing the employee's perception of benefits value

Sending the Message to Employees

Ask around. If your organization is like most, the people who work there won't have a clear picture of what their benefits are worth—or even have an approximate idea of their total remuneration value or total rewards. In most situations, medical and drug plans are among the most important benefits to employees regardless of age or family status. Yet for the most part, not until employees leave a firm and consider the option of continuing coverage through a COBRA option (availability required by federal law) do they learn that their medical and drug plan costs $400 to $500 per month. This is because most employers only make known the employee's share of monthly premiums. Employees are similarly surprised to learn that the true cost of a doctor's visit is $100 to $150, not the $20 copay. Clearly, employees focus on what they pay, not on actual costs or value of the benefits they receive.

This lack of understanding about employee benefits is one of the reasons health-care costs keep climbing. It's hard for people to buy cost effectively if they don't know or understand the total costs.

This suggests that there's a valuable recruitment and retention tool hidden right under managers' noses: explaining the value of benefits to job candidates and publicizing the value of benefits available to existing employees.

To maximize the organization's return on its benefits investment, both quantifiable and nonquantifiable benefits should be considered part of the strategic human resource and total rewards programs. These programs need to be designed to provide clear messages to employees.

A critical step in ensuring an effective ROI on the organization's benefits program is to be clear in the messages about benefits you want to send to employees. Some of these messages might include:

- We care about you and your family's health and well-being. Organizations offering excellent health benefits, for example, get more for their benefits investment when employees understand the true value of their health-care plan. An added focus on "well-care" benefits and prevention programs also sends clear messages of this type.

- We care about work-life balance. If that's your core message, identify and detail the organization's work-life benefits, such as flextime, paid time off, job sharing, and telecommuting—and why you have them.
- We need and expect you to stay with us. If your organization wants people to stick around, consider touting long-term benefits such as retirement plans, stay bonuses, or stock options.
- Your professional advancement is key to our success. Employers who offer training opportunities and tuition reimbursement get the best return on their investment when employees understand both the monetary value of these benefits and where in the organization the training may take them.
- Medical costs continue to rise and we must work together to solve the problem. We have seen organizations that covered 100 percent of their employees' health insurance. Employees saw this as an entitlement—until they were presented with the economic realities. After that, they were more comfortable with benefits cuts that still kept them in the 75th percentile.
- Executives may have special needs and we want to provide flexibility where possible. To attract and retain stars, some organizations offer richer benefits for executives including special executive flex plans that are used to allow choices and tax efficiency as well as serve as a retention vehicle.

Health and Well-Being

The very existence of a benefits program should be a loud and clear message to employees that the organization does indeed care about their well-being. "If we take care of our employees, they will take care of our customers," says Karen Shadders, vice president of people at Wegman's Food Markets, Inc. "If employees can't take care of their families, they cannot do their jobs. The focus is on freeing up people so that they can be more productive." The Rochester, New York, food chain gives most full-time and part-time employees free single health coverage and generous retirement benefits. "Our pay and benefits are at or above our competition's," Shadders says. "It helps us attract a higher caliber of employee."[3]

One progressive way of showing an interest in employees' well-being is to have disease-management programs, which are becoming increasingly prevalent. Numerous studies have shown a link between employer-sponsored programs to help people manage chronic disease and healthier employees who file fewer insurance claims. When people with high blood pressure, borderline diabetes, and other easy-to-identify conditions participate in disease-management programs, both the employees and their employers see positive results.

As you may be aware, there are privacy issues when it comes to medical conditions, but they can be surmounted by third-party administrators who aggregate a company's health data and—without knowing exactly which employees are being targeted—encourage people to get involved. Organizations that have budgets too small to invest in disease management, but that still want to show they care about their employees' health, should consider what we call "soft disease management." For example, if your organization seems to have a large number of cigarette smokers or overweight employees, contact your health insurance provider and ask about early intervention programs to help employees lose weight, kick their smoking habits, or enable them to take responsibility for improving their own health. These programs, run by third parties, are usually inexpensive and may help reduce an organization's insurance premiums while sending a positive message to employees. As a rule of thumb, you should expect to see an ROI in a disease-management program in about two years.

Financial Support for Benefits

Of course, financing is generally not a line manager's decision; however, every line manager should know the value of the organization's benefits programs. Managers who can talk with authority about their organization's benefits programs are likely able to influence employees much more than the HR department, a benefits manager, or an outside party. You can explain the purpose and value of these plans and what employees will need to contribute as well. And again, although you may not have a say in the type of retirement plan offered, you can discuss the differences between *defined benefits* (specific benefits at retirement, with investment risk as the employer's responsibility) and *defined contributions* (specific contributions each year, with the investment risk as the employee's responsibility) and let employees know that one is not necessarily less expensive than the other.

Work-Life Concerns

Flextime, time off, telecommuting, day care, elder care, and more—the employer-employee contract has changed dramatically over the years. These days, fewer people expect that benefits will be handed to them on a silver platter. That's why work-life benefits should be discussed the same way as other benefits are. Employees need to understand that the company offers and pays for these work-life benefits for the same reason it offers and pays for other benefits: because it values its people. And although a line manager may not be in a position to advocate for flextime or telecommuting, if these benefits exist, managers need to talk about them and help make them work for both the employee and the company.

Many employees today are interested in flextime because of the opportunities it gives them to manage their work life and family activities. Often, depending on the work itself, employees may highly value the ability to work from home, and employers gain significantly more productivity from these telecommuters. Likewise, paid time off factors can increase the value of a job to an employee. This is the case with McDonald's WOW compensation programs. The well-known restaurant chain, based in Oakbrook, Illinois, has strategically identified several of its compensation programs to stand above and beyond what other organizations in the same industry offer. These programs differentiate McDonald's as a preferred place to work within the quick-service restaurant industry; in doing so, the intent of McDonald's is to identify a few areas where the company can really shine, capturing the attention of current and prospective employees.

One such WOW offering at McDonald's is its sabbatical program, which is almost unique within the food-service sector. McDonald's offers all management and professional employees (from restaurant manager on up) a 100 percent–paid eight-week sabbatical after 10 years of employment. Moreover, an employee can earn another sabbatical with each additional 10 years of service. According to a McDonald's manager, "This benefit is the result of a strong belief from senior management that people want and need to be rejuvenated, and this is a great opportunity to recharge one's batteries." Further, he says, "While sabbaticals are not necessarily top of mind for new hires and people with a couple of years of experience, they are one of the most highly valued benefits by people who have been around for several years."

The Competitive Job Market

Managers need to know the competitive position of an organization's benefits programs in the job marketplace. You may need outside help to learn where your organization stands. Or perhaps you already know anecdotally—and that may be enough. For example, when one Hay Group client learned it was in the 95th percentile of the marketplace for health benefits, it polled its employees, asking if they'd rather stay in the 95th percentile but forgo other soft benefits and, in the longer term, even risk going out of business, or if they'd prefer to drop down to the 75th percentile, keep the soft benefits, and stay in business. Employees were willing to take a cut once they understood the situation and they knew how their benefits stood relative to the competition.

There's no easy answer to the question, "What's the competition doing in the way of payroll and benefits?" Instead, it may be better to put your efforts into learning about your people: where they're going, what they want, how they'll change in the coming years, how much they're willing to contribute to their own retirement and health-care plans, and how much the organization can afford to spend on total remuneration. Other organizations have other priorities, other budgets, and other employees. Although apples-to-apples comparisons may not always be possible, the more you know about where your organization stands in the mix—and what your employees expect from the organization—the better you will be able to talk about rewards and benefits.

Taking Stock of Your Company's Total Rewards

Before an organization can begin to build a strategic benefits plan, it needs to know where it stands regarding current benefits and total rewards. Our research has found that neither employers nor employees tend to know the value of their total rewards—that is, their total remuneration plus nonquantifiable benefits such as family days, birthday celebrations, career-development opportunities, and flexible work hours.

Although employees may feel good about employer-sponsored charity events or an employer's investment in people's careers, it may be tough to put a dollar figure on such benefits. Still, these benefits should be taken into consideration when identifying total rewards. As we'll see later, if you can't give them a dollar value, perhaps you can compare them to benefits at similar organizations. It's important to identify every nonquantifiable benefit as well, because you'll want to include them in discussions with employees later on.

As we mentioned in Chapter 5, the notion of total rewards is an important concept for any organization and certainly plays a large part in determining the mix of tangible cash compensation and intangible benefits. Figure 1-1, introduced in Chapter 1 and discussed further in Chapter 5, shows the total rewards model. Although most line managers may not be in a position to design benefits or total rewards strategies, they are often the first people employees approach with questions. To answer employee questions about total rewards, managers should do the following:

1. *Compile a list of all benefits offered:* Include both the quantifiable benefits such as health insurance, retirement plans, disability, paid time off, and tuition reimbursement and the nonquantifiable ones such as flextime, career development, work climate, and after-work activities such as softball leagues. Be thorough. You may want to conduct an informal survey or assemble a focus group to learn what people perceive as benefits. Do employees value the tuition reimbursement program? If it's seen as a benefit, it is a benefit regardless of what it costs. And if it's not seen as a benefit, it probably should be dropped.

From our experience with many employers and a multitude of focus groups and employee surveys, we've found that if employees are asked to rank the importance or value to them of current benefit programs, the first three items are always in the same order, regardless of actual program design: health-care plans, retirement plans, and paid time off programs. Beyond this, the type of benefit and its perceived value depends significantly on the age, financial situation, and family status of the employee.

2. *Examine each benefit and assign it a dollar value:* Be careful—remember that the actual cost is not always appropriate. For example, the actual cost of a retirement plan is not the annual cost, which varies greatly. Despite popular thinking, a traditional defined benefits plan may not cost an employer more than a 401(k) plan. How much the employer contributes to the former is based in part on the stock market—some years, the employer may not pay into the plan at all. Also, you don't know how much a defined contribution plan will cost until

you know what the organization will contribute to the plan and whether that amount depends on employee contributions or not.

When you understand how your company designs and structures benefits, you'll be better able to explain the value of the program to employees. Questions to ask your HR department include:

- How do we determine the value of our benefits programs?
- Do other organizations like ours offer these benefits?
- Do they offer more or less than we do?
- How do we adjust our basic benefits packages to keep competitive?
- How do benefits costs impact other rewards programs?

Only a thorough marketplace analysis will help you know where you stand relative to organizations of all sizes, in various sectors, and in many locations.

3. *Look at the message the total rewards program sends to employees:* Again, you may want to talk with a few employees about this. Do they get the sense that management cares about their health and well-being? About their children's education? About the community? What are their perceptions? Do those perceptions match the message management wants to send to its employees and the community?

The passion and vision of the executive leadership group can often be factors that help define the organization's benefits program. Jim Cantalupo, former CEO of McDonald's, drove consensus within his senior leadership group to make a significant change to the company's 401(k) employee contribution program. The senior team had serious concerns about the low rates of saving by employees in the company's core operations. This concern with the long-term financial outlook of its employees drove senior management to make a change in its 401(k) program. Though unheard of within the industry, McDonald's made the bold move to automatically enroll employees in the 401(k) program and invest 1 percent of their salary. At the same time, the company provided employees with a 1 percent pay increase to neutralize the effect of the imposed savings. In addition, the company matched the 1 percent employee contribution with a 3 percent contribution of its own, and then provided a one-for-one match on the next 4 percent that employees contributed to their accounts, with a total company contribution potential of 7 percent of salary. The program has been remarkably successful, with the participation rate for McDonald's restaurant managers increasing substantially.

4. *Match the results of your research with your total remuneration philosophy:* Don't just look at how the organization compensates people, but why it makes the choices it makes. For example, Southco, a global industrial hardware manufacturer, saved millions of dollars a year in overall benefits costs, in part by engaging employees in a discussion of where they wanted the company to invest its benefits budget. Also, a key part of the cost-saving initiative, according to Terri Francino, director of Southco's global benefits, was health-care consumerism. According to Francino, "We conducted extensive employee training in how to manage health-care costs. Programs such as mandatory mail order for recurring prescriptions and mandatory generics (when available) helped make employees responsible for bringing their own health-care costs down."

An effective communications strategy can be developed that explains how an adjustment in benefits brings the organization to well within the industry average while preserving competitive benefit plans. And although it may not be your job to develop such a strategy, that strategy will work best when line managers understand it and communicate it to their people.

Sometimes, employee attitudes and perceptions point to when a benefits plan will not be cost effective. For example, at an Internet start-up company where most employees were relatively young and didn't plan to spend their entire career there, a traditional defined benefits retirement plan wasn't perceived as valuable. The company's traditional philosophy of "spend your entire career with us and we'll reward you in retirement" didn't fly with its fluid workforce the way it would have with a more stationary workforce of people who planned to spend their entire careers there. After all, most employees didn't see themselves working there in three years, let alone three decades! So, an employer-sponsored retirement package held little value, regardless of how much the employer was willing to spend on it.

A major public-sector organization saved millions of dollars a year in overall benefits costs by identifying the variety of optional or flexible benefits in which its employees were interested. This analysis led to development of three very different health-care options from which the employees could choose. Though the plan options involved some critical pricing matters and assistance from a health insurer or health actuary to be sure the costs were correctly set, this flexible approach made employees feel they had more control; they selected the best plan for their family, and the premiums were aligned with need. But without a focus on educating the employees about the plan options and allowing them to relate choices with costs, a great deal of dissatisfaction might have occurred.

So, if you conduct an employee survey, or even a small, informal focus group, it's important to report your findings back to employees. "Here's what we heard you say—that you'd be willing to pay a little more for your health benefits to avoid having any of the benefits reduced. You understand that, even with this additional contribution, the health benefits will still be well within the competitive levels offered by other organizations. And we heard you say you'd prefer taking a cut in pay to avoid the risk of going out of business." After you share the results, explain what you're going to do, such as eliminate benefits that no one values, increase employee contributions to health or retirement plans, or select a new benefits vendor. Without these key communications, employees may resent that benefits are being taken away—even when the employees said they didn't want those benefits!

When some organizations look at total remuneration, they find they're low in base pay but not in benefits. Unfortunately, base pay adjustments often complicate the situation. For example, if an employee's pay is $10,000 below where it should be and she gets a $10,000 raise, the cost of her benefits that are typically tied to salary (life insurance, disability insurance, and 401[k] contributions, for example) will go up as well. This may put her total remuneration well above average, although that was not the employer's intent.

In sum, how do the results of your benefits research fit with the organization's competitive benefits philosophy—where it aims to be relative to other employers? After all, if your organization ranks last in total rewards, it may be difficult to put a good spin on it in your employee communications. But many organizations have hidden treasures—nonquantifiable benefits that people take for granted. How managers talk about those benefits, and how they set employee expectations, matter a great deal. Examine how your research compares with the messages the organization intends to send about its benefits. Since you need to be realistic, take a careful look at how the results square with the organization's financial ability to pay for those benefits.

Different Cultures, Different Needs

Once you have looked at your employees and examined their needs, the next step is to understand your organization's culture and its impact on benefits. As discussed in Chapter 3, Hay Group has concluded that there are four main organizational cultures. As you might imagine, these different cultures require different benefits programs.

Functional cultures are characterized by a chain-of-command work approach where people are typically hired for their entire career. This lends itself to a traditional balance of retirement and health benefits. In functional cultures, retirement plans are usually based on length of service. Therefore, a defined benefits plan is the most common design, as these plans are focused on providing career or long-service employees with significant benefits when they retire from the company. Health plans have limited choices and provide a competitive level of benefits with low employee contributions. Both short- and long-term disability insurance are important components of the culture, as are retiree life and health insurance, vacations, and executive retirement.

Process cultures have wider and flatter reporting and less hierarchical structures, with more diagonal reports and a real focus on teamwork. In these organizations, the employment contract focuses on employees' working hard and effectively while there, but without a focus on career employment for everyone. Therefore, process cultures emphasize defined contribution retirement programs such as 401(k) and profit-sharing plans, coupled with a de-emphasis on life insurance and retiree benefits. Technology companies that employ lots of expert technical staffers are good examples of process cultures.

Time-based cultures are fast-paced companies (including start-ups) with a "let's work incredibly hard to bring our product to market quickly and we'll all reap the financial rewards" attitude. The emphasis here is on getting market share in order to reap high profitability. In a time-based culture, turnover is generally accepted because the next great idea may come along with a new employee. Health benefits tend to have many more options and benefit programs are designed with a focus on flexibility and customization. There's often less emphasis on life insurance, retiree benefits, and vacations than in a functional culture, but a bigger emphasis on perquisites for busy professionals.

Network cultures bring people together for specific projects that have a limited life, such as making a movie. Typically, a network culture offers little or no retirement benefits, a flexible health plan (with a high degree of cost sharing), little or no company-sponsored life insurance, and little in the way of vacations and holidays.

It's not hard to see how employees in each of these cultures would value pay and benefits in different ways. At an organization where software engineers routinely work 70-hour weeks, for example, an occasional four-day weekend and a dinner-for-two gift certificate at a nice restaurant may go a lot further than it would at an organization where no one puts in more than 40 hours a week. At a traditional utilities company where employees often spend their entire careers, generous retirement benefits and average salaries may be valued more than big salaries and meager retirement plans.

The best way to fashion total remuneration is to consider the unique needs and culture of the organization, not follow a set of rules or standards imposed from outside. The following case is an example of how an organization's benefits program was tailored to its unique short-term mission.

Beaumont Foundation

At Beaumont Foundation, a charitable organization, no one was expected to work for more than five years because this was the original length of the foundation's charter. HR programs were geared toward encouraging people to join Beaumont and stay there for five years. Executives were able to articulate the foundation's total remuneration philosophy, and within that, a clear benefits philosophy and strategies in the context of its mission. The mission and the benefits strategy basically said, "We're here for five years, and we want you to be here for five years, too. During that time, we need to accomplish a huge task during this window of opportunity." This was a true example of a network organization, and its benefits programs focused on health care, minimal life insurance, standard vacation and holidays, and no retirement plans. "We really couldn't have a pension plan," recalls Chief Operating Officer Don Groninger, "so we decided to offer a Cadillac of other benefits packages."

Moreover, the foundation's total remuneration program had emphasis on base salary and variable pay, with a strong retention and "stay" bonus incorporated to encourage people to stay the full term. Additionally, simple ongoing perks such as lunch catered every Friday added to the comfortable work environment and the focus on employees.

Putting It All Together

As you begin the process of designing or redesigning the total rewards program at your organization, choose the redesign considerations most appropriate to your culture. For example:

- Decide whether focus groups work better or not than surveys as a way to identify employee needs and wants.
- When selecting the competitive market for comparison purposes, consider organization size, geography, and industry.
- Select the mix and focus of benefit plans that fits your total remuneration strategy and your organization's goals.

Once the plan is completed and fits the strategies for design and budget, develop an effective communications strategy. Remember, the communications process is a two-pronged effort: (1) initial launch and (2) ongoing communications.

Initial Launch: A comprehensive launch includes legal documents, plan summaries, and other communications that must be distributed. But there's more to a successful communications strategy than legal compliance. Most organizations should consider providing a total remuneration/compensation statement to their employees on an annual (or quarterly, if online) basis.

For organizations at midmarket level or better, total remuneration statements can be a powerful tool. They show employees how they are actually valued. They detail benefit dollars often come to be thought of as "hidden paychecks." These statements can also be adapted to show job prospects their potential total remuneration and serve as a way of attracting candidates.

As more organizations move toward a consumer-driven health-care model, employers will be offering employees (called "consumers" because they consume health-care offerings) a choice of health-care plans, which in turn will help contain overall costs. The tools for communicating these choices include easy access to databases through a user-friendly interface; and an Internet or intranet portal showing employees how their total remuneration may draw from a dozen or more sources, including insurance companies, hospitals, and educational databases.

Studies show that employees look to their employers to provide these tools for understanding. And when employers provide them—and announce their availability—employees use them to learn more about their benefits and manage those benefits.

Another key component of a successful launch of a new total remuneration policy is help with retirement and financial planning. People look to their employers for assistance in these areas, and employers are often in a good position to negotiate free or inexpensive financial counseling. Also, offering financial and retirement counseling is an easy way to reinforce the organization's message that it cares about its employees' financial health.

Ongoing Communications: The second phase of a benefits communications strategy is the ongoing messages employees see in their Web portals, in-boxes, mailboxes, and other places where they receive messages and are likely to pay attention to them. Organizations are reporting increases in participation rates and employee satisfaction, while also bringing costs down, when they use a combination of the following techniques to inform employees about their benefits on a quarterly or monthly basis:

- *Common Look and Design:* People pay closer attention to health-related information when it has a special look. Communications that arrive in distinctive packaging, use consistent stationery, or are branded in online communications get more notice than communications that arrive in standard business envelopes.
- *Regularly Delivered Messages and Updates:* Research shows that the most successful communication campaigns are those that strike the same message (and provide timely updates) on a regular basis, preferably quarterly.
- *Strategically Redundant Messages:* Organizations that deliver the same core messages via e-mail, standard mail, newsletter, Web portal, bulletin board—wherever people will see them—get bigger returns on their benefits investment. Some organizations are even using tools such as instant messaging to deliver reminders about benefits.

Some Success Stories

Organizations that have implemented successful changes in their benefits programs have drawn on many of the areas mentioned above. The following are some real examples of what organizations have done to successfully communicate new benefits programs.

American Modern Insurance Group

Elisabeth Baldock, senior vice president of human resources and learning at American Modern Insurance Group (AMIG), stresses good communications: "We have recently instituted total remuneration statements," she says. "The statements show the total value of the base pay, incentive, and benefits package, and they have been instrumental in getting people focused on the value that they are given in the compensation package." The investment in developing these statements is nominal compared to the value that they've brought. "If we save one job as a result of these compensation statements, it is worth it," says Baldock. "They pay for themselves." And whereas most organizations may use these types of statements only as a retention tool, AMIG also uses them as a recruiting tool: It includes remuneration statements in its job-offer letters. "Coming in the door, people not only know which benefits programs they get, but the value of these programs," says Baldock.

Although the statements are a critical tool for AMIG, they aren't the only one. According to Alisa Poe, AMIG's vice president of human resources operations, the organization wants the line manager doing as much of the implementation and communication of the total rewards program as possible because, as she puts it, "they are the most trusted people from the associate's perspective." The role of HR, she says, is to provide the tools and assistance. "But the most effective communications in this regard come from the manager."

St. Vincent's Medical Center

According to St. Vincent's Director of Benefits Jane Vassil, "a new benefits program is only as good as the communication program that introduces it." This New York City–based medical center arranged meetings with doctors, executives, employees, insurance representatives, and HR to introduce its new program. "The communications needed to be simple and direct. We showed pertinent comparisons between St. Vincent's benefits and those of other employers. The message went out across a number of platforms—mailings to employees' homes and PowerPoint presentations to small groups of employees—and they were tailored to different levels of employees who received different levels of coverage."

Avaya

A leading global telecommunications networking solutions provider, Avaya is a Lucent Technologies spin-off with operations in 49 countries and annual revenues in excess of $5 billion. Its 20,000 + employees did not fully understand the value of their medical and dental insurance, pensions, 401(k) plans, tuition reimbursements, sick days, and other benefits. The communications giant recognized the importance of communicating the value of its total rewards. If it didn't, it would risk losing good employees to organizations offering more base pay but less compensation overall.

In addition to retaining employees and attracting top-flight new talent, Avaya had another reason to explain its benefits: "Our focus is on a performance-based culture," says Bruce Lasko, Avaya's senior manager of global compensation and benefits. "We want employees to understand the business and understand their value." People in a performance-based culture must understand the value of their benefits as part of their total rewards, especially in an aggressive industry where benefits may account for up to 40 percent of one's total remuneration. Avaya executives wanted to tell employees about the monetary value of their benefits, and because benefits differed from employee to employee, they needed to find a way to reach each person individually.

Avaya created My Total Rewards—the name for its branded, easy-to-use total rewards online service center. Combining data from a dozen separate sources, My Total Rewards integrates Avaya's compensation and retirement, education, health and welfare, and other benefits programs. And it presents to employees the value of these programs in real dollars, in the context of their total rewards. When an employee logs on to My Total Rewards, he or she sees a complete personalized breakdown of the compensation package. In just one or two clicks, Avaya employees can find tables, pie charts, and simple explanations of their base pay, their targeted award amount, their benefits as a percentage of their total rewards, and a breakdown of the employee's and Avaya's costs for each benefit. Links to company policies, a frequently asked questions section, a glossary of benefits and compensation terms, and a list of company events make My Total Rewards a natural Web destination for Avaya employees.

My Total Rewards results are dramatic: More than 92 percent of employees have logged on to My Total Rewards at some point. Even more impressive is the number of employees who said their knowledge of the value of their benefits has increased. In the survey, employees were asked, "Before visiting My Total Rewards, were you aware of the value of your total rewards (compensation + benefits)?" A little more than half (53 percent) said yes. When asked, "Overall, My Total Rewards has increased my understanding of the value of my total rewards package," an impressive 91 percent agreed.

The Bottom Line on Benefits

Every organization is different—different employees with different needs, different cultures, and different missions. An effective benefits program aligns employee needs with the organization's goals. And it's based on careful research into what the organization offers, what it wants to offer, what employees want, and obviously what it can afford to offer.

Unless you're starting a brand-new company or launching a benefits program where none existed before, you won't be working with a clean slate. That means someone is likely to feel threatened. For instance, if you have one or two employees in your department who value their current traditional defined benefits retirement plan, you may need to explain why the organization is taking it away (or more commonly, redesigning it). When you make this type of change, it's critical to explain all of the changes and their impacts carefully, what they'll get in its place, and the consequences of not making the change. For example, recently IBM changed its defined benefit plan but failed to communicate it clearly and carefully. The new plan got bad press until IBM corrected its communications with the affected employees. You'll need to take some time to figure out how to package the good with the bad—how to talk about change to those affected by it.

Last, it may seem counterintuitive, but lobbing soft benefit after soft benefit at employees may do more harm than good because employees may not understand or appreciate their value. Doing this can foster an entitlement culture in which people expect handouts. The handouts will be appreciated only in the present moment. But taking the handouts away at a future point may make employees very unhappy.

Summary: A Checklist for Benefits

Ideally, every benefit—from dry-cleaning services and family day care to company-sponsored retirement plans and health-care benefits— should reflect the organization's benefits philosophy and be driven by its business strategy. Benefits should be thought out, not simply handed out. Based on our research and experience, we believe the best way to evaluate and maintain a successful benefits and total remuneration philosophy is to:

- *Analyze it:* Understand its clear and integrated philosophy, where it comes from, whom it serves, and why it was formulated.
- *Quantify it:* Know how it meets employee and organization needs and what its limitations are.
- *Compare it:* Know where it stands relative to other organizations with similar business models, cultures, and employee demographics.
- *Communicate it:* Do this clearly and often.
- *Monitor it:* Do this on an ongoing basis, because changes in industry, tax law, and other regulations may affect it.

CHAPTER 10

Remembering the *Management* in Performance Management

IN THIS CHAPTER, we tackle the often difficult task of measuring and managing an employee's value to the organization. This may be especially tough to do because different organizations expect different things of their employees, and each has a different way to measure and manage performance. In other words, when it comes to performance management, your last employer's methods may not tell you much about your current employer's ways. While there's no one perfect approach, performance management works best when it's tailored to an organization's needs and culture. We explore the common approaches and best practices that line managers use to measure and manage employee contributions.

The Rationale for Performance Management

Performance management is a process for establishing a shared understanding of what will be achieved and how it will be achieved; it's a way to approach managing people that increases the probability of both individual and organizational success. There are four reasons performance management is a valuable process for line managers:

1. *Increased Overall Organization Contribution:* When performance management is systematically executed and sustained over the long

term, it raises the organization's standard of excellence and improves everyone's performance.

2. *Increased Alignment of Employees' Efforts to Group Objectives:* When highly successful companies are compared to their less successful competitors, one of the differences to emerge is the prevalence of employee goals (see Figure 10-1 for a comparison of performance management and results). When employees know where the organization is going and how their work will help get it there, they're better able to deliver. A clear statement of company objectives helps managers ensure that employee efforts are focused on actions that will make a difference to the organization's performance.

3. *Increased Retention and Engagement from Your Employees:* Performance management is a key component in creating an engaging climate for your employees. An engaging climate is not just beneficial for retaining employees; it also leads to outstanding performance. In a recent study, we found top-performing teams had far more engaging climates than their typical counterparts. By using a robust performance management process, managers can clarify expectations, enhance employees' sense of being part of a larger whole, increase their motivation by setting stretch goals, develop their capability through coaching, and provide rewards for performance—all of which contribute to employee commitment.

4. *Increased Employee Competence:* A key component of performance management is addressing performance gaps and providing feedback and coaching to improve employee capability and performance.

FIGURE 10-1. RELATIONSHIP BETWEEN PERFORMANCE MANAGEMENT AND BUSINESS RESULTS

	Highly Successful Companies	Less Successful Companies
Performance-based Rewards	86%	30%
Clear Employee Goals	80%	26%
Working Together toward a Common Direction	70%	4%
Attention to Development	67%	27%

Source: D. Karvetz, The Human Resources Revolution (San Francisco: Jossey-Bass, 1988)

Higher capability across the employee population means higher probability of greater revenue and profits.

The Manager's Role

To own performance management, managers need to see it as an ongoing process, not a once-a-year event. Figure 10-2 is a useful model of the performance management process. The model shows that when performance management is working well, the three key components of planning, coaching, and rewarding and reviewing are not linear, but cyclical and ongoing. Managers have to move around the wheel many times during the year, with dialogue with their employees at the center of their activities.

The ongoing nature of performance management is underscored by Mary Eckenrod, vice president of Worldwide Talent Management of Cisco Systems. In characterizing Cisco's performance management and development process, Eckenrod says:

> [There's an] "ongoing process of aligning individuals' goals with organizational initiatives, and then collecting and sharing feed-

FIGURE 10-2. PERFORMANCE MANAGEMENT PROCESS

back to continuously improve performance and support talent development." During the ongoing review process, there were regularly scheduled events that provided a time to formally assess performance and develop plans for the future, including an Annual Performance Review and Development Plan, which reviewed individual key accomplishments in support of business initiatives and planned the next cycle of performance and development goals and deliverables.[1]

The one component of the process that truly needs to continue throughout the year is *coaching*. This is underscored by Dick Brown, CEO of EDS, a $20 billion global technology services company, who says that "a leader should be constructing his appraisal all year long and giving his appraisal all year long. You have 20, 30, 60 opportunities a year to share your observations. If, at the end of the year, someone is truly surprised by what you have to say, that is a failure of leadership. . . . By failing to provide honest feedback, leaders cheat their people by depriving them of the information that they need to improve."[2]

Let's take a look at each of the elements in the process model (Figure 10-2).

Planning

The planning phase sets the expectations between the manager and the employee. It's during this phase that the "what" and the "how" of the job are discussed and agreed upon (more on this later). Thus, it's critical that the manager ensure the goals are clear and there's commitment to those goals. While this phase is the initial meeting in the annual cycle, it may reappear throughout the year if goals, strategies, or conditions change.

One trap that many managers fall into during the planning phase is a failure to link the individual employee's accountabilities with the team's and organization's goals. A recent Hay Group study of performance management design and administration practices indicated that although 72 percent of organizations have clear strategic objectives, only 30 percent believe there's a linkage between strategic objectives and individual performance criteria.[3] Helping employees understand their contributions to the organization's goals can provide a sense of belonging to something greater than themselves. This help results in employees making discretionary efforts toward following the organization's priorities (as we mentioned earlier, discretionary effort is that little extra bit that employees choose to expend instead of doing the bare minimum).

Coaching

Many performance management efforts fail to be as effective as they could be because managers complete the planning phase and then take no further action until the end of the cycle, when they conduct a performance appraisal. The previously mentioned Hay Group study shows significant gaps in management coaching of performance. For example, results indicated that only 23 percent of employees received regular feedback on achievement of business results, 30 percent received regular feedback on required behaviors, and 27 percent received proactive coaching from their managers.[4]

Ongoing dialogue and coaching are critical components of a successful performance management process—that's why *dialogue* appears in the center of the model. Without constant focus on developing people, providing feedback, and supplying the needed resources, the process falters and the desired results don't materialize.

So what does coaching within the context of performance management look like? Effective coaching here is continuous and supportive, and it addresses both the "what" and the "how" of the job. Coaching addresses any performance shortfalls and reinforces positive behavior for sustained performance. It not only affects individual performance but also creates the engaging climate employees need to perform at their best. Additionally, it gives managers an opportunity to refocus employees, energize and motivate them, and provide guidance. The ongoing nature of coaching ensures that when it's time for the final review and reward phase, there will be no surprises. Employees and managers maintain positive working relationships and avoid difficult—and often disempowering—conversations at the end of the cycle.

The coaching part of the performance management process is often the most difficult (and as a result, the most overlooked). Giving critical but constructive feedback tests most managers. In fact, critical feedback can be thought of as the "heavy lifting" of leadership. Anyone who has ever struggled through a feedback discussion with a poor performer can attest to how uncomfortable it can be. However, without feedback, employees don't have the information they need to improve, and the organization's overall performance can slide toward mediocrity.

One way to help avoid negative dialogue in addressing performance shortfalls is in "holding others accountable" (see Figure 10-3). The phrase refers to a manager making others comply with his or her wishes where personal power or the power of the manager's position is used appropriately, with the long-term good of the organization in mind. It includes a theme or tone of "telling people what to do." Managers may find that by thinking about their own behavior along similar lines they'll be better prepared to address employee performance issues. Note that there are varying gradations of this competency, as shown in Figure 10-3, and that higher value-added levels of the competency appear at the top of the scale.

Coaching is a difficult skill to master. Covering it completely here would take far more space than this chapter allows. However, managers don't need to master all the nuances to be able to conduct effective coaching sessions. What's important to understand about coaching in the performance management process is that there are two types of coaching conversations—informal and formal. *Informal* coaching sessions should be part of the normal work routine. They should be spontaneous and immediate. Quite often they're the most important conversations for an employee. When managers recognize substandard behaviors or accountabilities not being met, they need to address them directly—and immediately. Likewise, when behavior or accountability exceeds expectations, it's equally important to recognize that as well.

Formal coaching sessions, on the other hand, should have a longer-term perspective and focus on the employee's long-term development and career growth. Managers need the "data" (demonstrated behaviors, results achieved or not) to support whatever constructive feedback and developmental suggestions they make. But they should also spend significant time discussing the employee's development and preparations for the next career step.

Reviewing

While reviewing is an integral part of coaching (managers need to monitor performance all the time and use that information wisely and strate-

FIGURE 10-3. "HOLDING OTHERS ACCOUNTABLE" COMPETENCY

1. **Wants Expectations Clear:** States concern that performance expectations are made clear and are understood.

2. **Gives Basic Directions:** Gives adequate directions, makes needs and requirements reasonably clear to achieve performance expectations.

3. **Sets Clear, Consistent Expectations and Goals:** Gives a detailed explanation of the goal: what it looks like for the individual and the group.

4. **Sets Limits:** Firmly says "No" to unreasonable requests, or sets limits for others' behavior. May structure situations to limit others' options, or to force them to make desired resources available.

5. **Demands High Performance:** Unilaterally sets standards, demands high performance, quality, or resources; insists on compliance with own orders or requests in a "no-nonsense" or "put my foot down" style.

6. **Holds People Accountable for Performance:** Confronts others openly and directly about performance. Reviews performance against clear standards and expectations.

7. **Takes Effective Action Against Performance:** Addresses performance problems in a timely way by assessing performance against standards and acting in a way to change performance for the better. Includes firing or moving poor performers to new areas to develop them

gically), it constitutes the year-end review. In keeping with the "no surprises" philosophy, managers need to ensure that they not only use the performance data they've gathered throughout the year but also balance those data in the year-end formal evaluation.

When it comes to the review phase, there are two potential pitfalls for managers: giving away high performance ratings even when they're not earned, and using the meeting only to look back and not forward. As mentioned before, managers have a tendency to avoid the difficult conversations that accompany poor performance ratings. When it comes time to assign a final performance rating for the year, the same applies. Avoid giving high ratings as a way to circumvent difficult dialogues with poor-performing employees. Those employees need to understand and appreciate the difficulty involved in achieving high ratings. Instead, providing them with the information they need to excel will help challenge them and raise the standard of excellence across the organization.

The second obstacle in the reviewing phase is in failing to use the final review as a starting point for the next cycle. Many managers, finding themselves overwhelmed with the administrative burden of the process, simply stop when they come to the final rating (some even opt out of communicating their ratings), and thereby they miss a great opportunity to look forward and to begin the planning phase of the next performance management cycle.

Rewarding

When most people think of rewards, they immediately jump to monetary rewards, incentive plan payouts, year-end bonuses, and pay increases. However, this is a limited perspective considering the breadth of tools available for recognizing employee contributions. While the rewarding phase usually does include year-end monetary rewards, it often also includes recognition and rewards throughout the year for work well done or for delivering performance that exceeds expectations. This is especially important, given the results of a 2003 Hay Group/Loyola University Chicago/WorldatWork study of compensation practices. This study indicated little differentiation in pay between top and average performers, with only 32 percent of organizations providing increases that might be considered "differentiated" between top and average performers (that is, at least a twofold difference in increase size between top and average performers).[5] To increase the differentiation, managers should reward employees as often as their superior performance demands; they shouldn't think of rewards as a single, year-end recognition.

Managers have a broad range of vehicles at their disposal to reward employee performance. These include, but aren't limited to, the following:

- Money
- Promotions and future career development
- New project opportunities
- Training
- Public recognition
- Increased exposure to the senior leadership
- Greater empowerment in making key decisions

Regularly recognizing and rewarding employees can have a significant impact on employee motivation. Unfortunately, when the rewards are poorly expressed and misunderstood, that can be equally demotivating. It's critical to link rewards directly to individual performance and organizational goals. As a manager, you need to ensure employees that rewards are directly proportional to performance. Without this perception, high-performing employees will likely feel disengaged, and no one will understand what high performance means because everyone's treated the same.

Clarity in Performance Management

The first step in the performance management process is to clarify your own goals and objectives. A recent Hay Group study shows how difficult that can be. The study showed a surprising lack of organizational clarity—that is, the extent to which employees understand what's expected of them and how those expectations connect with the organization's larger goals. In fact, the biggest single difference between great teams and typical teams was their level of clarity of understanding organization direction. Without clear goals, employees lack confidence in management. In particular, workers at lower levels strongly feel this lack of clear goals. Our rolling Hay Group Insight database examined the satisfaction levels for workers planning to leave their organizations within two years versus those planning to stay longer. This study revealed a key reason people leave their jobs: They feel their companies lack direction. Even among employees planning to stay more than two years at their companies, only 57 percent felt their organizations had a clear sense of direction.

Why do employees crave clarity? What could be more demoralizing for employees than the realization that all of that hard work hasn't achieved anything meaningful for either the organization or the department? Most employees want to do the right thing, but they can do it only if they know what the right thing is! Therefore, a key task in performance management is to create clarity for employees so that they understand what's expected of them. That will help increase the probability of success for them, for yourself as their manager, and for the organization as a whole.

Defining the "What" and the "How" of Performance

As we've mentioned several times, to be effective, performance management must link employees to the business strategy. That link helps them understand what they need to do as individuals and as team members to contribute to the organization's success. That's why performance management is about both the "what" and the "how" of performance. That is, it is based on business-related, value-creating outcomes (not activities)—the "what." And it must define the skills and behaviors necessary to achieve the desired outcome—the "how." Indeed, how outcomes are achieved is a critical determinant of the performance equation and is the stuff of which culture is created and nourished.

The "What" of Performance

Ideally, managers and employees engage in a planning process (see Figure 10-2) to jointly identify the performance levels expected and to commit to achieving those performance expectations. So, the key to performance planning is defining the "what" of the job: the specific goals or results that are expected. These typically fall into three categories:

1. *Accountabilities:* Ongoing responsibilities that don't change much from year to year
2. *Annual Goals:* Unique, value-added actions that support key organizational initiatives and objectives
3. *Developmental Goals:* Specific activities, assignments, or changes in behavior that improve personal capability or competence

The goals can be defined at the individual, group, and/or corporate level and are often a combination of the three. Regardless of how the results are defined, they should link individual, team, and organizational goals so that employees understand how they contribute overall. This helps keep everyone's eye on the prize and ensures that all individual and team work translates into better organizational performance. The best way to link these goals is to use a "cascading" goal-setting process. This process begins with the organization's goals and then defines goals for each department or work group in descending order, down to the individual level.

Aeromexico, based in Mexico City, had worked with a strategy consulting firm that delivered a 249-page report listing key performance indicators (KPIs) for measuring progress by the enterprise. The good news was that the KPIs gave the top team the metrics for measuring success. The bad news was that there were 100 KPIs, and they weren't prioritized. So the organization held many team discussions to determine which KPIs connected most directly with organizational priorities and where they fit in the business cycle. Then each executive team member settled on five chief goals. By clarifying key objectives and linking them to team efforts, the teams greatly increased the odds that the goals message would "cascade" down the line.[6]

Type "SMART goals" into any Web browser, and you will come up with literally millions of hits. That's enough to make you think that there's nothing new left to say on the topic. Every management course on the topic uses the acronym SMART; as mentioned in Chapter 4, the specific letter associations may vary slightly, but the typical meaning is:

- *Specific:* Be sure to be clear on what you are trying to achieve.
- *Measurable:* Ensure you have good data on how you're doing.
- *Achievable:* Don't try to achieve too much; ensure you have resources to achieve your goal.
- *Relevant:* Align individual goals with broader organizational goals.
- *Time Based:* Set deadlines for when you intend to achieve the goals.

But the world is constantly changing and business demands are ever changing along with it. In that spirit, we offer our take on SMART:

• *Specific:* Specific is good, but as Ralph Waldo Emerson said, "A foolish consistency is the hobgoblin of little minds." Circumstances change during the life of a performance objective, and sticking to yesterday's objective may be counterproductive. Specific goals are appropriate, but the goals should be framed in the context of the big picture. Employees need to understand why a goal was selected so that if circumstances change they can make the right decisions rather than play it by the out-of-date book.

• *Measurable:* Measurable is also good (in fact, essential), but this should not be used as the driver in setting targets. You want to motivate people to achieve what matters, not what is easy to measure. An example of this is seen frequently in education. Teachers' performance can be observed and measured. You remember who your good teachers were, right? Nevertheless, measuring performance is difficult. Using grades and test scores has obvious flaws, but they are used nonetheless, much to the consternation of dedicated educators. If something is important enough, you can probably come up with a way to measure it. A goal that's not measurable has very limited impact on motivation because people need feedback to know how well they are doing; otherwise motivation won't occur.

• *Achievable:* Achievable is very important because goals perceived to be unreachable have a negative impact on motivation. However, there's equally strong evidence to suggest that goals that are too easy lead to low performance. Putting the appropriate amount of stretch in your objectives is critical.

Research suggests that goals that people expect to achieve with only minimal effort have (at best) a zero impact on performance. There is little or no intrinsic reward associated with achieving simple goals. As the required effort increases and the likelihood of success decreases, the motivational impact goes up. If the goal is meaningful, people will attempt to achieve it in order to earn both the intrinsic and the extrinsic rewards.

However, once people start to believe that the goal will not be achieved, even with a solid effort on their part, they stop trying. The overall impact is still positive, as many others remain motivated, even by a difficult goal. But as the effort goes up and the probability of success continues to go down, more and more people will give up. Eventually, most will believe that the goal is unattainable and not worth the effort so they'll stop trying. Worse yet, they become cynical, and performance drops further and faster than if no goal had been set at all.

The situation is further complicated by the fact that organizations have different philosophies toward their performance management processes, and these suggest different shapes for the performance curve. One organization may have a performance management philosophy oriented toward a star system. This means that significant achievements are celebrated, the brightest and the best are retained and rewarded, and everyone else had better watch out. In the star system, goals are "stretchy." It may be a strong cultural fit if only 30 percent of employees will hit the target, as long as most of the population believe they can be one of that 30 percent, that it is important to them to be so, and that coming in at 90 percent of target does not mean that they are about to be fired. Conversely, your performance management philosophy might be about removing the deadwood from the organization. You want to set goals that identify the low performers (say, the bottom 20 percent) and weed them out. In this case, you'll want to set goals that at least 80 percent of the employees will achieve.

The challenge for a manager is to set targets that will fall into the motivational zone (realistic, yet stretching) that are also consistent with the organization's philosophy for performance management. Most typically, when a majority of the population (say, 50 to 65 percent) believe they have at least a 50:50 chance of achieving the target, this will be acceptable and motivating. But be careful: This is not a standard prescription that will apply in all cases.

Managing pay to relate to performance is an important objective. When the organization wins in the marketplace, individuals will likely benefit, especially in terms of faster career progression and higher incentives. If performance is high, the funding should be there to achieve this. As a manager, you should be motivated to beat the competition, not necessarily the other organizational units of your business.

• *Relevant:* Relevance refers back to alignment, an important objective. By relevant, we mean that people in pursuit of a goal should feel that the goal is important to the organization and within their control to achieve it. If this is the case, it's a good goal.

• *Time Based:* Any useful objective will have a time frame for completion (and maybe for starting). Without having a specific time frame, it is impossible to say if the goal has been met or not.

Does SMART mean equitable? Not necessarily. Consider an example from the world of sports—competitive diving. In diving, the level of difficulty of a dive is factored into the final rating of performance. A competitor executing perfectly a moderately difficult dive may earn a score of only 9, whereas a competitor executing near perfection on a much more difficult dive may earn a score of 9.5.

Now, consider area sales managers who are selling the same line of products but in different territories, with different potential sales, and with different customer mixes. Should they be given the same targets? Probably not. For sales jobs, goals typically relate to incentive compensation. Incentives should motivate sales managers to perform at their best; thus, goals should represent an optimal degree of stretch for each sales manager. Given the differences in territories and customers, selling $10 million in area one is as challenging as selling $12 million in area two.

The "How" of Performance

The "how" of performance management focuses on the values of the organization and/or of the competencies or behaviors necessary for outstanding performance. These critical competencies and behaviors paint a picture of success that's clear, objective, understandable, and relevant to the job. They also help focus employee development on improving in a way that is critical to the continued success and profitability of the organization.

Why do we care about the "how" of performance? Research suggests that outstanding performers (those who demonstrate the right competencies in the job) are far more productive than average performers—in some cases, as much as 140 percent more productive![7] By including how better performance is to be achieved, managers are much more likely to bring about long-term improvement.

Competencies

Hay Group, starting with the pioneering work of Harvard psychologist David McClelland, has a long-standing record in identifying the attributes or competencies that predict outstanding performance in specific jobs and roles.[8] In the early 1960s, McClelland began to research what factors might predict outstanding performance, aside from the traditional selection standards of intelligence, technical skill, and experience. Using a specialized interview methodology that captured what people actually do in the course of their work, McClelland was able to identify those competencies that separated top performers from the rest, even though both groups may share common job-relevant expertise and experience, as well as IQ.[9] Daniel Goleman, drawing on Hay Group's database of competencies in the workplace, popularized the power of this methodology in his best-selling 1995 book *Emotional Intelligence*.[10]

As applied to the workplace, a *competency* is an underlying characteristic of an individual that leads to effective performance in a job. For example, hurling a 90-mile-per-hour fastball is a competency associated with a major league pitcher. Differentiating competencies among employees helps distinguish superior from average performers. In other words, there's a difference between a 60-mile-per-hour fastball and a 90-mile-per-hour fastball. As we discussed in Chapter 2, research has shown that there are significant differences in output between superior and average performers. Moreover, this performance variation increases for jobs of greater complexity—with the most pronounced differences in sales jobs, where there can be greater than a two-times difference in performance variation between average and superior performers.[11]

Threshold, or essential, competencies are required for minimally adequate or average performance. Again, if your fastball isn't fast enough, you won't get into the major leagues. To apply this concept in the world of business, consider the challenge many organizations face in moving successful "doers" into the role of "manager of doers." This attempt often plays out in unexpected ways. In sales, for instance, organizations traditionally draw their star performers into the management ranks under the assumption that star-level sales delivery equals the capability to manage the delivery of sales. Lo and behold, many former stars fail to deliver under these different work circumstances. It turns out that threshold competencies for both typical and outstanding sales managers are analytical capability, drive for results, and persistence—the very competencies that drove their success as individual contributors. Outstanding sales managers, however, often demonstrate additional competencies: the ability to motivate and energize others, the ability to provide balanced feedback for performance improvement, and the ability to enhance the capability of others to deliver on their own. The threshold and differentiating competencies for a given job are useful guidelines for selection, succession planning, performance appraisal, and management development.

Competencies can be demonstrated through behavior and reasoning. At a very basic level, they manifest themselves as personal dispositions (underlying needs, drives, or thought patterns that direct an individual's behavior, as in the needs for achievement, affiliation, and power.[12]) The relevance and impact of such motives on managerial behavior are well documented.[13] Competencies can also be expressed as relatively stable personality traits (curiosity, patience, perseverance, interpersonal sensitivity, and so on), attitudes, values (for example, "If I want to be a good manager, I really should coach and develop my direct reports"), and content knowledge or skills (for example, finance, manufacturing, industry-specific skills).

The particular manner in which a competency acts as a differentiating characteristic has practical implications for getting people into the right jobs. For instance, as alluded to in Figure 10-4, above the "water line" knowledge and skill competencies (which can be assembled from a well-written résumé) are relatively easy to develop, assuming the pres-

FIGURE 10-4. COMPETENCY "ICEBERG" MODEL

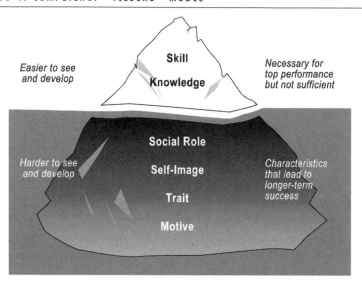

ence of threshold capabilities. Classroom or on-the-job training is often the most cost-effective way to develop these job-specific abilities. But deeper motives and trait competencies (as with conceptual ability or strategic perspective) are more difficult to assess and develop. It's typically more cost-effective to select and/or promote on the basis of these latter characteristics. Quoting from a *Financial Times* article on this very topic, "It's easier to hire a squirrel than to teach a turkey to climb a tree."[14]

What do these competencies look like? Let's say that the competency of "teamwork and cooperation" is a key differentiator for a given job. The phrase implies the intention to work cooperatively with others, to be part of a team, to work together as opposed to working separately or competitively. Teamwork and cooperation could be defined by the five levels shown in Figure 10-5. To adequately assess someone relative to this competency, managers use direct observations of the employee in action.

The following tips can be useful when summarizing performance relative to set competencies:

- Be thoroughly familiar with the competencies and objectives to be evaluated.
- Record key situations in which a competency was demonstrated or an objective achieved. Include the context (when, where, etc.),

FIGURE 10-5. SAMPLE TEAMWORK AND COOPERATION COMPETENCY

1. **Cooperates:**
   - Supports team decisions, is a good team player, does his or her share of the work.
   - Keeps other team members informed and up-to-date about what is happening in the group.
   - Shares all relevant or useful information.

2. **Expresses Positive Attitudes and Expectations of Team or Team Members:**
   - Expresses positive attitudes and expectations of others in terms of their abilities, expected contributions, etc.
   - Speaks of team members in positive terms, either to the team member directly or to a third party.

3. **Solicits Inputs:**
   - Genuinely values others' input and expertise.
   - Displays willingness to learn from others, including subordinates and peers.
   - Solicits ideas and opinions to help form specific decisions or plans.

4. **Encourages Others:**
   - Publicly credits others who have performed well.
   - Encourages and empowers others, making them feel strong and important.

5. **Works to Build Team Commitment:**
   - Acts to promote good working relationships regardless of personal likes or dislikes.
   - Builds good morale or cooperation within the team, including creating symbols of group identity or other actions to build cohesiveness.

the action (what the employee did or didn't do), and the outcome (the result or impact of the action or inaction). Record your observations promptly. You don't want to find yourself having to remember or re-create events later.

- Be specific in documenting behaviors. Avoid general words such as *good* or *fine*.
- Avoid allowing what you've seen in one situation to influence your observations of other situations.
- Document both the presence and absence of desired behaviors.
- Ask for feedback from others who work closely with the employee.

Using Multi-Rater Feedback

Many organizations collect multi-rater, or 360, feedback on employees because they realize that feedback from other sources offers another perspective. For example, it's not unusual for employees to discount the feedback they receive from their supervisor, feeling that the supervisor doesn't appreciate their accomplishments or understand them enough to offer meaningful, constructive feedback. Performance feedback from sources other than the manager can be good input and provide employees with a better picture of what they should or shouldn't do in given situations. Multi-rater feedback can be very useful for development; however, for performance management purposes, multi-rater feedback has its limitations. The 360 feedback has a potential for bias and for inaccurately reflecting changes in behavior or development.

Although multi-rater feedback can be a powerful tool, it's certainly no silver bullet for a poorly designed performance management system. Most organizations aren't ready to make the leap from pay decisions based on a traditional appraisal to one influenced by multi-rater feedback. Multi-rater feedback is best used to support employee development, while traditional appraisal is best for pay decisions. For example, multi-rater systems that include rater-written comments (even though they are anonymous) can paint an accurate picture of behaviors that the employee has or hasn't demonstrated, and that managers may not have seen. This information is useful in developmental coaching sessions, providing employees a clearer idea of what they did or didn't demonstrate in a given situation.

Challenges and Solutions in Measuring Performance

We've covered the manager's role in the performance management cycle and have highlighted some pitfalls that are inherent in the process. However, one step requires more discussion: reviewing.

Unfortunately, accurately assessing employee performance isn't as easy as it sounds. There are challenges that arise whenever managers attempt to assess performance. Although each of the challenges listed in Figure 10-6 have recommended remedies, managers should evaluate the cause of the problem and determine an appropriate solution based on the particular circumstances.

FIGURE 10-6. RATING CHALLENGES AND REMEDIES

1. The Halo/Horns Effect

- *Challenges:* Tendency for good or bad performance in one area of work to "color" the assessment in other areas of work (if Jim is a strong "analytical thinker," he must be a strong "conceptual thinker" too). Often results from a general discussion of job performance, which does not include specific objectives and measures.
- *Remedies:* Careful observation throughout the year and review of all relevant information. Take a balanced or weighted approach to reaching a final assessment based on each individual area of work.

2. Primacy and Recency

- *Challenges:* People tend to overemphasize recent events. It is not easy to remember significant events that occur during an entire year.
- *Remedies:* Informal discussions throughout the year and continual review of performance expectations. Review of all relevant documentation and information from your employee. Keep track of changes in behavior and growth throughout the year and ensure that you are neither masking poor performance nor "playing old tapes."

3. Contrast Effect

- *Challenges:* A performance assessment of one employee inappropriately influences an evaluation of another employee. An employee who has replaced a poor performer is likely to look good by comparison but still not meet the requirements of the position.
- *Remedies:* Focus on the employee's results rather than on how he or she compares with those of other employees.

4. Leniency vs. Strictness

- *Challenges:* Tendency to appraise more leniently or strictly than is warranted.
- *Remedies:* Be aware of this tendency. Remember that an employee can be developed further only with honest and constructive feedback. Rely on the steps in the process to help you make an honest and balanced assessment.

5. Cultural Tendency and Inflation

- *Challenges:* Tendency to provide ratings that are in the middle (central tendency) or are toward the top (inflation) of a rating scale.
- *Remedies:* Rate individuals using the entire scale or performance dimension. Stay focused— base your ratings on observable performance results and observable behaviors. Remember that an employee can be developed further only with honest and constructive feedback.

6. Personal Biases

- *Challenges:* People have a tendency to be more impressed by people they like and those who are similar to them in appearance and attitudes. Your own needs can influence your judgment.
- *Remedies:* Be aware of your own motives and biases. Have clearly identified objectives and measures against which a person can be assessed.

7. Isolation/Relativity

- *Challenges:* The challenge of rating someone with minimal opportunity to observe actual performance.
- *Remedies:* Create/force real opportunities throughout the year to observe actual performance. Use self-appraisal and multi-rater feedback tools to increase understanding of actual performance.

8. Tenure Challenge

- *Challenges:* The challenge of rating someone new or with longer tenure in the job.
- *Remedies:* Compare the individual's performance against the job standards for fully competent performance. Stay focused/base your ratings on observable performance results and observable behaviors, rather than where the employee "should" be relative to tenure.

Forced Ranking and Forced Distributions

In simple terms, forced ranking systems generally require management to rank employees in order from best to worst. In forced distribution systems, employees are assigned to a rating category, which designates a fixed percentage of employees to be contained in the category (for example, 15 percent of employees can be included in category 1, 65 percent in category 2). In many systems, the lowest performers may be terminated. Managers claim that these systems enable them to provide more meaningful distinctions in distributing rewards, help them motivate employees to improve performance, and eliminate rating inflation.

Some of these benefits can be attained; however, managers need to ensure the organization has the right conditions to make these systems work. These conditions include:

• *Objective, Credible Measures:* Before implementing a forced ranking or forced distribution system, managers should ensure that the measures used to make ranking decisions are objective and credible, especially if employees in the lowest category are to be terminated or placed on probation. The measures should be true, reliable, and meaningful standards of performance. Without good measures, forced ranking may be perceived as unfair to employees, and it can increase legal exposure for organizations that terminate employees based on forced-ranking results.

• *Communication and Coaching:* Employees need to know where they stand relative to the measures and how the forced-ranking results will be used. Managers need to communicate the process results and coach employees to improve their performance. Organizations with forced ranking or forced distribution systems often have environments characterized as "highly charged" or "high performance." A word of caution: With this type of culture, there's a potential danger of inciting fear in employees. And fearful employees may not direct their discretionary time productively.

• *Calibration:* The organization should have a system in place to ensure consistency in rankings across the organization, especially for employees in similar jobs or job families. Common approaches include conducting calibration meetings to ensure consistency across departments in the criteria used and ranking decisions made and having "+2 reviews" where the manager of the employee's manager reviews all assessments across the group for consistency.

The bottom line is that you have to ensure that your organization has the right conditions for forced ranking or forced distributions to be effective. As GE's Jack Welch stated, "Our vitality curve works because we spent over a decade building a performance culture that has candid feedback at every level. Candor and openness are the foundations of such a culture. I wouldn't want to inject a vitality curve cold turkey into an organization without a performance culture already in place."[15]

Finally, forced ranking systems may suggest a false sense of precision in the assessment of employee performance. They may also create unintended consequences, such as team members competing with one another instead of with the actual competition.

Forced performance distributions, while more practical than forced rankings, also present challenges for managers. The rating distributions should be reflective of the real distribution of performance. We have found the most practical use of performance distributions is as a guideline for managers rather than as an absolute control. The key is to use the tool to begin the dialogue of what real performance looks like within the organization.

Managing the Middle

It's understandable that so much attention is paid to an organization's top performers and its low performers, but don't forget about the other 50 to 75 percent of employees: the ones who make up the backbone of most organizations. The key is to reinforce the notion that the middle is not a bad place to be, and this starts with the labels that are associated with the middle. Words like *average* and phrases like "meets expectations" do not convey the middle as a good place. Just as people tend to think of C as average in terms of school grades, there is negative connotation attached to it. Many companies try to broaden the performance category terms, or even use terms that communicate the value of the middle. For example, in Yahoo's performance management system, the descriptive term for the middle is "Performs Well." Libby Sartain, Yahoo's chief people officer says, "They're the workhorses; they get the job done and we want to keep them."[16]

In addition to using appropriate terminology, it's important to clarify performance gaps for various groups of employees. For bottom performers, this means there should be direct discussions on gaps in performance and what's needed to close those gaps. For top performers, the focus is on giving them what they deserve in terms of both pay and opportunities that are not available to anyone else. But for those in the "mighty middle," the focus should be on making them feel valued, as part of the organization, by emphasizing development and employee commitment. Martin Cozyn, head of HR for Nortel Networks, for example, says, "If you're labeled top, we'll treat you special," he says. "If you're core, we'll give you every opportunity to grow."[17] Providing the middle people with a vision of a "better place to be"—a path to the top for those who want it—can lead to employee engagement, which, as noted earlier, often yields greater discretionary effort by individuals and results for the organization.

Summary: A Checklist for Managing Performance

The task of managing performance can be daunting, but with proper focus and execution, it can provide the organization with great benefits: benefits that the market recognizes. Approximately 35 percent of an institutional investor's valuation of a company is attributable to nonfinancial information that gauges the ability of management to deliver results, including things such as strategy execution, management credibility, and management expertise.[18] Having a strong performance management system, and effectively managing performance, clearly fall in this category.

How does a manager reap these benefits? The following checklist provides a start:

- Know how to translate organizational "must-wins" into departmental "must-wins."
- Make sure employees know what they need to do, day to day, for the organization to succeed.
- Provide ongoing feedback and constructive criticism—no surprises at year-end review!
- Consider the challenges of reviewing and assessing, and prepare yourself for painful, difficult discussions.
- Reinforce that the middle is a valued place to be.

CHAPTER 11

A (Career) Path to Employee Satisfaction and Business Success

ONE OF THE MOST POWERFUL TOOLS managers have in their rewards tool kit is the opportunity to offer employees a fulfilling, long-term career with the organization. This is the key reason many employees are at the organization in the first place. In fact, our ongoing research and experience with client organizations suggests that, although pay may factor into why people leave their employers, employees are deeply concerned about their opportunities for personal development and growth.

This chapter covers the key aspects of well-developed career paths and the importance of supportive reward structures and programs that reinforce employees' growth and development and help organizations thrive.

Grow Your Own Talent

Most employees know they're responsible for managing their own careers. They know that their futures depend on their continually improving their skills. If employees aren't expanding their capabilities and career-advancement opportunities, they're risking compromising their employability—within their current organization or elsewhere. It's your role as a manager to create opportunities for people by broadening their experiences and making them more valuable to the organization and to themselves. In return, these employees will likely stay with the organization longer.

Dennis George, vice president of information technology at Bridgestone Americas, a $10-billion subsidiary of Bridgestone Corporation, directs a workforce of 300 professional information technology professionals. According to George, "The best managers create an environment for people to forge their own careers and where people can prosper long term. We've recently invested resources to create a more visible job family structure so that teammates can see what their future career opportunities are and what they need to do to get to the next level.

"Although we don't want to paint a box around a job, we do want to enable our team members to see what typical job expectations are, to understand the required competencies and skills to succeed, and for teammates and managers to have a dialogue on where they should be focused from a career perspective.

"While the best managers have always done this, we feel that the tools that we've developed will support all of our managers and team members in creating more conversations as well as a higher quality dialogue around potential career opportunities."

Hay Group Insight's employee opinion database suggests, however, that many employees aren't getting the advancement-related support they seek from their managers. According to our Hay Group Insight database of employee opinions, fewer than half of employees surveyed consider their managers to be doing a good job of counseling them in their career development. To keep more of their best people, organizations would do well to focus managers on helping the development of their employees and ensuring that they are being positioned for and placed in roles that align with their skills and capabilities.

One of the criteria used in our assessment of *Fortune* magazine's America's Most Admired Companies, which Hay Group has conducted annually since 1997, is *employee talent*, or the extent to which a business is perceived to hire, nurture, and develop talent and to provide for the succession to senior positions from within. Organizations on *Fortune* magazine's list of America's Most Admired Companies do a better job at identifying and developing more leaders and higher-quality leaders than do the companies that don't make that list. And because of their successful develop-from-within track record, the Most Admired Companies do this at a lower overall cost, enhancing their overall return on their rewards investment. In Figure 11-1, we show a comparison of compensation levels in organizations that appear at the top of the Most Admired category with their less-admired peers in the same industry sector (as defined by Fortune). Quite simply, organizations that get this part of the rewards equation correct pay less—5 percent less, as shown in Figure 11-1—than other organizations for their talent. Put another way, managers and professionals at the America's Most Admired Companies place great value on the future growth and opportunity component of their organizations' total rewards.

The result, hardly surprising, is that most organizations understand that it's less expensive and more effective to "grow their own" talent than to headhunt for costly external talent. Plus, the direct savings in reward costs is enhanced by significant savings in recruitment costs. It is, therefore, critical to factor this component into the total rewards management program. Opportunities to save 5 percent on reward costs are few and far between.

Skills-Job Alignment

Even in the best organizations, most learning and development is focused on progressing people through *functional silos*—for example, trainee accountant to finance director or market analyst to marketing director. While this approach is probably appropriate at lower levels, development of effective leaders demands a breadth of experience that

FIGURE 11-1. HIGH-PERFORMING COMPANIES PAY 5% LESS THAN OTHERS

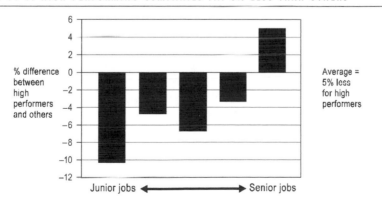

usually can't be achieved simply by progressing through a specific department or function. The real challenge for managers is how to develop employees in small, lean, or flat organizations where it's not so easy to offer a functional career path. When organizations address this issue, it's often by bolting extra accountabilities onto an existing role, either giving a senior staff position a small business to run (in addition to a staff role) or making a line manager lead a multifunctional project team (while continuing to act as a line manager).

The reality is that much development of this kind, if it takes place at all, is done for the sake of the business and not for the benefit of the manager. Ultimately, such moves may benefit neither the manager nor the organization. The main idea of a career path is to allow employees to progress from job to job while growing naturally in their skills, capabilities, and competencies (what we call *input criteria* because these are the things people put into their work). At the same time, a career path allows employees to grow in their expected job accountabilities (what we call *output criteria* because that is what the employer gets out of the employee). Effective career progressions avoid the shock of a job that stretches an employee too far.

A key aspect of effective employee development is ensuring alignment of the nature of the work and the skills and capabilities of the employee. This chapter provides a framework to help you effectively align work and employee capability.

The Architecture of Roles

Most organizations use generic terms to refer to the nature of a role: a *managerial role*, part of the *senior management population*, or an *executive*, for example. People assume that while different senior management roles require different functional knowledge, they're still all basically the same. In fact, development and performance processes usually involve assessing senior managers against a generic set of desirable "leadership" behaviors.

Still, people who experience a significant change in their roles—say, finance director to general manager, general manager to HR director, or production manager to program director—will tell you that the jobs "feel" very different, that they don't seem to be able to make things happen the same way as they did before. That's because, within a generic "senior management" population, there actually are critical differences from role to role and different demands on the individuals performing them.

There are two characteristics that determine different types of roles across all sectors and all geographies: levels of work and nature of roles. Let's consider each in turn.

Levels of Work

For most organizations, identification of the levels of work (or management levels) is largely intuitive; titles such as technician, team leader, manager, senior manager, and director come to mind, each signifying a level of work. However, it's important to recognize opportunities to add value to large and complex organizations. In the largest and most complex organizations, there are six levels of work across the management populations, divided between operational and strategic functions. See Figure 11-2 for descriptions of these levels. However, the levels per se don't explain the differences in the "feel" of jobs. To fully understand the situation, we explore the second characteristic that determines the types of roles.

Nature of Roles

There's a fundamental distinction between *line* and *staff*—in other words, between positions that are in the line of fire if revenue, cost, or profit targets aren't met; and positions that support those roles that are directly accountable for achieving line results. The different nature of these roles can be described as follows:

- *Planning and Policy:* The jobholder provides advice and guidance to support the achievement of business results through the development of functional capabilities and the interpretation of policies.
- *Business and Operations:* The jobholder is directly accountable for business results achieved through direct control of the organization's resources.

However, a third category has become prevalent in matrix organizations. These roles, which may be called program managers, brand managers, or business managers, are similar to the business and operations roles listed above, in that they are clearly associated with a business target, but they lack the direct authority of the business and operations

FIGURE 11-2. SIX LEVELS OF EXECUTIVE WORK

	Level	Description
Strategic	Global Enterprise Leadership	Singular roles in the organization, guided by stakeholders (e.g., owners, government) to set the direction for the organization and ensure successful continuity, consistent with its charter. Constrained only by general laws of nature, science, business philosophy, and cultural standards.
	Enterprise Leadership	Thinking about the organization's overall policies and strategies. Goals are very broadly defined (e.g., increase international operations). Often confronting the unknown.
	Strategy Formation	Thinking required to set the broad strategy for a business that is integral to the core purpose of the total enterprise. Necessarily long-term, considering and integrating discontinuous change in terms of products, markets, and technologies. In functional roles the contribution will include both setting enterprise-wise functional policies and developing corporate objectives and strategies.
	Strategic Alignment	Thinking to position a business or function within a broadly defined business strategy. Scanning the environment and anticipating the impact of external forces—up to 5-year horizon.
Operational	Strategic Implementation	Focused on the variable application of policy locally—turning functional policy into reality. Thinking requires considerable degree of interpretive, evaluative, and/or constructive thinking to address issues that are noticeably different from what has been encountered previously.
	Tactical Implementation	Thinking is toward clearly defined functional objectives within established policy frameworks but requires solutions that represent improvements on current practice.

LEVELS OF WORK

positions and handle more ambiguity in realizing their objectives. We define this third category as follows:

- *Coordination and Commercial:* The jobholder manages and coordinates internal resources and/or develops relationships with external partners to deliver measurable business results.

The Role-Type Matrix

When we bring the characteristics of line and staff together, we see an architecture of management roles that can be found to dominate all large, complex organizations. The top level of a major freestanding global business is reserved for the CEO. The next level is the executive team running businesses of this kind. By definition, this level contains relatively few positions. The bulk of management populations, therefore, are in the third level and within this level, fall into essentially 18 role types, which describe 95 percent of all management jobs found in organizations of all kinds.

Different Competencies for Different Management Roles

As discussed earlier in this book, rewards are not limited to cash. Providing developmental opportunities is one highly effective way of recognizing and rewarding the accomplishments of employees. Employees want to learn and develop themselves. Personal development enhances a person's range of career options within the organization, and typically it raises the individual's market value from a career perspective. Since there's such a shortage of talent in many organizations, one of a manager's most critical functions is to implement this nonpay reward. A. G. Lafley, chairman and CEO of Procter & Gamble, agrees: "The people we hire, and the focus we put on their development as leaders, are critical to P&G's ability to innovate and compete," he says. "Nothing I do will have a more enduring impact on P&G's long-term success than helping to develop other leaders."[1]

"Development" isn't simply moving people into different jobs. It's helping them acquire the skills and know-how that the organization values relative to its business needs. With a long-term view, this added capability can lead to greater earning potential. But in the short term, learning new things and applying them are intrinsically rewarding to most people.

One key to good development lies in identifying the capabilities that the organization values, the capabilities employees have and don't have, and the opportunities that enable people to take advantage of their current strengths while developing new ones. Not just any new job will meet this objective. Given that management roles vary by size and scope (as previously described), it follows that different roles at varying levels of complexity require different skills and behaviors. This involves a degree of common sense, of course. Obviously, general managers do some things very differently from, say, finance or marketing managers.

Wouldn't the successful completion of certain managerial tasks also require a certain set of characteristics? Recent Hay Group research confirms just that.[2] Despite similarities, there are important behavioral differences depending on the type of management role and the operational-to-strategic focus of those roles, as outlined in the previous section.

As discussed in Chapter 10, the most common management roles share a set of threshold (or minimum) competencies. From our ongoing research and work with clients, for effective managers there is a common degree of:

- Analytical and conceptual thinking skills
- Concentration—the ability to stay focused
- A knack for influencing others
- An ability to listen to the concerns of others

But beyond this core set of behavioral building blocks, there are critical differences in the competencies needed for different management roles. This raises serious questions about traditional management-assessment methods, especially those that overemphasize the qualities of the person while paying little attention to the accountabilities of specific management roles. A strong case can be made for rethinking how organizations select, develop, and promote their leaders. By better understanding the demands of specific roles and the competencies required for performance in those roles, organizations can reduce the risks associated with job placement and, over time, improve performance.

Understanding the unique competency requirements associated with a role is especially crucial for organizations that reward high potentials by moving them to different roles to further their development. What competencies are critical to success in alternative new roles? And what are the individual's development needs in relation to these possible roles? These factors should be considered in recommending such developmental opportunities. A new assignment is rewarding and developmental only when the individual possesses the threshold competencies to be effective in addition to the potential to develop the critical competencies to be outstanding.

Competency Distinctions Across Management Roles

The differences between the *planning and policy* group and the *business and operations*—although built on common threshold characteristics—are significant. Excellent leaders in advisory roles consistently display certain characteristics that are much less noticeable in the delivery group. Some of these characteristics fit our assumptions of what makes an outstanding staff leader. For example, they include:

- Substantially higher conceptual capability than delivery or coordination colleagues, especially at the highest levels below the board of directors
- Certain kinds of people skills; in particular, an understanding and ability to interpret others' perspectives at a high level
- High levels of customer service toward line managers
- Heavy emphasis on developing others, including peers and—at the top of organizations—chief executives and board members
- Striking levels of integrity, putting the good of the organization and its stakeholders above all other considerations (not that delivery jobs are entirely lacking in this characteristic, but they display it much less clearly)

Figures 11-3 and 11-4 identify accountability profiles and differentiating competencies delineated by levels of work and type of role.

Performance in these jobs appears to be founded on organizational understanding, empathy with customers (especially internal customers) and staff, conceptual thinking, and a strong moral sense of rightness and propriety. This is how value is added. By contrast, the delivery roles—in which managers retain direct control over resources—display different characteristics:

- Focus on results, including setting goals, establishing thorough cost-benefit analyses, and being attracted by entrepreneurial risk
- Much broader awareness of the organization in the markets or environment in which it operates, including threats and opportunities

(text continued on page 192)

FIGURE 11-3. ACCOUNTABILITY PROFILES AS A FUNCTION OF ROLE TYPE AND LEVEL OF WORK

		Advisory Roles	Collaborative Roles	Operational Roles
Strategic	**Strategy Formation**	Focuses on the alignment and integration of strategies for a function that is a critical driver of business success. Partners in determining firm strategy and providing strategic advice that supports achievement of critical business objectives.	Develops and delivers strategically important programs critical to the organization's mission through coordination and direction of diverse resources over whom direct control is not exercised.	Focuses on the achievement of bottom-line results where global and/or business-critical objectives must be achieved. Typically more complex general manager or sales roles.
	Strategic Alignment	Focuses on the alignment and integration of policy in a strategically important and diverse area. Provides advice and guidance that support the achievement of major business objectives. Seen as thought leader internally.	Defines and delivers specific and measurable long-term programs and results through a complex network of resources and partners over whom direct control is not exercised.	Focuses on the achievement of bottom-line results where product and market developments demand significant change to current business capabilities. Typically general manager or sales roles.
Tactical	**Strategic Implementation**	Focuses on the translation and application of policy in diverse, although usually related, areas.	Delivers specific, measurable results across a broad, complex area through a network of diverse resources and partners over whom direct control is not exercised.	Integrates and balances operational or sales resources to extend current business capabilities, ensuring that market demands are met in the short and medium term. Manages a large, complex operating unit to objectives.
	Tactical Implementation	Focuses on the translation and application of policy in a specific functional area.	Delivers measurable results in a discrete, defined area through a network of internal and external resources and partners over whom direct control is not exercised.	Manages defined resources to ensure achievement of clearly specified objectives such as volume, cost, quality, and service to meet schedule and customer requirements.

FIGURE 11-4. DISTINGUISHING COMPETENCIES BY ROLE TYPE AND LEVEL OF WORK

		Advisory Roles	Collaborative Roles	Operational Roles
Strategic	**Strategy Formation**	N/A	• Networks/builds relationships • Takes a strong leadership role • Greater level of organization commitment, models loyalty • Encourages development and provides feedback • Integrity	• Competencies from previous level *plus* • Strategic focus with broader, longer-term view • Higher levels of developing others • Sophisticated influence on strategies based on in-depth understanding of others and organization's politics
	Strategic Alignment	• Broad and strategic business perspective (understanding the organization in the market) • Complex influence skills based on deep understanding of people, organization, and business • High integrity	• Seeks information to support decisions, negotiate, and influence others • More likely to seek input of others • Integrity	• Competencies from previous level *plus* • Focuses on providing strong visionary leadership • Willing to apply rules flexibly
Tactical	**Strategic Implementation**	• Continues to focus advice and service on the larger organization • Continues to model loyalty to the organization • Coaches and develops others • More likely to take a leadership role than at previous level	• More initiative than previous level • More likely than other collaborative managers to set challenging goals	• Competencies from previous level *plus* • Demands high performance from the team • More likely to act consistently with values and beliefs
	Tactical Implementation	• Focuses on service to the larger organization • Models loyalty to the organization • Manages subordinates one-on-one rather than as team • Accepts need for flexibility	• Demonstrates responsive rather than proactive initiative • Demonstrates pattern recognition more than insight	• Focuses on business results • Focuses on own team, coaching, supporting, gaining input • More likely to take on challenges than peers in other roles

- Self-confidence, willingness to embrace both risk and challenge
- Strong visionary team leadership displaying charismatic and symbolic gestures
- Flexibility in achieving results, including taking some risk with the organizational rules
- Strong orientation on results and focus on strong people leadership, including coaching, holding people accountable, and promoting teamwork

The *coordination* group contains roles that are highly collaborative in nature and includes significant matrix roles with responsibility to manage across product lines, business sectors, and geographies. The differentiating competencies for these roles are:

- Intentions to persuade, convince, influence, or impress others in order to get them to go along with or to support the business agenda
- Ability to understand and diagnose the power relationships in the organization
- Willingness to share information candidly, accurately, and openly with peers, managers, and subordinates, including business performance information
- Ability to work collaboratively and cooperatively across organizational lines to serve customers and achieve organizational strategies
- Tolerance for ambiguity and the ability to perform effectively in the face of uncertainty or lack of clarity

Navigating the New Organizational Landscape

Although there are no easy answers for how to develop these career paths, three principles are worth considering:

Principle 1. Understand the demands of the role—both its job accountabilities and its associated behavioral requirements: Most of us understand that roles become more complex as managers move up the organization. What we may fail to acknowledge, though, are the differences among roles at the same level of complexity. The reason is that we don't fully grasp a job's content or the interaction of a role with others in the organization. Consider the example of a head of finance of a growing manufacturing firm who was promoted to the head of operations. (Figure 11-5 outlines this scenario.) Although the complexity of leadership challenges was similar, the roles were very different. The finance position was clearly an advisory role. It required someone who understood the impact of the position on the business and who could work behind the scenes as a trusted adviser with expertise in a specific area. The operations position required a business-focused, results-oriented approach—someone who could roll with punches thrown by market and industry changes. Most important, the head of operations had to be a people person—someone who could manage and lead a wide variety of individuals and departments.

Within months after her promotion, it was clear that the new operations head lacked these competencies. She was rigid and divisive; she had no people skills. Frustration rose. Performance fell. In less than a year, she was replaced. No one came out a winner. The leadership team struggled with the loss of a respected colleague. The operations head left with a sense of failure and regret. Organizational growth was slowed. All of this occurred because of a lack of understanding of the different demands that different roles place on leaders.

Before moving someone to a new role, it's important to have a thorough understanding of the implications—not just the type of management role or the technical skills it requires but also its size and scope.

FIGURE 11-5. CHANGE OF POSITIONS WITHIN ORGANIZATIONAL LANDSCAPE

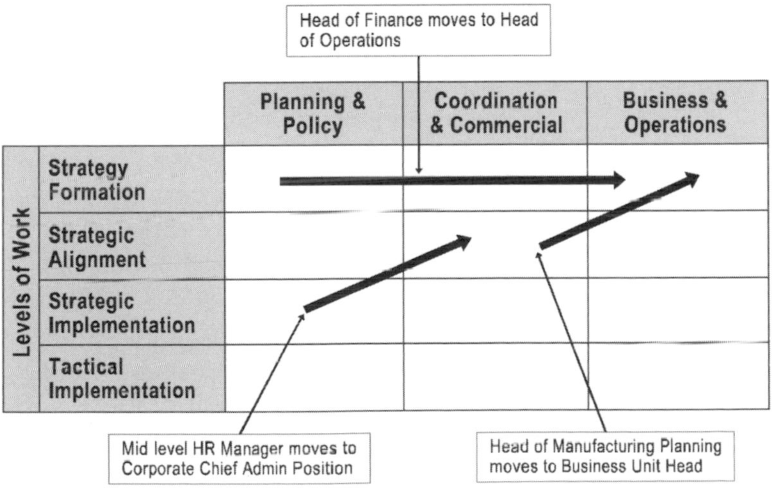

How much accountability is demanded? Is it strategically or tactically focused? What are the managerial demands? How does it impact business results? A more careful understanding of the demands of a high-level business delivery role, and the shift in behavior required of the jobholder, may have led to some critical questions regarding the feasibility of this career move. For instance:

- Does this person have the stamina and resilience to cope with being ultimately held accountable for results?
- Does this person have the confidence to withstand the public and frequent exposure of this type of position?
- Does this person have the skills and experience to manage diverse groups and organizations?
- Can this person be a visible enterprise leader, capable of working with and motivating large teams?
- Can this person effectively juggle and manage multiple streams of work and projects simultaneously?
- Can this person seamlessly reprioritize business concerns, often based on conflicting demands?

At the same time, you need to assess the context of the role within the larger organization. How does it interact with other elements of the organization? What formal and informal relationships are needed? How are results achieved—through direct control or the ability to influence others outside those formal relationships?

Principle 2. Know your management talent and how these managers stack up against current and likely next positions: All too often, as in the case of the misplaced operations head mentioned above, organizations don't have a good understanding—beyond past experiences and successes—of what makes an individual a good manager. Consider the case of a mid-level HR manager for a global telecommunications firm who was promoted to a corporate chief administrative executive role with matrixed resources across global geographies. As with the former example, he had been highly successful in his previous role (see Figure 11-5). And he had some experience working in a corporate environment, but in a less strategic position. He, too, quickly found himself struggling in the new role. The move from an advisory to a collaborative leadership role with cross-cultural and cross-business coordination demands, and from somewhat tactical to highly strategic, was too much. Lacking the networking, relationship-building, and negotiation skills needed in the new role, he failed to perform to expectations.

Such pitfalls are common in organizations until they begin to develop a deep understanding of their managers. What types of management roles have they held? Which competencies helped them to be successful? Which do they lack? What are their developmental needs? What are their personal and professional goals? How do they view themselves? How do others view them?

Principle 3. Evaluate and manage the risks of leadership moves: Once the job and the person are fully understood, the risk of moving the person to another position can be more accurately assessed. Although there are no set rules, there is a rule of thumb: In most cases, move no more than one step up in level and one step across to another type of role. It's not that bigger steps can't be taken. They can, but with more risk. As one general manager noted, "It's like stretching a rubber band. At some point—you're never sure where—it just snaps." In assuming that high-potential employees can take on just about any new role (they are, after all, the best talent), many organizations unintentionally stretch them to their breaking point. Often, these high flyers lose both self-confidence and the motivation to stay with their employer. To avoid such breakdowns, use a stair-step approach—although slower, it is often more effective. And even that needs to be carefully considered.

In another case, the head of manufacturing planning for a growing technology firm was recently promoted to head a business unit. A highly successful "coordination" leader—when she told the division president to embrace a new technology, the president listened—she had little experience running a multifaceted business unit. She wasn't comfortable coaching people, was an ineffective team leader, admitted she didn't fully understand the complexities of her organization, and tended to focus on her first love—implementing manufacturing innovations. Although she had really only moved one position laterally (from coordination to operational leader) and one level up (from aligning her group to the overall business strategy to actually setting strategies), she struggled. However, she recognized her limitations and, more important, was motivated to improve her game. With the employer providing targeted coaching, she learned critical new behaviors that boosted her people skills.

When you're promoting managers, such focused development is

important in limiting the risks. The particular development required depends on the individual and the role. It may come in the form of short-term project management. It may include external coaching and/ or internal mentoring. And it may require relatively straightforward skills training.

Moving from an operational position to a collaborative role can be even more difficult. Although it may appear to be a promotion, at least on paper, it often feels like a step down. Initially, such leaders often experience the loss of the formal control they had in their previous roles. Suddenly, they find themselves "leading from the rear." Gone are many traditional leadership "power tools"—large staffs, high visibility, and direct control. Instead, they must use their ability to read people, politics, and processes, and to use their influence—often behind the scenes—to accomplish their goals.

Such moves require a good understanding not only of the role but also of the organization and its culture. Managers who successfully make this transition tend to be emotionally mature. They understand why people behave the way they do, and they also understand their own behavior.

Succession Planning and Career Mapping

Clearly, a better understanding and alignment of roles and competencies helps organizations identify, select, develop, and promote managers at all levels. By understanding how demands vary with the level of work and the type of role, you can better select people with the right competencies for specific roles.

When using "career pathing" as an integral part of a rewards strategy, consider how you'll manage job transitions. When changing management roles, pay attention to how a move may impact the financial reward system. For example, to support development, it's common for people to move laterally in an organization, or even downward from a senior advisory role (for example, director of finance) to a first-level line deliverer (managing other people's delivery). Under conventional reward systems, this kind of job change can result in reduced salary ranges or incentive opportunities. While you could make individual exceptions for such a job change, if you plan to make this type of development an integral part of your rewards system, you may want to consider a structural change to the pay system.

Many organizations have significantly reduced the number of levels or grades in their pay structure to better support lateral mobility and development. These systems come in many forms and labels, with broadbands and career bands being common. Under these approaches, discussed in Chapter 7, people are expected to assume multiple roles within the same band to broaden their skills and competencies before moving up to the next higher band. Pay opportunities are sufficiently broad to accommodate these changes.

This knowledge can help organizations map careers so that managers can move ahead in "doable" steps. It also allows them to tailor their development—including their coaching and mentoring programs—to meet the needs of individual executives as they move from one type of role to another, or as they make the transition from tactical to strategic focus. Indirectly, our knowledge of roles and development also impacts how to pay people. Management that is more willing to invest in people development may actually be able to invest less in pay. However, getting an appropriate return on this development investment requires that organizations understand the different roles and competency requirements. This reward strategy has the advantage of being more difficult for competitors to replicate compared to, say, matching an organization's compensation levels. Indeed, some organizations can acquire a certain mystique by providing highly desirable development opportunities that are hard to get elsewhere. Investing in development also has direct implications on how conventional pay systems are structured, as described earlier with the broadbanding example. Pay and development need to work together.

Laurence Johnston Peter, U.S. educationalist and author of *The Peter Principle*, among other works, theorized that employees will advance to their highest level of competence in an organization, and then be promoted to—and remain at—a level at which they are incompetent. But given the new research about work and people, there's no reason that the infamous Peter Principle should ever again be blamed for a failed manager. By more carefully assessing, analyzing, and understanding the person and the role, organizations can select, develop, manage, and promote leadership talent more effectively.

Implications for Reward Management

As we indicated at the beginning of this chapter, organizations that can offer and effectively manage career development can realize significant savings in their tangible rewards budgets. But the real challenge for managers, if they are to influence this component of the rewards package, is to encroach on the turf of fellow professionals and begin to impact such things as job design, job-person matching, and career pathing. It also means leaving behind the certainties and comfort of such things as market pricing. Navigating the new map may require more lateral moves or unique job designs. In moves of this kind, the market price of the new position may be similar to the market price of the previous position, but the effective management of rewards means that, in some way, managers need to reflect the value of the resource the organization is seeking to create rather than the market value of existing roles.

Managers need to understand typical career routes and ensure that tangible pay progresses as careers progress. They need to reinforce high-potential programs with rewards structures and supporting guidelines that don't simply rely on well-established grades to communicate the rapid progress individuals are making. If individuals are to value career development, they must understand the benefits they're likely to obtain from moves that aren't immediately attractive.

Summary: A Checklist for Managing Career Paths

Keep the following items in mind when you think about career paths and which jobs to put your people in—that is, aligning employee skills with the nature of roles:

- Understand the levels of work and the nature of roles; know the "architecture of jobs."
- Remember the different competencies for different management roles; people who are highly adept at advisory roles may not be so successful at delivery roles.
- Bear in mind that development means more than moving people into different jobs; it's helping them acquire skills and know-how that the organization values.
- Consider that a new assignment is only rewarding when the individual possesses the threshold competencies to be effective, in addition to the potential to develop the competencies required to be outstanding.

CHAPTER 12

The Importance of Communications

BECAUSE REWARDS CAN BE a sensitive workplace issue, communicating about pay, incentives, and benefits is among the most difficult and important tasks management has to do. Our Hay Group Insight employee opinion database suggests that two-thirds of all employees are satisfied with the organization where they work, and more than 70 percent like the work they do. But only about 35 percent are satisfied with their pay. Interestingly, this percentage doesn't vary much between employees in high-paying companies and those in low-paying companies. Research conducted by WorldatWork in its Knowledge of Pay Study found that simply better communications about how the compensation system works have a greater impact on employee satisfaction with pay than do increases in actual pay. In addition, employee engagement is improved with employees' increased knowledge of the pay system, which includes the organization's compensation strategy, job evaluation and market pricing processes, and salary administration procedures.[1] For many employees, there's a built-in disconnect between what they receive as pay increases and what they think they deserve. Unfortunately, managers are often either unwilling or unable to deliver the truth.

This chapter provides background and perspective on how to develop an effective reward communication strategy that will greatly enhance the ROI of an organization's compensation program.

Managing Expectations

When management introduces a new rewards program, the corporate grapevine usually preempts formal communications. Fear abounds. The specter of cutbacks and freezes clouds people's perceptions. But good communications and even better implementation can thwart rumors and calm fears. Moreover, communications about pay can minimize the disruption that a new program might otherwise foster while maximizing the upside to the organization and employees alike.

For example, financial services organization Northwestern Mutual puts a lot of effort into explaining its pay program, according to Allan Kluz, director of compensation and benefits. "The key for us is balancing effective communications without making it look like propaganda." Kluz says that business unit leaders handle a lot of the actual communications. HR provides them with the tools and the key points, "but business unit leaders really make it their own—and much of HR's time is spent in working with managers to understand the programs better so they can more effectively communicate them."

Will good communications put an end to complaints about programs that slow salary increases or substitute performance-based incentives for entitled merit increases? Probably not. But good communications can blunt much of the criticism by making a sound argument for change, by documenting the decision-making process, and—this is key—by using managers as the primary messengers.

According to Elisabeth Baldock, senior vice president of human resources and learning at American Modern Insurance Group (AMIG), "The company's philosophy is that the line manager should do as much of the implementation and communication of the compensation program as possible." When it comes to salary planning, rewards, and everything else around the total cash piece, says Baldock, "the responsibility and accountability for communicating and implementing is the line manager's." HR's role, she explains, is "to provide the tools and assistance necessary to make them successful."

At AMIG, managers handle all of the communications regarding compensation, including base salary increases, incentive targets, and understanding their benefits programs. HR provides the talking points and offers assistance on how to talk with their employees. "We push business literacy," says Baldock. "Everyone is copied on the pre-earnings PR release," she says. "Everyone is encouraged to listen to the earnings reports." And there's openness in AMIG employee communications. According to Baldock, "We have a strong belief that our associates need to be armed with as much information and knowledge about our business as possible, because they are our window to the customer." The CEO's rationale for this openness, says Baldock, is that "the more people know what we do on a day-to-day basis, the more successful we'll be. We're all sellers of what we do."

At many organizations, managers feel especially challenged when compensation programs are changed. The managers often are personally affected by the changes—such as with a new incentive plan—and at the same time they must implement the changes affecting their subordinates.

Senior management and HR can improve the chances of successfully implementing change when they involve line managers in the process. There are several reasons for this. First, employees generally trust and believe their supervisors more than they do senior management. Second, HR is often perceived as not understanding the operational side of the business or of being only a mouthpiece for senior management. In fact, if line management *isn't* involved with the communications, employees may get the idea that line managers had no input or that they don't buy into the changes.

In some organizations, this might mean recruiting managers from various levels to work on the steering committee for the change project, thereby adding manager representation on issues ranging from program design to communications and implementation. According to Caterpillar Corporation's head of compensation and benefits, Greg Folley, "things started changing a couple of years ago when senior leaders began a systematic change-management program with a philosophy to bring leaders and managers inside the tent early on." "Before," says Folley, "the compensation program design was completed before line management was brought in. Then they saw the finished product. Only the HR function and senior executive group did the design work. We used to press a button, say to our line managers, 'Go communicate!' Now, our managers are active partners in the design of our compensation programs, and they take full responsibility for communicating them." Caterpillar's philosophy, Folley says, is that "our managers are leaders of our organization and that they have the accountability to take ownership and make the compensation programs their own."

Some organizations even purposely include their most vocal internal critics as part of the process, assuming that will get them to buy into the new program. (Many employees are so accustomed to hearing only negative comments from certain people that when they hear something positive, they assume it must be a good idea!) When the nature of the change or the culture of the organization precludes this level of involvement, managers should be given prior notice, or "heads up" communications. They also should have a chance to ask questions and be prepped on how to answer employees' questions. Most of the time, when employees have questions, they go directly to their managers, not to HR. And few things limit the effectiveness of program launches more than preventable manager disaffection—not to mention eroding employees' confidence in their managers because those managers are ill-equipped to respond.

Most compensation-change initiatives have perceived winners and losers, and it's important for managers to recognize this inevitability. For example, employees accustomed to guaranteed pay increases will understandably feel threatened by a new policy that hinges pay increases on performance. Similarly, introducing performance-based incentives often presents a problem when they bring with them the possibility that some people will earn less than before.

Often, top management introduces these programs with the attitude that top performers, who matter the most, will be happiest—and that is how it should be, of course. Those poor performers who lose out will either improve or move on, voluntarily or otherwise. At risk, however, are the solid and competent performers, some of whom operate on the fringe of the superior performance but go unrecognized because of imperfections in the measurement system.

The clues to managing the expectations of nonmanagement employees are the corporate culture and the specifics of the change. Recognizing these factors is very important. After all, when a manager has to break news that is perceived as bad news or deliver a message that breeds uncertainty, there are smart ways and not-so-smart ways to go about it.

An Opportunity to Gain Employee Trust

Managers can look at communications and change implementation as onerous, thankless tasks. Or, they can see these as the employee relations opportunities that they are. Employees who are dealt with professionally and openly will react better to changes than those who feel stonewalled or taken by surprise, no matter what the news may be.

At Caterpillar there was once a mentality where, according to Greg Folley, "Everyone ran for the hills and let the Compensation and Benefits people carry the message." "But," he explains, "you can stop them from running for the hills through an 18-month change-management plan and an extreme amount of management involvement and communication. Now, HR works with managers, and they know they have the responsibility and that success or failure depends on them."

At the beginning of most new or redesigned compensation projects, organizations want to know how the program should be rolled out and what communications will cost. That's usually a difficult estimate because the answer depends on the nature of the change the organization ultimately adopts, as well as logistical issues that govern levels of effort needed, resources, and cost. The message complexity matrix shown in Figure 12-1 is a tool that can help organizations reach an early comfort level about what their communications needs might be. As the figure shows, there is conceptual complexity and logistical complexity involved in sending the message of a new or different program to employees.

FIGURE 12-1. CONCEPTUAL AND LOGISTICAL COMMUNICATIONS MATRIX

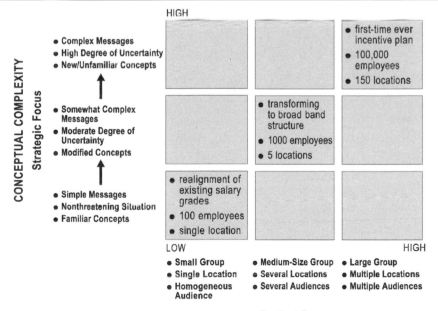

Conceptual Complexity

On the vertical axis of the Figure 12-1 matrix, we see various levels of conceptual complexity that should be charted relative to an organization's culture. Generally, the factors governing conceptual complexity are:

- *Complexity of Messages:* How involved are the messages that need to be sent, in terms of either the plan's mechanics or the rationale for it?
- *Perceived Threat:* How much anxiety and concern might the compensation change engender in groups that are affected by it?
- *Familiarity:* How familiar are managers and employees with the concepts and mechanics of the programs being changed? For instance, implementing an annual incentive plan in an organization that's never used variable pay will likely take more time and effort than introducing a new incentive plan in an organization used to variable pay and whose employees understand the risk-reward equation.

Logistical Complexity

On the horizontal axis of Figure 12-1, we see various levels of logistical complexity. These include:

- *Group Size:* How many people need to receive the information?
- *Location:* How many different locations are involved?
- *Audience:* How many different audiences need to be addressed?

Obviously, a small, single-location organization with a relatively homogeneous workforce represents logistical simplicity. On the other hand, a large organization with a diverse workforce in multiple locations scattered around the globe represents a huge logistical challenge.

Strategic Planning and Change

The desired outcome of clear communications and sound implementation isn't to make people happy—it's to make the new program work. But at the same time, it's never a good idea to force a new program down people's throats. Nor is it wise to let communications lay out the program mechanics. Making the program work requires strategic planning. Strategic communications planning consists of the following activities:

Confirming the Change Objectives

Before any communications planning can begin, the organization needs clarification on what it hopes to gain by the compensation change. Communicating these objectives—cutting costs, improving safety, enhancing quality, growing revenues, etc.—will be a big part of the communications program itself. Managers may also want to explain what's not changing, when the planned changes will happen, and when employees will find out more about the initiatives.

Developing the Communications Objectives

Before rolling out a new compensation program (and even before the design phase goes too far), organizations must decide what they want their employees to know, think, feel, and do as a result of the change. For example, if the objective of the program is to reward assembly workers for making fewer line errors, you may want them to know they're allowed to stop the production line when they suspect an error; you want them to feel empowered—and to make independent decisions.

A primary but often overlooked objective of any communications plan is to show (not just tell) employees that the compensation change makes good business sense, that it will benefit the organization, and therefore that it will benefit most employees. Early on, communications experts can help by determining if a good case for the program change can be made. If not, then perhaps the design needs reconsideration.

Below are a few sample communications objectives that are usually part of the communications strategy:

- Ensure that employees understand and embrace the reasons for the program.
- Boost confidence in top management's decision-making process.
- Gain buy-in—convince all involved that this new program is better and more fair than the earlier one.
- Encourage active support of the change.
- Ensure understanding of all aspects of the program, including mechanics and timing.
- Link the change positively to other initiatives.

Delineating the Target Audiences

Different audiences require different communications. Obviously, managers need to know more about the new program because they have to administer and explain it. They also need to understand their own compensation if it differs from that offered to their subordinates. Other primary audiences include members of HR departments, who typically act as trainers or facilitators in the rollout and orientation process and who provide program support throughout the year.

Note that the communications may have secondary audiences, or unaffected employees who may be facing similar changes down the line. Additional audiences, such as the media, may deem certain actions newsworthy, and press the organization for comments.

Of course, it's critical to know how many people constitute the audiences and where they are. Even in the electronic age, the logistics of communications are complicated by distance and demographics.

Creating the Messages

Determine what you can say that will get your points across to the various audiences you have delineated. Declarative statements, in and of themselves, aren't enough. You'll need to show, not just tell. For instance, a message to legitimize the process cannot simply be: "We spent many hours working on this project." Rather, you need to explain who did what, talk about why the organization feels it's important to do this, and acknowledge the help of outside consultants (if applicable), as well as any external data used in creating the program. You also need to explain how the program will work—again, best done with use of examples, in clear, simple language.

Picking the Key Messengers

Use the right people to give the right messages. For instance, it is almost always wiser to have a top leader lay out the strategic context of a change, as opposed to an HR representative or even the employees' managers (although managers should reinforce the concepts). Every organization is different. Take the time to figure out the best use of leaders, managers, and support personnel in the communications process. In some cases, even an outside third party may be appropriate, especially if that person has been involved with previous initiatives that went well.

Overcoming the Barriers to Effective Communication or Implementation

A plan that doesn't consider the factors that could block communications or implementation is likely to not perform as desired. For instance, if there's a huge management credibility issue, the initial efforts should be to repair this situation. If work-related stress is causing a lot of "noise" in the system, consider ways to ease that stress before introducing the new program. Some ways that help overcome communications barriers include:

- *Ensuring That Messages Overlap:* Send your message through a variety of media—the company newsletter, a payroll stuffer, a bulletin board announcement, a home mailing, the company intranet. As a rule of thumb, it's better to spread your communications net too wide than not wide enough.

- *Changing the Timing:* If people have grown accustomed to Friday afternoon announcements, shake things up with a Monday morning announcement—and say why this communication is anything but routine.

- *Using Innovative, Attention-Getting Vehicles:* For example, use brightly colored special announcement envelopes to get people's attention.

Choosing the Right Communications Vehicle to Drive Your Message

Analyze how your organization typically communicates and what seems to work best. Does everyone use the company website? At Avaya, they do. That's why the company's benefits communications strategy worked so well (see Chapter 9). Does everyone read the company newsletter? If so, use it as a communications vehicle. But don't stop there. You know your company, and you know what will work best.

You may want to consider small group meetings led by senior managers, HR representatives, or outside experts. At these gatherings, many employees learn about the new plan at the same time—perhaps over a company-sponsored pizza lunch. For far-flung branches and business units, a videotape or video conference with the top executives kicking off the program can be powerful, too. After all, it might be impossible, financially and logistically, for your CEO to be there in person. (That's another advantage of video presentations for far-flung organizations: Video can be used to reach employees in a lot of locations in a short time to minimize grapevine chatter.)

Regardless of how well thought out or how indispensable your communications plan, you will not deliver it if you can't get your hands on the resources required. For example, while an organization with no internal video production capability and no budget for outside help may have a great idea for a video about the new compensation plan, it should shelve the idea until it has the resources to make a video. You need to be realistic: Determine who in the company has the skills—and the time— to work on the communications plan.

Tactical Planning

Rarely do optimal conditions and practical timing collide. Fiscal deadlines, the need to preempt the grapevine, and windows of opportunity created by regularly scheduled meetings are just a few of the factors that force organizations to condense or rush their communications plans. However, when the timing is thought out and part of the strategic planning process, there's always a better chance for a solid communications effort.

A good strategic plan informs the tactical plan, which is the blueprint for action. The elements of the tactical plan are:

- Confirm the audiences and their particular needs.
- Refine the message.
- Select the messengers.
- Determine the preferred media.
- Create the plan.
- Establish the timetable.
- Assign the accountabilities.

Depending on the complexity of the communications plan, the tactical plan can be as simple as the example shown in Figure 12-2, which assumes a small, informed group of people responsible for communications. However, in a more complex situation, or when a large group is accountable for production and delivery, or in organizations whose practices demand it, a more detailed plan that includes review periods and milestones is required.

Implementing the Plan

While many rollouts can be the joint work of HR, the communications department, and outside consultants, managers and executives often play

FIGURE 12-2. TACTICAL COMMUNICATIONS PLAN

Deliverable/ Vehicle	Purposes	Content/ Messages	Messenger	Audiences	Timing	Accountability
Web	Initial Communications to All Employees	• Provide brief overview • Manage expectations • Distinguish "eligible" group/note plan for others	Joint from Senior Leadership	All Employees	TBD	Communications Team
Video Broadcast	Provide Endorsement from the Top	• Make strategic connection • Offer brief overview of benefits	Benefits Director	All Employees	December, March	Consultants
E-Mail	Update Executives and Managers	• Report on progress of program & training orientation process • Reminder of upcoming activity • Reinforce management role	Core Design Team	Executives & Managers	October	Consultants
Presentation	Provide Endorsement from the Top	• Make strategic connection • Offer brief overview of benefits • Define performance management	Benefits Director	All Employees	November	HR
Presentation	Update Executives and Managers	• Report on progress of program & training orientation process • Reminder of upcoming activity • Reinforce management role	Business Heads and/or Core Team	Executives & Managers	December	HR

prominent roles in the implementation. As noted earlier, line managers are the preferred messengers for most communications to employees.

As a manager, you may be called upon to carry important messages to employees, often via a prepared presentation deck. Beyond presenting the basic slides, have a talk with HR (take an HR manager to lunch) or the outside consultants (let them take you to lunch). Ask for talking points or a script to ensure that they tell about all the relevant details. HR or the outside consultants may have compiled a list of frequently asked questions (FAQs) to help line managers respond to employee questions in a consistent manner.

"We give managers a standard presentation to give to employees," says Carl Smith, Caterpillar's corporate compensation manager. "They get talking points with suggestions on what to advise their employees based on their job level or type of situation. Some supplement what we give them and others don't make it a priority. This shows up in employee opinion surveys," he notes. "Managers who make it a priority usually get better results from the employee opinion surveys." At other organizations, managers receive discussion protocols, like the ones that follow that can be used to help direct conversations with individual employees about salary increases, range adjustments, and other compensation issues.

Discussion Protocols

Scenario 1: A large increase in salary to bring outstanding new performers up to minimum:

- "Our new grade structure shows that your compensation is below/well below the minimum salary we attach to this job. We're going to fix that."
- "The minimum for your job is $x; the midpoint is $xx; and the maximum is $xxx. Your performance has been judged outstanding [elaborate, if appropriate], which even if you were at the range minimum, would warrant a higher than average merit increase. So, we're happy to give you an xx percent increase to bring your salary up to $xx."
- "Because you are still relatively low in the salary range, if you continue to be an outstanding performer, you should be able to look forward to continued 'higher than average' increases over the next few years. Of course, as you approach and possibly exceed

the range midpoint, increase percentages, even for top performers, are not as high. But that's a ways off. And promotion is also a way to achieve your career objectives and earn more money." [If there is also a variable pay plan, this is a good time to emphasize the organization's reliance on it to help deliver additional pay and recognition to high performers.]

Scenario 2: Average increase in salary for solid performer in middle of the range:

- "Our new grade structure shows that your compensation is within the range and nearing the target compensation we associate with this job. Your performance has been judged as solid [elaborate, if appropriate]. The minimum for your job is x; the midpoint is xx; and the maximum is xxx. Our new compensation structure and salary increase policy says that outstanding and competent performers who are lowest in their salary range should get the largest raises. Since you're closer to the range midpoint, your increase can't approach the highest we give—but because of your performance, it still is competitive internally and externally. I'm pleased to provide you with an xx percent increase, which will bring your salary up to xx."

- "Because your pay is not yet at midpoint, as long as you continue to be a competent or high performer, you should be able to look forward to continued 'higher than average' increases over the next few years until you near the midpoint of your pay range. As you approach and possibly exceed the range midpoint, increase percentages, even for top performers, are not as high. But remember, a $40,000 employee who gets a 6 percent increase is still earning just $42,400, while a $60,000 employee who gets only a 3 percent increase is earning much more at $61,800 per year—still a sizable gap. And promotion is also a way to achieve your career objectives and earn more money. Of course, achieving the highest performance rating would add to your increases."

Scenario 3: Low/no increase in salary for outstanding performer high in the range:

- "Our new grade structure shows that your compensation is well above the midpoint salary we attach to this job. This doesn't mean you are overpaid. It just means that the combination of your hiring salary [possibly] and your increases over the years continue to reward you well. You now are compensated as a seasoned performer and you are earning a salary that is very competitive in the external marketplace and within our company. The minimum for your job is x; the midpoint is xx; and the maximum is xxx. Your performance has been judged as outstanding [elaborate, if appropriate] and since you're paid well above the range midpoint you already earn about 30 percent more than others in your range—the rate of salary increase growth slows down. However, because of your strong performance, I'm pleased to provide you with an additional lump sum portion to make you 'whole' relative to your performance. The salary increase portion of xx percent will increase your salary to xx."

- "Although we cannot provide you with an increase this year since you are above the range maximum, I am pleased to be able to give you a lump sum performance bonus of xxx—which is equivalent to xx percent of your annual base salary."

- "Because you are so [close to/over] the salary range maximum, your increases may only be at this level over the next few years. Eventually, as the salary ranges are adjusted more than your annual increases, you will be in a position in the range to receive [bigger increases/standard increases instead of the lump sum performance bonus]. Promotion is also a way to achieve your career objectives and earn more money."

Summary: A Checklist for Reward Communications

When explaining a new compensation plan or changes to your current plan:

- *Manage expectations:* Early and clear communications can offset employee fears and stifle grapevine rumors.
- *Engage line managers in communications:* Studies show that employees trust their direct managers more than anyone else in the organization.
- *Train line managers:* They'll need to know more than PowerPoint factoids; instead, give them talking points and discussion protocols so they can speak with employees one-on-one, if needed.

- *Identify your target audiences:* Different audiences need different kinds of communications.
- *Overreach rather than underreach:* It's better for employees to learn about a compensation change through e-mail, snail mail, a small group meeting, and a bulletin board posting rather than not learn about it at all.

Recognition: The Most Meaningful Reward?

HAY GROUP INSIGHT employee opinion surveys have suggested that too few organizations take advantage of the motivational power of non-monetary rewards. Only about 50 percent of employees surveyed—management as well as nonmanagement—report that their contributions are recognized when they perform well. That's a pity because recognition could well be the most meaningful reward an organization could offer its employees. In this chapter we address the importance of recognition and the role it plays in motivating employees.

The Prevalence of Recognition Programs

The Motivation-Hygiene Theory proposed by Fred Herzberg, a clinical psychologist, in 1966 helps shed light on the importance of recognition. According to Herzberg, compensation will, at best, prevent employees from being dissatisfied with their work environment. Recognition, how-ever, satisfies. No wonder recognition is instrumental in reducing turn-over, in increasing productivity, and in creating a positive work environment.[1]

Organizations do seem to be getting more serious about employee recognition. Approximately 89 percent report having some form of recognition program in place, and 48 percent are increasing the scope of their recognition programs over the previous year.[2] In tougher economic times, when organizations face budget constraints yet want to reward employees for their work, they tend to produce more recognition programs because they are less costly. As money for merit increases and bonuses became tighter for many organizations, they started looking for noncash ways to reward their employees.[3]

Progressive-thinking organizations understand the power of tying recognition to corporate and HR strategies. Some have added an awareness of recognition programs to their existing curriculum of courses offered to managers to encourage employees to excel. Indeed, these programs can play a pivotal role in enhancing the employer's brand and promoting the organization as an employer of choice. At the very least, the hope is that employees will find it hard to walk away.

Many organizations have indeed grasped the role that recognition plays in the rewards portfolio. Recognition programs have evolved from primarily tenure-based "thank you" programs to ones focusing on employee engagement, recognizing "above and beyond" performance, and reinforcing desired behaviors and desired work climate. Most recognition programs have both formal and informal components. They have become much more strategic over time, with 70 percent embodying a written strategy linked to the business plan; about two-thirds of them also have measurement criteria.[4]

Organizations are getting more serious about recognition programs. Most organizations have formal budgets for these programs, with the median cost constituting about 1 percent of payroll.

The following case study illustrates the recognition efforts of one corporation but its actions are typical of many others.

Case Study: Prudential Financial Services

Prudential Financial Services, with more than 30 million customers globally, is one of the oldest and largest U.S.-based financial services organizations. Prudential Financial views employee recognition as key to achieving its business strategy. The company has a formal function dedicated to providing expertise and capabilities in this area. Terri Sarni is the director of recognition services: "This is not a feel-good kind of thing," she says. "Prudential Financial recognizes people for things that are most important to the company—it's all about business."

According to Sarni, "We use recognition as a strategic tool for shaping behavior and performance to move the organization in a desired direction. We do this by aligning recognition with business needs, promoting employee behaviors that support the business, and educating managers on recognition practices—all of which keep employees engaged.

"However, business isn't only about money; it's also about providing meaning and dignity to employees on the job. At Prudential Financial, one of the ways we do that is through formal and informal recognition practices. Formal practices are highly structured programs with established award criteria, a nomination process, a selection committee and a celebration mechanism to recognize the winner. In contrast, informal practices are spontaneous ways to say 'thank you' to employees for a job well done."[5]

The Power of Recognition

Many managers would agree that rewards and recognition naturally go together—so much so that many compensation and benefits departments today are being renamed "Rewards and Recognition." So why is it that only about half of all employees believe their contributions are recognized? Because there's room for improvement when it comes to recognition.

Employee efforts that get recognized also get repeated. If companies can recognize the employee's discretionary efforts that align with the organization's success, and can capitalize on those efforts through recognition, it's not hard to see how superior performance can be continued, and at a fairly nominal price. The important thing to remember is that recognition programs are not incentive plans. They are after-the-fact interventions. Indeed, recognition rewards should be given for specific events, not for sustained individual performance. Performance management should assess and acknowledge the latter.

Often overlooked as a powerful motivator, recognition can be used to reward desired behaviors that are consistent with company culture, values, and strategies. Recognition is not a replacement for performance management, but rather a process for improving performance through people. Recognizing events, activities, and efforts after the fact may not drive improved performance, but it will reinforce it. Think of it as an investment in the improvement process that should be made without an expected gain. Yet, as can be found among the organizations in *Fortune* magazine's annual America's Most Admired Companies, recognition often delivers gains beyond expectation. These companies are known for making the most of nonmonetary rewards, and they are highly desirable employers for that reason, among others.

To be most effective, recognition programs should be embedded in the organization's total rewards strategy. Perhaps the most important rule regarding recognition is that it shouldn't stand alone—it's not a one time initiative. Companies see the real power of recognition when it's integrated with the HR strategy and overall rewards strategy and is delivered regularly in small doses.

Recognition plans, just like compensation plans, should align with organizational objectives, not with out-of-date traditions. The most effective programs are designed with the direct participation of managers, who need to consider what behaviors and deeds should be recognized and how they should be recognized.

Behaviors to Recognize

Ideally, the behaviors you want to recognize should align with the corporate mission and core values. Beyond that, it's common to recognize completion of special projects, the meeting of quality/productivity benchmarks, or simply going above and beyond expectations. Very often, continuous service to the organization is reason for recognition, as evidenced by today's abundance of service award programs. Also consider whether the program should emphasize innovation, effort, or goal attainment. Your organization's reward philosophy should determine this.

Another consideration is the emphasis or orientation of the recognition program. For example, should the program reward team or individual efforts? Very often, groups of employees form a team to solve a specific business problem, such as a system implementation, and are recognized for their collective efforts. On the other hand, an individual who proposes an important process improvement may be recognized for an outstanding individual contribution. Although both approaches work well, you don't want the recognition program to create competition among employees.

Degree of Formality

How formal should the recognition program be? There are three basic types: day-to-day recognition, formal recognition, and informal recognition. As a general rule, the more formal an award, the fewer number of recipients. To be most effective, recognition programs typically include a combination of these programs.

Day-to-day recognition includes spot-recognition awards (whether cash or noncash). These awards also typically involve some form of paper award, either a certificate or a letter with a "thank you," "caught in the act," "great customer service," or "helping hand" theme. Often, winning these awards involves a lot of peer-to-peer interaction, including nominating coworkers as recipients.

Informal programs have few rules, very broad guidelines, minimal documentation, and no formal approval process. Formal programs, on the other hand, typically include a prescribed process for nomination and selection. Nominations may be made by peers, customers, supervisors, department heads, or even nominating committees.

At McDonald's, the recognition program is formal. The Ray Kroc Award goes to the top 1 percent of restaurant managers. Managers must meet a rigorous combination of quantitative, qualitative, and operational criteria to qualify. This selective group of 130 employees receives a cash award and a trip to the Oakbrook, Illinois, headquarters for a banquet and reception with senior McDonald's executives. The Ray Kroc Award sticks with people—it's a badge of honor in the organization. Likewise, McDonald's sponsors a President's Award, which is awarded to the top 1 percent of staff. Like the Ray Kroc Award, recipients are treated to a banquet/reception and are also given cash.[6]

Eligibility to Receive Awards

As mentioned earlier, it's not good to create internal competition for recognition, nor is it advisable to allow recognition to turn into a popularity contest. But eligibility should be clearly established. Some considerations include:

- Should there be a minimal service requirement?
- Should there be a limit on how many times an individual can be recognized?

- Should management be eligible?
- Should there be an option to create department-specific recognition programs?

Frequency, Size, and Types of Awards

How often recognition awards should be given is largely up to the organization. Obviously, on-the-spot awards can happen at any time, but frequent, regular awards (for example, monthly, quarterly, annually) are more effective. Generally the smaller the award, the more often it is given. However, trying to provide regular recognition without diluting its meaning is a delicate balance. "Recognition needs to be focused and targeted so that associates know exactly what they are doing right to have the most impact, " says Lis Baldock, senior vice president of human resources and learning at AMIG. "You don't want to get to a point where you are celebrating the fact that everyone wore shoes today." Nonetheless, the power of simple recognition is not lost on AMIG's managers. According to Baldock, "At AMIG, we have found that a simple thank you can be as powerful as a formal recognition program."

There are also consistency concerns. Carl Smith, corporate compensation manager at Caterpillar Corporation, says, "We've shied away from cash and other tangible awards purposely because there has been some disengagement in the past because the rules and criteria varied from department to department. That is, some managers would be quite lenient and provide rewards for nonsignificant contributions while others would recognize it for more milestone achievements."

Tiered recognition awards can be a way to keep a culture of recognition alive. For example, monthly recognition award winners can be nominated for an annual recognition award, which typically is significantly larger (in size and value).

Noncash Awards

There are entire books devoted to the possibilities of noncash awards. In fact, the list is limited only by one's imagination. Common awards types include merchandise and/or gift certificates, entertainment certificates, educational opportunities, cumulative earned value credits, symbolic recognition awards (plaques, certificates, etc.), and social awards such as luncheons and parties. Some of the most powerful recognition programs, however, don't cost the organizations a single dollar. That's because employees often value a simple, personal gesture from the company's senior leaders.

Carl Smith, at Caterpillar Corporation, agrees. "We have dozens of recognition programs across our organization. Our managers can hand out spot cash rewards. But we find nonfinancial recognition is typically the most powerful, especially when it is given by our leaders. We get more mileage from public recognition from a manager when it's done in small groups or privately. It's inexpensive and it goes a long way."

Likewise, says Alisa Poe, at AMIG: "Our CEO writes a note to everyone who gets a service award. We even ordered notepaper for senior managers because we see handwritten notes as very meaningful rewards. We do have some formal recognition programs—our Midland Valuable Players Program allows managers and fellow associates to recognize people around our core values. But the most powerful recognition tool we have is the recognition that our senior managers provide our associates. The key to recognition for us is that it is fresh and meaningful and informal.

"Our managers also tend to move around to different parts of the business, and they bring with them different experiences on how recognition can effectively work. Departments have their own programs and share them with others. They tell one another 'Here's what works, and here's what doesn't. As a result, we have better ideas across the organization and more alignment across our departments."

Case Study: TDK Electronics

TDK Electronics Corporation uses employee recognition as a key tool in building a positive work climate and in retaining top talent. TDK has an ongoing reward and recognition committee comprising employees from all employee groups and departments. The purpose of the recognition program is to find fun and unique ways to thank employees who go the extra mile in accomplishing their work or exhibiting great team behavior.

"Employees like this program very much, and management is especially appreciative of the program because it creates an efficient avenue for thanking employees and increasing their motivation to do a good job," says Jill Gray, TDK's director of general affairs. The program provides all managers with a set of "hats off" paper certificate awards that they can provide to employees on the spot for doing something good. And to make it more fun, any employee who has collected four of these certificates is eligible to play "the game" at the next employee meeting. TDK identifies some type of game (roulette wheel, fishing, or bowling, for example) for the meeting and then gives those who've qualified a chance for a prize—typically something as simple as a beach towel, sunglasses, lunch bag, or movie passes.

Gray says the program has received high marks and the committee's creativity and excitement flows over into the employee base. "It is now part of our culture. TDK's rewards and recognition program has never been very expensive in the first place," she said. "The purpose of rewards and recognition is not to compensate employees for their extra effort on the job; it is a small token for a large amount of thanks and gratitude to our teammates."[7]

Summary: A Checklist for Recognition

Often thought of as a subset of communications, recognition can become a powerful part of your rewards program. Roy Saunderson, president of the Recognition Management Institute, sums up the impact of recognition programs this way: "I can't sit here and say that recognition programs by themselves contribute to the bottom line, but there is considerable research that shows that a philosophy of putting people first, creating a creative culture, caring for people and listening to people does have a direct measurable effect on the bottom line."[8]

To be effective, recognition should:

- Align to organizational objectives and reflect the company's mission, vision, and values.
- Be an integrated part of the rewards program.
- Provide managers with an opportunity to identify desired behaviors and deeds that make the organization a success.

Notes

Chapter 1. Why This Book Is Important

1. Jeffrey Pfeffer, "When it Comes to 'Best Practices'—Why Do Smart Organizations Occasionally Do Dumb Things," *Organizational Dynamics* 25 (1996): 31–35.

2. Krista Anderson and Guorong Zhu, *Organizational Climate Technical (OCSII) Manual* (Hay Group McClelland Center for Research and Innovation, October 2002).

Chapter 2. Ensuring an ROI on Your Rewards Programs

1. K. Dow Scott, Ph.D., Thomas D. McMullen, and Richard S. Sperling, "Fiscal Management of Compensation Programs," *WorldatWork Journal* 14, no. 3 (3rd Quarter 2005): 13–25.

2. Ibid.

3. K. Dow Scott, Ph.D., Thomas D. McMullen, and John Nolan, CPA, "Taking Control of Your Counter Offer Environment," *WorldatWork Journal* 14, no. 1 (1st Quarter 2005): 25–34.

4. John A. Byrne and Jack Welch, *Jack: Straight from the Gut* (New York: Warner Books, 2001), 144.

5. Jac Fitz-enz, *The ROI of Human Capital* (New York: AMACOM, 2000), 231–239.

6. John E. Hunter, Frank L. Schmidt, and Michael K. Judiesch, "Individual Differences in Output Variability as a Function of Job Complexity," *Journal of Applied Psychology* 75 (1990): 28–42.

7. Krista Anderson and Guorong Zhu, *Organizational Climate Technical (OCSII) Manual* (Hay Group McClelland Center for Research and Innovation, October 2002).

8. Richard Henderson, *Compensation Management in a Knowledge-Based World* (New York: Prentice-Hall, 2005).

9. K. Dow Scott, Ph.D., Thomas D. McMullen, Richard S. Sperling, and Marc J. Wallace III, "Linking Compensation Policies and Programs to Organization Effectiveness," *WorldatWork Journal,* 12, no. 4 (4th Quarter 2003): 35–44.

10. K. Dow Scott, Ph.D., Thomas D. McMullen, and Richard S. Sperling, "Fiscal Management of Compensation Programs," *WorldatWork Journal* 14, no. 3 (3rd Quarter 2005), 13–25.

11. K. Dow Scott, Ph.D., Thomas D. McMullen, Richard S. Sperling, and Marc J. Wallace III, "Linking Compensation Policies and Programs to Organization Effectiveness," *WorldatWork Journal* 12, no. 4 (4th Quarter 2003), 35–44.

Chapter 3. The Link Between Rewards and Business Objectives

1. Hay Group Presentation at WorldatWork Total Rewards Conference, "Ensuring Culture Change at Arbella: A Case Study in the Effectiveness of Rewards," May 13, 2002.

Chapter 4. Performance Measures That Motivate

1. Gary P. Latham and Edward A. Locke, "Goal Setting: A Motivational Technique That Works," *Organizational Dynamics* 8, no. 2 (1979): 68–80.

2. Joshua Kurlantzick, "Serving Up Success," *Entrepreneur Magazine*, November 2003, 86–89.

3. John Chambers, "CEO of Cisco Systems," *San Francisco Chronicle*, February 29, 2004, I-1.

4. Louis Gerstner, *Who Says Elephants Can't Dance* (New York: Harper Business, 2002), 231.

Chapter 5. Getting Employee Commitment with "Total Rewards"

1. Jody Hoffer Gittel, *The Southwest Airlines Way: Using Power of Relationships to Achieve High Performance* (New York: McGraw-Hill, 2003).

2. Evren Esen, 2005 U.S. Job Recovery and Retention Survey Poll Findings, Society for Human Resources Management, November 2005, p. 2.

3. Bureau of Labor Statistics, *Occupational Outlook Quarterly* 47, no. 4 (Winter 2003–2004), 44.

4. Accenture, "Employee Recruiting and Retention Ranks as Top Priority for Senior Executives," press release, July 2005. Refer to www.accenture.com.

5. Daniel Goleman, Ph.D., "Leadership That Gets Results," *Harvard Business Review* 78, no. 2 (2000): 78.

6. The Conference Board, Research Report 12-1302-01-RR, "Managing Culture in Mergers and Acquisitions," 2001.

7. Alan Deutschman, "Inside the Mind of Jeff Bezos," *FastCompany Magazine*, August 2004, 52.

8. IQPC.com, International Quality and Productivity Center Cubic Award Winners, 2004, Most Innovative Corporate University.

9. Jennifer Merritt and Louis Lavelle, "It's Time to Plug Talent Leaks," *BusinessWeek Online*, February 2, 2005.

10. Samuel Greengard, "The Five Alarm Job," *Workforce Management Magazine*, February 2004, 43–48.

11. K. Dow Scott, Ph.D., Thomas D. McMullen, Richard S. Sperling, and Marc J. Wallace III, "Linking Compensation Policies and Programs to Organization Effectiveness," *WorldatWork Journal* 12, no. 4 (4th Quarter 2003): 35–44.

12. Brenda van Leeuwen and Jo Pieters, "Building Philips' Employer Brand from the Inside Out," *Strategic HR Review* 4, no. 4 (May/June 2005): 16.

Chapter 6. Putting a Price Tag on Work

1. Alvin O. Bellak, "The Hay Guide Chart-Profile Method of Job Evaluation," *Handbook of Wage and Salary Administration* (New York: McGraw-Hill, 1984), Chapter 15.

2. Patricia K. Zingheim, Jay R. Schuster, and Marvin G. Dertien, "Measuring the Value of Work," *WorldatWork Journal* 14, no. 3 (July 2005): 42–49.

3. Edward E. Lawler III, *Strategic Pay: Aligning Organizational Strategies and Pay Systems* (San Francisco, Calif.: Jossey-Bass, 1990).

4. Patricia K. Zingheim, Ph.D., Jay R. Schuster, and Marvin G. Dertien, "Measuring the Value of Work," *WorldatWork Journal* 14, no. 3 (3rd Quarter 2005): 42–49.

5. Hay Group, "What Are You Paying For?" Hay Group Working Paper, 2005, www.haygroup.com.

6. Howard Risher, "Making Managers Responsible for Handling Pay," *Workspan* 46, no. 3 (March 2003): 8–12.

7. Stephen Fournier, "Keeping Line Managers in the Know," *ACA News* 43, no. 3 (March 2000): 46–48.

8. Ibid.

9. Elayne Robertson Demby, "Weighing Their Worth," *Human Resource Executive*, March 2005, http://www.workindex.com/editorial/staff/sta0506.asp.

10. K. Dow Scott, Ph.D., Thomas D. McMullen, Richard S. Sperling, and Marc J. Wallace III, "Linking Compensation Policies and Programs to Organization Effectiveness," *WorldatWork Journal* 12, no. 4 (4th Quarter 2003): 35–44.

11. Ibid.

12. Donna Graebner and Kevin Seaweard, "Bringing It All Inside: Job Evaluation and Market Pricing at JCPenney," *Workspan* 47, no. 8 (August 2004): 30–35.

Chapter 7. Base Salary Management: Building the Foundation

1. K. Dow Scott, Ph.D., Thomas D. McMullen, Richard S. Sperling, and Marc J. Wallace III, "Linking Compensation Policies and Programs to Organization Effectiveness," *WorldatWork Journal* 12, no. 4 (4th Quarter 2003): 35–44.

2. Ibid.

3. Ibid.

Chapter 8. Reinforcing Results with Variable Pay

1. Marshall W. Van Alstyne, "Create Colleagues Not Competitors," *Harvard Business Review*, September 2005, 24.

2. Ibid.

Chapter 9. The Hidden Value of Benefits

1. Jim Jubak, "Welcome to the Bankruptcy Economy." Refer to: http://moneycentral.msn.com/content/p93643.asp.

2. Gretchen Weber, "Preserving the Starbucks' Counter Culture," *Workforce Management,* February 2005, 28–34.

3. Elayne Robertson Demby, "Two Stores Refuse to Join the Race to the Bottom," *Workforce Management*, February 2004, 57–59.

Chapter 10. Remembering the *Management* in Performance Management

1. Jennifer Chatman, Charles A. O'Reilly III, and Victoria Chang, "Cisco Systems: Developing a Human Capital Strategy," *California Management Review* 47, no. 2 (Winter 2005): 136–167.

2. Ram Charan, "Conquering a Culture of Indecision," *Harvard Business Review* 84, no. 1 (January 2006): 108.

3. Tom McMullen and Jeff Meyers, Hay Group research conducted at 2003 WorldatWork National Conference, San Diego, CA. Study made available to survey participants.

4. Ibid.

5. K. Dow Scott, Ph.D., Thomas D. McMullen, Richard S. Sperling, and Marc J. Wallace III, "Linking Compensation Policies and Programs to Organization Effectiveness," *WorldatWork Journal* 12, no. 4 (4th Quarter 2003): 35–44.

6. Hay Group, "Managing Performance," Hay Group Working Paper, 2001.

7. John E. Hunter, Frank L. Schmidt, and Michael K. Judiesch, "Individual Differences in Output Variability as a Function of Job Complexity," *Journal of Applied Psychology* 75 (1990): 28–42.

8. Lyle Spencer and Signe Spencer, *Competence at Work* (New York: John Wiley & Sons, 1993), 3–16.

9. David C. McClelland, "Testing for Competence Rather Than Intelligence," *American Psychologist* 28 (January 1973): 1–14.

10. Daniel Goleman, *Emotional Intelligence: Why It Can Matter More Than IQ* (New York: Bantam Books, 1995).

11. John E. Hunter, Frank L. Schmidt, and Michael K. Judiesch, "Individual Differences in Output Variability as a Function of Job Complexity," *Journal of Applied Psychology* 75 (1990): 28–42.

12. David C. McClelland, John W. Atkinson, Russel A. Clark, and Edgar L. Lowell, *The Achievement Motive* (New York: Appleton-Century-Crofts, 1953).

13. P. Vitale, "Competency Analysis of Executives, Managers, and Technical Professionals in the Companies of ENI Gruppo, S.p.A." Paper presented at The Third International Conference on Competencies and Human Capital, Castelgondolfo, Italy, June 10–12, 1998.

14. "Beware of Turkeys That Fly and Top Performers Who Walk on Water," *Financial Times*, October 1994, 17.

15. Jack Welch, *Straight from the Gut* (New York: Warner Business Books, 2001), 144.

16. Alix Nyberg Stuart, "Motivating the Middle," *CFO Magazine*, October 1, 2005, 62–70.

17. Ibid.

18. Sarah Mavrinac and Tony Siesfield, "Measures That Matter," in OECD, Ernst & Young, ed., *Enterprise Value in the Knowledge Economy: Measuring Performance in the Age of Intangibles* (Boston Ernst & Young, 1997), 49–72.

Chapter 11. A (Career) Path to Employee Satisfaction and Business Success

1. William Holstein, "Best Companies for Leaders," *Chief Executive*, November 2005, 24.

2. Guorong Zhu, Steven B. Wolff, Ruth Malloy, and Signe Spencer, "Executive Competencies: Unraveling the Myth of the Generic Leader," Hay Group Working Paper, 2006.

Chapter 12. The Importance of Communications

1. Jeremy Handel, "Survey Knowledge Shows Pay Knowledge = Pay Satisfaction," *Workspan* 45, no. 7 (July 2002): 78–79.

Chapter 13. Recognition: The Most Meaningful Reward?

1. Frederick Herzberg, Bernard mausner, Barbara Bloch Snyderman, *The Motivation to Work* (New York: John Wiley & Sons, 1959), 3–38.

2. Lane Abrahamsen and Greg Boswell, "Employers Turn to Recognition to Motivate Employees," *Workspan* 46 no. 12 (December 2003): 24–26.

3. Ibid.

4. Ibid.

5. Barbara Parus, "Recognition: A Strategic Tool for Retaining Talent," *Workspan* 45, no. 11 (November 2002): 14–18.

6. Amy Zuber, "McD Honors Winners of First Ray Kroc Award," *Nation's Restaurant News*, March 20, 2000, and Michael Arndt, "Scenes from McDonald's Confab of the Faithful," *Business Week*, May 19, 2000.

7. Jeremy Handel, "Recognition: Pats on the Back Motivate Employees," *Workspan* 44, no. 12 (December 2001): 36–38.

8. Lynn McKibbin-Brown, "Beyond the Gold Watch: Employee Recognition Today," *Workspan* 46, no. 4 (April 2003): 44–46.

Index

About the Authors

Doug Jensen (doug_jensen@haygroup.com) is a vice president and National Executive Compensation Practice leader in the Walnut Creek, California, office of Hay Group. He's also responsible for managing Hay Group's relationship with strategic and global companies. He has 33 years of experience in all facets of human resources, with special emphasis in total rewards and executive compensation. Prior to joining Hay Group, he was the director of compensation and benefits for the Pillsbury Company; before that, he held compensation and benefits positions at Frito-Lay, Inc., and First National Holding Company of Atlanta. He holds a master's degree in human resources and a bachelor's degree from Stanford University.

*   *   *

Tom McMullen (tom_mcmullen@haygroup.com) is a vice president and U.S. Reward Practice leader based in the Chicago office of Hay Group. He has over 20 years of human resources practitioner and consulting experience working with clients on broad rewards issues. His work focuses primarily on total rewards and performance management program design, including rewards strategy development, incentive plan design, employee pay, and job evaluation. Prior to joining Hay Group, he was in senior compensation analyst roles with Kentucky Fried Chicken Corporation and Humana, Inc. He holds a master's degree in business ad-

ministration and a bachelor's degree in mathematics from the University
of Louisville.

*   *   *

Mel Stark (mel_stark@haygroup.com) is a vice president and the Regional Reward Practice leader in the New York Metro office of Hay
Group. In his practice role and in his personal consulting, he is focused
on adding clarity to clients' operations through cultural diagnostics, job
analysis, work measurement, accountability mapping, and organization
design. Building commitment in clients' employees is also stressed
through the effective implementation of holistic rewards programs. He
holds a BA from The American University in Washington, D.C., and
has earned an MBA from Bernard M. Baruch College and an advanced
professional certificate in organizational behavior and development
from New York University's Graduate School of Business Administration.

About Hay Group

Hay Group is a global consulting firm that works with leaders to transform strategy into reality. We develop talent, organize people to be more effective, and motivate them to perform at their best. With 82 offices in 47 countries, we work with over 7,000 clients around the world. Our clients are from the private, public, and not-for-profit sectors across every major industry, and thus they represent diverse business challenges. Our focus is on making change happen and helping people and organizations realize their potential.